RETHINKING MIDDLE EAST POLITICS
State Formation and Development

Simon Bromley

Polity Press

Copyright © Simon Bromley 1994

The right of Simon Bromley to be identified as author of this work has been asserted in accordance with the Copyright, Designs and Patents Act 1988.

First published in 1994 by Polity Press in association with Blackwell Publishers.

Editorial office:
Polity Press
65 Bridge Street
Cambridge CB2 1UR, UK

Marketing and production:
Blackwell Publishers
108 Cowley Road
Oxford OX4 1JF, UK

ISBN 0 7456 0907 4
ISBN 0 7456 0908 2 (pbk)

British Library Cataloguing-in-Publication Data
A CIP catalogue record for this book is available from the British Library.

Typeset in 10 1/2 on 12 pt Sabon
by Pure Tech Corporation, Pondicherry, India
Printed in Great Britain by Page Bros, Norwich

This book is printed on acid-free paper.

Contents

To Vanessa

Preface

The original project for this book came about as a result of the coincidence of my growing dissatisfaction with radical analyses of Middle East politics at the time of the second Gulf War with David Held's suggestion that I write a short primer on the region's politics. The current book is both more and less than we had envisaged at the outset. It is more in the sense that I soon found that a great deal of rethinking was necessary, both in relation to the particular development of the Middle East and in terms of general social and political theory, in order to grasp the region's development in anything like its full complexity. This study is thus a much more discursive and analytical work than I had originally intended. A certain price has been paid for this in so far as the book provides somewhat less information of a sheerly narrative kind than had been planned. Although this is a loss, my feeling is that the theoretical gains are on the whole worth it.

Throughout the writing of this book I have incurred many debts, both intellectual and personal. My intellectual debts to scholars of the Middle East will be obvious to the reader, and it would be invidious to single out particular influences. However, given the sharpness of some of the criticisms levelled in what follows, I want especially to emphasize how much I have gained from those with whom I strongly disagree.

I have also been lucky to have had the constant advice of Justin Rosenberg. His ability to decipher my arguments for me, and patiently to persuade me that I cannot write the first thing that comes into my head, is as necessary as it is amazing. This would be a far more enigmatic work, to put it politely, without the benefit of his judgement. Paul Cammack and Fred Halliday provided much useful advice on an early essay which rehearsed some of the main themes of the present argument. Ray Bush generously read the entire manuscript shortly before the final revisions were done and suggested many valuable clarifications as well as giving me the benefit of his expertise on Egypt.

At Polity Press, David Held and Gill Motley were as helpful and forbearing of missed deadlines as ever. David also read the manuscript and made many good suggestions for revision. Jennifer Speake did an excellent job at the copy-editing stage.

My cat, Rosa, has lengthened the gestation period of this book by more than I care to admit. I can't always understand her comments, but I'm sure they are intended to be constructive.

Last but by no means least, Vanessa Fox has tolerated and supported my incessant preoccupation with the project for too long. Vanessa (and Rosa) attempted to make me more normal – but once again they did not always succeed. Vanessa also 'waded' through a late draft and did her best to improve the clarity of my writing. Many thanks go to her for much love and support.

Simon Bromley
Sheffield, England

Introduction

The arguments of this book are addressed to a number of different audiences and are conducted on a number of different planes. It is, therefore, necessary to make clear at the outset what it seeks to do and (perhaps as importantly) what it does not attempt. The central argument of what follows is conducted on two fronts. In the first place, I analyse and criticize a range of debates on the character of political and socio-economic development in the Middle East in order to begin the constructive task of defining a new (and I hope better!) approach. These debates include both general theorizations of the region and particular models of Middle East politics. Rather than attempt to provide an exhaustive review of thinking on the Middle East, the selection of debates has been governed by two criteria: first, my sense of the dominant intellectual traditions in contemporary academic writing on the Middle East in the West; and second, contributions which (whether negatively or positively) enable me to address what I take to be the central analytical question – namely, the process of *state formation*.[1] This provides the second, substantive focus of investigation: how do we theorize the linked processes of state formation and capitalist development in the modern world? Any originality that this book might have lies in its attempt to reformulate the central questions involved in

1 As will become clear, I take it for granted that the literature produced by modernization theory and by dependency theory are of little assistance in understanding the Middle East. But since I regard these as now old debates, I do not further rehearse criticisms of them here.

analysing politics in the Middle East, by means of an inquiry into the nature of state formation. For this reason, it is simultaneously an intervention in a set of more general debates in contemporary social and political theory, debates concerned to specify the historical and structural character of modernity. Yoked together, these theoretical and substantive concerns provide the axis around which the constructive analysis is conducted and give the book its concrete focus – the comparative character of state formation and development in the modern Middle East.

Thus this book is both an attempt to rethink Middle East politics and socio-economic development and an intervention in some more general debates about how to understand the social development of the modern world. For reasons that I set out in chapter 1, the study of the modern Middle East is a particularly fertile terrain from which to address the latter. This specific conjunction of the particular and the general is, therefore, deliberate; and it is motivated by a firm belief that theoretical advances can only be reached through substantive investigations, for in the end there can be no other test of a theory than its capacity to provide better and fuller explanations than its rivals.

The special need for new kinds of work on Third World politics has been more widely recognized as the now sterile debates between modernization and dependency theories have run their course. Neither of these models proved adequate, though the latter in particular did inspire a great deal of valuable work. The reason for this failure was simple and obvious: neither was able to develop a coherent theory of the process of state formation. Given the importance of this process for the socio-economic development these theories sought to explain, and given also the centrality of the state to social and material reproduction across most of the Third World, this turned out to be a fatal limitation.

After this book was substantially completed I came across an essay which also argued the need for 'a new analytical tack' with exemplary clarity. Geoffrey Hawthorn noted that Third World politics is still 'waiting for a text', in the sense both that we lack an accepted theory for understanding and explaining it and that few of its ruling elites have found a satisfactory script by which to act. Rather than search for a new theory akin to those that have already failed the test both of inquiry and of practice, Hawthorn suggests that we begin our rethinking by noting that all late-developing societies face two common problems: first, that of consolidating state power rapidly and in difficult circumstances; and second, that of sponsoring socio-economic development in adverse international conditions. Once we recognize this, we can see why models based on societies where these processes have already been accomplished, and which therefore presume a high degree of stability and of institutional development, are unlikely to be very useful. Finally, Hawthorn contends that:

> To grasp the politics of any one Third World country and thereby to make illuminating comparisons between the politics of several is to understand how those in power (and those who seek it) have framed the common ambition to capture and define the social and political space and economically to develop; how they (or their predecessors) have framed constitutions and formed institutions to realise these ends; and the ways in which, imaginatively and practically, these and other more or less institutionalised institutions have actually been used. . . . to see what the two Third World projects are, and to understand the kinds of predicaments which those who try to realise them can produce, is to understand more, and to understand more on these people's own terms, than if one persists with the increasingly anachronistic abstraction of older social theories. (1991:42)

This is very well said. Hawthorn's identification of the two central features of Third World politics – in my terms, state formation and the sponsoring of development – is both accurate and shifts our attention away from a fixed, institutional account of the state towards an examination of the *processes* of state *formation*. But should we leave it there? Hawthorn appears to be unsure. My answer in this book is 'no'. For while Hawthorn is surely right to argue against the kind of theorizing that was modernization and dependency theory, and to plead the case for historical and comparative study, I think that our work has to be grounded in some determinate theory of what the character of modern social development is. Without this I do not see how we can organize the myriad data that history and comparison present to us, how we can fashion specific hypotheses about the causes and consequences of state formation and development and how we can assess the character of Third World politics and economics.

The basic claim of this book, which its constructive and substantive elements seek to explore and to develop, is that by focusing on the historical character of surplus appropriation, by detailing the specific social relations which have governed these processes and by considering their patterns of reproduction and transformation by social forces, we can explain a very large part of what appears to be significant about the development of the modern Middle East. At the outset, this is no more than a working hypothesis. And the only worthwhile basis for assessing this claim is not by recourse to second-order (or meta-theoretical) inquiry, but in terms of whether the theoretical approach and methodology here adopted is consistent and can furnish better and fuller explanations than those currently on offer.

These primary concerns dictate the organization of the book and the selection of questions for inquiry. In chapter 1 we review two alternative traditions of analysis of the Middle East and attempt to develop a third alternative. The two cases subject to critical review are, first, a variant of culturalist accounts in which it is Islam that gives the Middle East its distinctive characteristics, and, second, the kinds of argument found in mainstream social theory deriving from Max Weber. As an alternative to both of these, I suggest that historical materialism provides a better way of approaching the study of the Middle East, enabling us both to avoid essentialist arguments about culture and to move beyond the comparative and descriptive nature of Weberian sociology. On the basis of this new perspective, chapter 2 turns to the substantive task of explaining the internal decline of the Middle East and its dependent incorporation into the capitalist world. This involves an analysis of a number of related issues, separated for the purposes of exposition, including the nature of decline in the Middle East, the process of European expansion into the region, the evolution of the Eastern Question and the project of imperialist and nationalist state formation immediately after the First World War.

With chapter 3 we enter the politics of the modern Middle East, the era of state formation proper as the newly demarcated territories were transformed into states. In order to define the nature of state formation in the region, a number of existing approaches to Middle Eastern politics are critically reviewed and the main aspects of the international environment of the process are sketched. This allows the formulation of a number of guidelines for the substantive investigations to follow. In chapter 4 these studies are organized on a comparative basis as the main features of state formation and dependent development are examined in Turkey, Egypt, Iraq, Saudi Arabia and Iran. In chapter 5 I turn from a comparative to a thematic focus, and attempt to draw out some of the main patterns of change in the region in order to re-address three areas of contemporary debate concerning the state and democracy, the nature of the region's political economy and the place of Islam in Middle East societies. Finally, a short Conclusion draws an end to the discussion with some suggestions as to how the general framework deployed here might be further extended and refined in future research.

As should now be apparent, I have attempted to write neither a history, nor a comparative or thematic treatment of the state and politics in the Middle East, nor even a political economy of the region. There are already a number of very good texts which cover this ground.[2] This also means that some features of the region which have often received extended treatment in these other kinds of study are ignored, for example the Arab-Israeli conflict or the more recent wars in the Gulf. I believe that my analysis has significant implications for the re-evaluation of these questions, but this is not the place to pursue those debates. Instead, I have tried to rethink politics and development in the region at a more general level, by isolating what I take to be the central features of capitalist development in the modern world and by working through the historical particularities of their instantiation, reproduction and transformation in the Middle East. If correct, then the general shift of theoretical and substantive concern argued for here must have implications for the rewriting of the history and the politics not only of the Middle East but also for other parts of the world. In the Conclusion I suggest what some of these implications might be.

2 It is somewhat invidious to identify particular texts, but three might serve as examples: Malcolm Yapp's recent histories (1987 and 1991), Roger Owen's study of state power and politics (1992) and Richards and Waterbury's political economy (1990).

1
Understanding the Middle East

Three ways of understanding the non-European world

Analysis of the societies of the non-European world has generally operated with a series of categories derived from the analysis of the West. This can take one of two different but related forms. In the first case, non-European societies are negatively evaluated *vis-à-vis* the West, and their (lack of) development is explained by listing those features which are taken to account for the dynamism of the West, and then by asserting their absence elsewhere. Simple and clear though this procedure may be, it does not make for good logic or history. Logically, it cannot but assume precisely what it needs to prove: namely, the existence of a single, evolutionary path to modernity. And this in turn imparts a disabling circularity to historical accounts of the *absence* of development in the non-European world. In reply, it might be argued that this path is not an assumption but a fact, and that one cannot prove the existence of something which did not take place – a non-European path to modernity. After all, by definition, the breakthrough into sustained, if not yet sustainable, economic growth only occurred once and it took place in the West, from where it conquered the rest of the world. Whether it would have developed elsewhere at some later date, without the Western impact, we can never know. Irrespective of the logic of this defence, it merely exposes the second problem commonly associated with this style of argument. As it offers a description of non-European societies in terms of what they are *not*, it inevitably provides strictly residual, even circular, accounts of their history. The West developed because it had the following features – and the non-European world remained undeveloped because it lacked them. But what is the evidence that it was *this lack* that accounts for the fortunes of the non-European world? Why, its absence of development. The teleology is complete.

A second form of argument resists positing an evolutionary path to modernity in the West, arguing instead that it is not the absence of epochal change that requires explanation but the 'European miracle'. To some extent, this was the path adopted by Max Weber. More recently, this contingent development has been explained in a number of different ways (see, for example, Jones, 1981; Hall 1985; Mann 1986; and Gellner 1988). Most accounts involve some mixture of factors such as the particular ecology of north-western Europe, the presence of extensive market relations, the existence of a state separate from civil society, the persistence of a competitive state system and the ideological input provided by the Christian Church. What these otherwise varied accounts share is a recognition of the political and cultural embeddedness of economics in pre-modern societies. Before the advent of modernity, there does not exist an institutionally separate realm of production and distribution. That is to say, as Karl Polanyi argued in *The Great Transformation*, in pre-modern societies the 'economy, as a rule, is submerged in . . . social relationships' (1944:46). Understood thus, it is the emergence of a separate, unhindered, purely economic sphere that is in need of explanation.

In Weber's case, it was the process of Occidental rationalization that was both unique and central to modernity. Following the mainstream of European social and political thought from the Renaissance to the Enlightenment, Weber tended to depict the world of the Orient as a form of irrational despotism. His various accounts of 'rationalization' are an attempt to show how calculability, above all economic rationality, emerged in Occidental history. In the fields of science, art, administration, the state and the economy, Weber contrasted the formal rationality of the West with the affective and traditional modes of activity typical in the Orient. The somewhat differently focused work of historical and comparative sociology can be illustrated by reference to John Hall's emblematic study of the causes and consequences of the rise of the West, *Powers and Liberties* (1985). Hall argues that China did not develop because the imperial state placed a capstone on economic advance; that Hindu India stagnated as a result of the hierarchical culture of the Brahmans, which prevented the emergence of an autonomous economy and contributed to political instability; and that in the world of Islam, tribalism combined with a rigid doctrine 'to make political rule alien, transitory and predatory', such that the economy never 'gained real autonomy' and the state never provided market-supporting services for society (1985:110, 101).

In these kinds of account, then, it is the disembedding of the 'economy' and 'rationality' that provides the central narrative of modernity. Theoretically, it is characteristically argued that social power comes in three kinds, based on access to the means of production, violence and cognition – the rule of producers, warriors and clerics – and each of these powers can, in the appropriate circumstances, organize, and be dominant within, the social order as a whole.[1] 'Modernity' begins when production and cognition can free themselves from the restraints imposed by the warriors and the clerics (see, especially, Hall 1985; and Gellner 1988). Once free from political and religious control, 'trade' and the 'market', or rationality and science, function as essentially unilinear vectors of modernity, as if the latter can be adequately understood as a *quantitative* expansion of production and science.

What such perspectives cannot provide is an account of *why* pre-modern societies had the character that they did, and hence they can no more supply an adequate *theory* of the process and results of disembedding.[2] This problem arises directly from the methodology adopted. For if we ask of a given society, why in this case was, say, religion dominant, we are offered a historical description of its dominance in the case in question or, at best, a claim that religion (clerics) provides a wider range of services to society than any other actor. This reply involves an apparently

1 In fact, Mann reckons that there are four types of social power, but this complication does not affect the basic argument.

2 Gellner's argument in *Plough, Sword and Book* (1988) is something of an exception here, in so far as he is at pains to insist on the novelty of the break represented by modernity and seeks to account for the generic stasis of agrarian social orders. Beyond this, Gellner's originality lies in his argument that cognition is also socially embedded, normally serving the functional requirements of communal order and reproduction. Thus Gellner adds that the continuous productive innovation of a market economy presupposes a process of cumulative cognitive expansion, whose discovery is both fortuitous and irreversible. Perhaps surprisingly, many of the main features of Gellner's account of the stagnant character of pre-modern society are consistent with Marx's treatment of pre-capitalist societies in the *Grundrisse* – though Gellner certainly does not share this judgement.

obvious appeal to the facts. But, in fact, it rests on the empiricist *assumption* that, in Maurice Godelier's formulation, 'the visible order of things furnishes a self-evident demonstration of their reasons for being, that their order makes them intelligible' (1986:127). This is such a powerful ideology, one that is so aligned with our every-day commonsense experience, that it takes a considerable effort to see that it is in fact just an assumption, as much in need of proof as any other.

Unlike the synthetic, empiricist approaches sketched above, it was questions like this that preoccupied Karl Marx. Marx did, indeed, ask why the 'economy' occupied a specific position within a given social order, and why it subsisted within other kinds of social relations. And he reasoned that the dominance of a particu-lar type of social relation in any given case could not be accounted for by its general characteristics, properties it possesses in different contexts, but must rather involve some aspect of its functioning specific to each case where it is, in fact, dominant. If we could discover what this aspect was, then we could *explain*, rather than merely *describe*, the dominance of the phenomenon concerned. The hypothesis on which Marx fixed was that in each case the specific functioning of dominant social relations concerned their ability to organize the production of society's material infrastructure. As Godelier has put it: 'social relations dominate the overall function-ing of a society and organize its long-term reproduction *if – and only if – they function at the same time as relations of production, if they constitute the social armature of that society's material base*' (1986:208). Let us emphasize that this is merely a hypothesis, whose validity can only be established empirically and historically. It was never intended by Marx to be used as a supra-historical theory. The crucial difference between this perspective and those sketched above is that it does not begin by privileging Western societies and then move on to explain non-Western development as a deviation. Rather, it applies a common methodology of explana-tion to all social orders.

Islam and modernity

These general considerations about the social theory of the West and non-European societies have a particular relevance in the case of the Middle East. In the first instance, it was through the contrasts drawn between the Orient and the Occident that the self-definition of modernity, as well as the typifications of the Islamic world, were simultaneously accomplished. At root, the West was universal, rational, pluralist and secular, while the Orient wallowed in particularism, tradition, despotism and religious obscurantism. In turn, this self-definition became part of the unwitting conceptual baggage of the contemporary social sciences, especially as mediated through the thought of Max Weber, in so far as modernity came to be formulated in terms of such abstractions as rationalization, science or industrial society. By these and other means, Orientalism – itself one specific component of a more general Eurocentrism – became a seemingly ever-reproduced feature of Western discourse about both itself and the Islamic world. For these reasons, the critique of such thinking must go beyond the mere identification and rejection of Orientalist depictions of the Islamic world. It is not sufficient to discard Orientalism for the apparently universal categories of social science, since the latter are to a considerable extent the mirror image of the former.

Thus, from modernization theory through to more recent musings on post-modernism, much of the social science debate on the character of the Middle East has remained caught in the snares of this formative intellectual history, counterposing Islam and modernity, without ever becoming fully aware of its complicity with the ideological prejudgements of modernity. At its simplest, one argument runs that Islam is either incompatible with or poses a challenge to the institutions and the project of modernity (Ahmed 1992). A somewhat subtler claim to the effect that Islam is compatible with, yet not really of, modernity has also been made (Gellner 1992). How, then, are we to make progress in this deeply contested terrain?

Clearly, a great deal turns on how these assertions implicitly understand the social reality which terms such as 'Islam' and 'modernity' seek to grasp. What are the assumed features of societies described as Islamic? What contrasts are offered to distinguish pre-modern and modern societies? How is the transition from the Islamic to the modern understood? Too often, the answers to such questions, when made explicit, are so crude as to be scarcely credible as serious explanations, and yet too clever to be dismissed as merely ignorant polemics. (After all, arguments about social development being blocked by a poverty of semantic resources would look pretty silly trying to explain the non-emergence of capitalism in ancient Greece. Yet they have acquired a unique respectability in studies of the Middle East.)

This state of affairs has, of course, been the subject of a justly celebrated critique by Edward Said, *Orientalism* (1985). Said defines Orientalism in a number of different ways (Ahmad 1992). On occasion he speaks as if there really was a unified cultural and intellectual tradition in the West, beginning with the Greeks and culminating in the Enlightenment, that could be known through its texts and that has always been bent on subordinating the non-European other. This Orientalism is characterized by a style of thought, a distinctive ontology and epistemology, based on a categorical distinction between 'the Orient' and 'the Occident', which runs from Aeschylus to Marx. The other major definition of Orientalism is in terms of the culture of colonialism.[3] Thus, Orientalism is sometimes related to the set of institutions and practices which accompanied European colonial expansion into the 'Orient', and it can thus be regarded as:

> the corporate institution for dealing with the Orient – dealing with it by making statements about it, authorizing views of it, describing it, by teaching it, settling it, ruling over it: in short, Orientalism as a Western style for dominating, restructuring, and having authority over the Orient. . . . [In this way] The Orient was viewed as if framed by the classroom, the criminal court, the prison, the illustrated manual. Orientalism, then, is knowledge of the Orient that places things Oriental in class, court, prison or manual for scrutiny, study, judgement, discipline, or governing. (1985:3, 41)

In Said's account, then, Orientalism is more a product of a European culture than a knowledge of the Orient, and as such it contrives to produce a new reality adequate to its own ways of knowing. The vicious circle is completed, Said avers, when 'the modern Orient . . . participates in its own Orientalizing' (1985:325); that is to say, when the elite of the Arab-Islamic world becomes ensnared by an Orientalist cultural imperialism then the circular, self-confirming character of its ideology reigns supreme. Both the West and local elites remain impervious to the real voices and aspirations of the region.

---

3 Said in fact offers a third definition: Orientalism as an area of modern academic knowledge, but this is really parasitic on the other two versions.

Notwithstanding its rhetorical power and undoubted importance, Said's account is open to a number of objections. In terms
of his substantive acceptance of the unity of 'Western' culture, Said
replicates the idealist construction of European history, and thereby antedates the origins of Orientalism by failing to distinguish,
on the one hand, the ethnic and religious provincialisms common
to all cultures, and on the other, a specifically Eurocentric 'theory
of world history and, departing from it, a global political project'
(Amin 1989:75; see also Rodinson 1987). Equally, the theoretical
procedure adopted, an analysis of Orientalist 'discourse' – understood in Foucauldian terms as a set of statements with both their
own internal procedures for validating knowledge and their intrinsic
relation to power – inevitably attributes a homogeneity to the
phenomenon that it does not in fact possess, and falsely attributes
an essentialist will to power to Western ways of knowing. The
result is a position that is difficult to distinguish from cultural
relativism, thereby laying Said open to the charge of producing an
'inverted Orientalism'. The way in which this combination of substantive and theoretical propositions leads to a damaging loss of
analytical cogency has been well put by Aijaz Ahmad:

> What gave European forms of these prejudices their special force in
> history, with devastating consequences for the actual lives of count-
> less millions and expressed ideologically in full-blown Eurocentric
> racisms, was not some transhistorical process of ontological obses-
> sion and falsity – some gathering of unique forces in domains of
> discourse – but, quite specifically, the power of colonial capitalism,
> which then gave rise to other sorts of powers. (1992:184)

Finally, and perhaps most damagingly of all for our purposes,
Said's claim that the Orient has been constructed by the West and
that it is now starting to participate in its own Orientalizing can
direct attention away from an analysis of the social and material
reality of Middle East societies. In so doing, it is in some danger
of encouraging an apologetic view in which the forces at play in
the region are seen to operate very largely beyond its control.

Thus, while Said has identified a genuine problem in the study
of the Middle East, *Orientalism* does little to provide us with the
tools with which to build an alternative understanding of the
region itself. What follows is a modest attempt to assist in that
task. To this end, I will begin by outlining the different phases in
the historical relationship between Europe and the Middle East and

by relating this to the main themes of Eurocentric treatments of the Orient. Next, I will critically review a range of writing on the Middle East, moving from (more or less) 'Orientalist' writing to less distorted forms of social and material analysis. And, finally, on the basis of this critique, I will present a historical materialist framework for analysing the development of the Middle East. The aim of this perspective is to refuse the temptation to offer residual and descriptive accounts of non-European history and to avoid essentialist and ahistorical judgements about 'culture'. In this search for a more adequate understanding, we need to avoid the use of such reified terms as 'Islam' and 'modernity' as explanations for social orders putatively identified as Islamic or modern. In their place, we must try to think historically the precise sets of social relations and material practices that constitute and transform these societies. Obviously, these relations and practices are not static, as they only exist in so far as they are contingently reproduced by diverse social forces. It is only a historical study of these structures that will enable us to escape the 'Orientalist' worldview.

From Orientalism to Eurocentrism

Contacts between 'Europe' and the 'East' pre-dated the emergence of Islam and the later consolidation of the Islamic empires. By way of trade and conquest, Europeans had already developed extensive relations with the East. At this time, and in fact for much of the subsequent history of Islamic–Christian interaction, the very terms of the conventional opposition between the 'West' (the Graeco-Roman world and its heritage) and the 'East' (Egypt, Persia and Mesopotamia) are misleading. Not only did the long-distance trade of the tributary social formations involve significant interaction in the Mediterranean basin, but also much of the Greek heritage (as well as the considerable corpus of Islamic scientific knowledge) entered European culture through Latin translations of Arabic texts. Moreover, levels of economic development were comparable across these areas until the late seventeenth century: Asia produced some 70 per cent of world industrial production around 1700 with 60 per cent of the world's population; although standards of living were generally higher in Europe – due to greater agricultural productivity – they were of a similar order, and the variations within each continent were far wider than any aggregate differences between the two.

In medieval Europe, the Western definition of the Islamic world was powerfully shaped by the Crusades. These were 'a manifestation of the Christian Holy War, fought against the infidels in the East, in Spain and in Germany and against heretics, schismatics and Christian lay opponents of the Church for the recovery of property or in defence' (Riley-Smith 1977:74). Legitimated by the papacy, the Crusades began in the eleventh century and declined in the fourteenth, but papal authorizations and grants of crusade indulgences continued until the late eighteenth century. As Rodinson has noted: 'What began as localized warfare grew to a mobilization of all of Europe. Europe joined the Spaniards in their struggle – the Reconquista – and the Normans marched to Italy to fight Islam' (Rodinson 1987:6). In part, this was based on the economic expansion of the Italian commercial cities throughout the Mediterranean world. At first, economic transactions with the Muslim East were carried out through intermediaries such as Greeks, Syrians and Jews, but as commercial relations developed European merchants established direct contact.

At this stage, ethnic and religious provincialisms existed in both the Christian and the Islamic world, but in neither case were these linked either to legitimating theories of world history or to universalist claims about the appropriate forms of social organization. In fact, the threat from the Mongols and the discovery of a pagan world, together with divisions in the Christian world, later led to a greater tolerance of Islam. The subsequent Ottoman advances into Europe briefly revived concern about the Turks (indeed the Knights of St John continued war against the Turks until 1798), but this threat was now seen in primarily secular, rather than theological, terms.

The sharp, theoretical dichotomy between 'West' and 'East' was only formulated in the modern political theory of the Renaissance. And in the subsequent development of European thought during the Enlightenment, in the work of Montesquieu, Smith and Hegel, a composite category of 'oriental despotism' was refined that has subsequently served to account for the different trajectories of 'Occidental' and 'Oriental' history (see Anderson 1974b).[4] For this Orientalism equally defined *both* the backward, stagnant nature of the 'East' *and*,

---

4 In Marx's hands this became the 'Asiatic mode of production', a notion whose theoretical status in Marx's work seems to bear an inverse relationship to the volume of commentary on it. We return to this, thankfully briefly, later.

by contrast, the rational, dynamic character of the 'West'. The origins of 'Orientalism' were thus intimately related to the process of self-definition that accompanied the transition to capitalism in Europe and the ensuing European conquest of the globe.

As to the popular dissemination of such views in the eighteenth century, the translation of *Arabian Nights* by Antoine Galland between 1704 and 1717 was of immense importance:

> the Muslim world no longer appeared the province of the Antichrist, but rather an essentially exotic, picturesque world where fantastic genies could, at their whim, do good or evil. . . . [the liberal sexual attitudes of Islam for men] were now becoming highly exciting to a society increasingly preoccupied with eroticism. (Rodinson 1987:44, 49)

Thereafter, the distinctive emphases of Eurocentric thought have resonated through Western discourse on the East. The Oriental matrix of ancient Greece has been marginalized, Christianity has been perceived as the key to the cultural unity and dynamism of Europe and the Orient itself has been constructed in racist ways based on a religious essentialism (Amin 1989). Itself part of the culture of the modern capitalist world, the specifically Middle East variant of a more general Eurocentrism was rooted in the interactions and conflicts that comprised the fall of the Islamic empires in general and the Ottoman domains in particular. Sharpened by imperialism, and aided by the comparative study of religion and language and a pseudo-scientific biology, the Romantic nationalism within Europe fashioned the idea of '*homo islamicus*, a notion widely accepted even today' (Rodinson 1987:60).

The subsequent imperialist domination of parts of the Ottoman (Turkish) and Safavid (Persian) empires was secured before the discovery of oil. Of course, both 'Islam' and 'oil' have been important in shaping the West's relations with the region, but the pattern of conflict and exploitation is at once broader and deeper than this conventional imagery supposes. As already noted, the modern Middle East was not a region existing outside of, and developing independently from, Europe, only entering the Western orbit with the finding of oil and the formation of the state of Israel. This much is obvious. Yet all too often, the active, determining role of the European powers in the political, economic and cultural formation of the region is neglected in favour of a simplistic emphasis on resources and religion. And while Maxime Rodinson may be right to suggest that the political challenges to Eurocentrism resulting from decolonization, together with the development of a nominally universal social science, betoken a fundamental crisis of such ways of thinking, it is hard not to recognize these assumptions in a great deal of current commentary about the Middle East. Indeed, as I have suggested above and as will be seen in more detail below, the social sciences have embodied not a little of the 'Orientalist' wisdom.

The intransigence of Islamic civilization

For the most part, 'Orientalist' writing about the Islamic world is marked by a pronounced tendency towards culturalist forms of explanation. The significant features of culturalist analysis are threefold: first, it defines culture as the key moment of a social order, the determinant of its evolution; second, it then reifies non-European, in this case Islamic, culture by treating it as an unchanging tradition which condemns the society to relative stagnation; and third, it offers an idealist form of explanation by positing a unique dynamism to the culture of the West, namely Christianity. A notable reinvention of this thesis, cast in a strongly culturalist form, is to be found in the scholarly innovation in Islamic historiography represented by the work of Patricia Crone and Michael Cook (Crone and Cook 1977; Crone 1980; Cook 1983; and Crone and Hinds 1986). These authors have offered a bold and challenging reinterpration of early Islamic history, but in their seminal study of *Hagarism: The Making of the Islamic World* (1977), a sweeping verdict on its subsequent evolution is entered in the following terms:

> Whether the foreign goods were accepted or rejected, the Muslims acknowledged only one legitimate source of their cultural and religious ideals: the Arabia of their Prophet. For barbarians who had conquered the most ancient and venerable centres of human civilisation, this is a *tour de force* without parallel in history; but by the same token the fate of civilization in Islam could only be an exceptionally unhappy one. . . . Islamic history is marked by a striking narrowness and fixity of semantic resources. It was of course compounded from the same trio of classical, Hebraic and barbarian elements as was the history of Europe. But whereas in Europe the three sources remained distinct, Islam rejected the first and fused

the other two; and as a result its resources are heavily concentrated in a single and specifically religious tradition. . . . [And] just as the single source of the Islamic tradition accounts for the austerely unitary character of so much of Islamic history, so also the plurality of sources of the culture of Europe is a precondition for its complex historical evolution. (Cook and Crone 1977:106, 139)

There it is, then; history determined by a fixity of semantic resources. A judgement all the more forced, given that the account offered of the *formation* of the Islamic polity and tradition is considerably more nuanced (see Crone 1980).

The work of the sociologist Bassam Tibbi goes further than most in setting such judgements within a broader theory of modern societies. Tibbi argues that the global spread of the European process of civilization has been based on a Western, scientific and hence technological culture that is different from and alien to the pre-industrial cultures of the non-Western world. Islam, understood as a cultural system, is defined as the religion of the Koran, finally and fully revealed, and omnicompetent in social affairs by virtue of its status as law. In this cultural system, 'Law, in this case the *shari'a*, is the complex of theological and worldly regulations of Islam. Arabic is the medium of articulation in this sociocultural system. Islamic educational institutions [*madrasa*] are in addition the place in which this religiocultural tradition, practised in Arabic, is passed on' (1990:58).

Adopting a structural-functionalist model of social change, Tibbi sees secularization in terms of a *'functional differentiation of the social system* as well as a *redefinition of the sacred* to suit the altered situation' (1990:125). Accordingly, the Islamic societies are portrayed as stagnant from the time of the collapse of the Arab empires in the thirteenth century, and are then seen as responding to an externally imposed, secular dynamic originating in Europe. Tibbi argues that in these circumstances the component elements of Islamic culture – the *shari'a*, Koranic Arabic and the *madrasa* – have all constituted and continue to constitute formidable cultural barriers to social change. For despite the adoption of radical nationalist and socialist, secular ideologies in the period of Middle East state formation, 'there was neither a process of secularization nor a theological reformation' (1990:125).

The asymmetrical contest between the West and the Islamic Middle East is divided by Tibbi into three phases, as follows:

1. . . . [between the 1790s and 1930s, there was] a revitalization of
Islam as an indigenous culture so that it could assert itself against
the expanding new power, Europe . . . [which] had both *modernist*
components (the integration of modern science and technology in
Islam) as well as *millenarian-nativist* components (a return to prim-
eval Islam as a defensive culture against the alien). 2. . . . [between
the two World Wars] new Western-educated elites evolved who
were better able to lead the anticolonial struggle. The ideologies of
secular nationalism and socialism replaced the political ideology
of Islam. 3. . . . [and after 1967] the suppression of secular ideologies in favour of a resurgence of Islam as a political ideology.
(1990:125)

Thus it is the cultural rigidity of Islam in the face of Western-
inspired projects of social transformation and the rapid social
change thereby engendered which accounts for the assertion of
political Islam. And the project of the latter is a populist opposition
to the failure of the secular regimes. In turn, Islamist movements
receive an additional impetus from the international consequences
of the failure of socio-economic development, namely the widening
economic gap between the Middle East and the West.

   Descriptively illuminating as it is, the problems with this account
are twofold. In the first place, while a functional differentiation of
the social structure may well characterize modernity, it does not
explain anything simply to posit such an evolution: the concept of
differentiation is too bland to tell us anything specific about the
changing forms of social relations and material practices. The
precise *social* character of Western development remains obscure.
And if we ask why there was no change in the Islamic world, then
we come to the second difficulty with the argument. The Islamic
world saw no differentiation because of the rigidity of Islam as a
cultural system. But what is the evidence that it was *this* that
blocked social change? The lack of development, of course. As with
culturalist formulations in general, the argument is obviously circular and hence tells us nothing. The contrast drawn may be real
enough, and the thesis of cultural blockage may even be true. But
to establish the truth of the comparison we need independent
argument or evidence relating to the fixity of Islam. No more than
Crone and Cook does Tibbi seek to supply it, and they are not
alone. In fact, this kind of claim has long been the mainstay of
Anglo-American political science and sociology when confronted
with the Middle East. As Lisa Anderson has pointed out in respect

of the former, when the expectations of modernization theory fell
from favour, 'political scientists working on the Middle East took
up the study of "tradition" ' (1990:61).

This cultural and political 'intransigence of Islamic civilization'
(Crone and Cook 1977), as contrasted with the complexity and
dynamism of the Christian case is, of course, a mainstay of European social and political thought. Indeed, though played out in
differing registers, this is the chord that has been struck loudest in
Western discourse on the Middle East. And in one very particular
sense it registers something which is undoubtedly true: namely, that
capitalism developed in the West and conquered the rest of the
world; and that the Islamic empires stagnated, declined and were
overrun. But a great deal turns on precisely how this difference is
reckoned and accounted for.

Broadly speaking, it is possible to identify two ways of explaining
the divergence between the West and the Islamic world. On the
one hand, there is the culturalist position instanced above, which
when explicitly theorized is usually underpinned by a more or less
functionalist model of social order and social change. On the other
hand, there is a tradition of materialist analysis, originating with
Ibn Khaldun, passing through Karl Marx and Max Weber, into the
work of contemporary students of the Middle East. However,
while Marx and Weber to some extent share a common materialism, we shall see that their respective frameworks can be developed
in different directions and with important points of contrast. The
Weberian tradition, itself the point of departure for much comparative sociology, represents an ambiguous departure from the
culturalist position. And it is to the nature of this development that
I now turn.

Islam in the path of rationalization

We have seen that culturalist accounts of Islam and the West are
both idealist and circular, instances of the first kind of analysis of
non-European societies noted at the outset. The work of Max
Weber and Ernest Gellner, by contrast, is on an altogether different
plane. While their analyses are not without problems, which I shall
try to explore below, Weber and, especially, Gellner provide challenging accounts of the place of Islam in the modern world.
Though culturalist strains persist in their arguments, materialist

explanations are also to be found. However, notwithstanding the considerable insight of Weber and Gellner's work, a satisfactory explanation of the place of the Islamic world in modernity eludes both thinkers. The reason for this, I will argue, lies in both their inability to break with abstract, ahistorical treatments of 'Islam' and 'modernity' and their refusal to theorize (as opposed to describe) the changing forms taken by social relations in different kinds of society. Weber and Gellner, then, represent the second kind of analysis of non- European societies noted at the beginning of this chapter.

Max Weber, rationality and Islam

On one reading of his *œuvre*, it was Max Weber who definitively fixed (for the modern social sciences) the question of the distinctiveness of the West in cultural terms. In his Preface to the *Gesammelte Aufsatze zur Religionssoziologie* Weber asked: 'What chain of events in the West and only here led to the appearance of cultural phenomena which nevertheless – as we at least like to believe – developed in a way which was of universal importance and value?' Weber never offered a settled, clear and unambiguous answer to this question. Moreover, his scattered writings on rationality and rationalization – generally taken to form the central theme of his comparative sociology – seem to imply many sites of rationalization, each with its own distinct mode of rationality. Despite this, Rogers Brubaker has suggested that what Weber calls the 'specific and peculiar rationalism of Western culture' is 'not simply a conceptual mosaic' (1984:30). Brubaker identifies three themes which span Weber's discussion of rationality: first, rational conduct is based on the knowledge provided by systematic and empirical science and its application in technology; second, a rationalized social order is characterized by the '*Versachlichung der Gewaltherrschaft*', the 'objectification' or 'depersonalization' of power; and third, rationality involves control understood as the calculated application of rules in fixed procedures.

Furthermore, Weber did not give a univocal answer as to the origins of Occidental rationality. At times, as in *The Protestant Ethic and the Spirit of Capitalism*, he argued that Protestantism, and especially its ascetic sects, fosters a premium on public conduct towards, as well as a psychological impulse for, orderly, sober, this-worldly activity; in short, the Protestant ethic generates the spirit of capitalism (Marshall 1982). On other occasions, Weber offered a more eclectic account of the institutional preconditions for the operation of market rationality (Collins 1986). Conventionally, the two strands have been reconciled by noting Weber's (highly debatable) claim that without the additional spark provided by the (Protestant) spirit of capitalism, the mere presence of its institutional preconditions nowhere gave rise to capitalism in its modern form. In either case, however, it is capitalism that is seen as the main driving force for rationalization in the modern world, and Weber's model of capitalist rationality (itself taken from neoclassical economics) serves as the template by which other forms of rationalization are typified. This comes close to rendering the whole case for Protestantism circular.

In general, as Derek Sayer has argued, Weber:

> in effect . . . generalizes Marx's model of alienation with the result that capitalism becomes a special case – if a uniquely 'fateful' one – of a more encompassing 'expropriation' which is the foundation of the discipline which sinews the modern subject into the 'machines' of modern society. Severance of the material means of a given human activity from its agents (which, just as for Marx, implies their isolation as solitary individuals) is the generic basis for all institutional rationalization. (1991:135)[5]

Overall, then, Weber's writings appear to oscillate between an attempt to define the 'specifically constructed' but universally significant '*rationalism*' of Western culture and a comparative historical approach concerned to explain the specificity of modern *capitalism*. Prophet of universal rationalization, or synthetic, comparative historian: these have been the poles around which interpretations of Weber's sociology have turned. What is less ambiguous is Weber's statement that his methodological device of the 'ideal-type' consciously emphasizes 'what is and was in opposition to Western cultural development'. Accordingly, the typification of the Oriental is, in large measure, the mirror image of the Occidental.

The result of this is that Weber's substantive categories of historical explanation prejudge what needs to be explained (see Mommsen 1974 and Hindess 1977). For their construction as ideal

---

5 Sayer does not appear to recognize that by generalizing a historical argument, Weber is in danger of reifying the process of social change that he seeks to explain.

types builds into concepts which are meant to be explanatory features which are also taken to describe the Occidental world. This difficulty carries over into Weber's studies of religion: on the one hand a counterpointed footnote to *The Protestant Ethic and the Spirit of Capitalism*, or on the other a genuinely comparative study. Anthony Giddens has noted that Weber's studies of religion 'were intended as analyses of divergent modes of the rationalization of culture, and as attempts to trace out the significance of such divergencies for socio-economic development' (1976:5), but whether the characterization of such modes is truly comparative or merely a set of negative, residual contrasts with ascetic Protestantism remains unclear.

Weber argued that Hinduism is ascetic but 'other-worldly', hence it could not provide an ethic oriented to worldly activity; that Confucianism is 'this-worldly' but not ascetic, thus it could not direct worldly activity towards a systematic calculation of gain; and that only Protestantism is ascetic and this-worldly, and thereby able to rationalize worldly activity towards capitalist ends. The religion about which Weber had least to say was Islam, but what he did say is none the less extremely interesting (see, especially, Turner 1974). Islam, on Weber's account, is this-worldly but not ascetic. At the level of values and belief, of culture, Weber argued that the ethic of the Koran was accommodating towards a hedonistic attitude, especially towards women and property, and thus that no ascetic, this-worldly ethic could emerge to direct economic activity towards rationally calculable (hence capitalist) ends.[6] On this account, the obstacle to rational, capitalist development lay in the beliefs, and hence the worldly activities, of practising Muslims. (This last, incidentally, is a judgement which later scholars in other ways much influenced by Weber, for example Ernest Gellner, have resoundingly opposed.)

By contrast, however, and in practice representing the main emphasis of his treatment of Islam, Weber also offered an explanation of Islamic societies based on the character of prebendal feudalism and patrimonial bureaucracy, or 'Sultanism'. This materialist account stands independently of, and is not fully of a piece with, the culturalist account (Turner 1974). In this materialist version of the argument, it was the character of patrimonial domination in

---

6 These characteristics are in turn held to derive, not from Islamic monotheism, but from the tribal and warrior-like nature of the social matrix in which Islam was forged.

the Abbasid, Mamluk and Ottoman empires which frustrated the development of rational, capitalist forms of economic activity. According to Weber, the central contradiction of 'Sultanism' was as follows: the more the ruler relied on mercenaries or slaves (prebendal feudalism), the more they could subjugate the masses and extract perquisites of office; the more such overlords demanded, the more the ruler had to exploit the masses while posing as the people's leader; and thus charismatic protests against central rule were endemic. Leaders came and went with some regularity but the underlying structure remained intact. The insecurity brought about by the devolution of tributary power in the form of tax-farming resulted in a decline of the monetary economy and a general ruralization. Investment in *waqf*s was a typical expedient, given the insecurity of property rights, since the ruler could only touch these by disregarding the *shari'a* and the *ulema*. Once Ottoman expansion was stopped by the Safavids, the Portuguese and the Russians and the Hapsburgs, then parasitic exploitation set in. This was aggravated by the devaluation of the currency once Spanish silver and gold entered the eastern Mediterranean. Thereafter, the janissaries and the *ulema* opposed all reform in the Ottoman Empire, resulting in stagnation.

Here, Weber is offering a materialist account of the stagnation of the Islamic empires and their inability to generate capitalist forms of activity. This is so in two senses. To begin with, Weber is concerned to explore the role of Islam, understood as a set of social practices, in the reproduction of the social order as a whole. Islam is seen as giving shape and form to processes inherent in patrimonial, agrarian societies. And secondly, the specific cultural features of Islam are themselves explained not by reference to an unchanging 'tradition' but by the totality of its social location. As Turner has put it: in 'patrimonial conditions of social control, the urban piety of Islam was not the product of calculability and rational mastery of life; it was almost wholly geared to the problems of personal security and communal order' (1974:110).

To be sure, the thrust of Weber's case is still that patrimonial domination, buttressed by sacred law and justice dispensed by the *ulema*, is arbitrary and 'irrational'. In this sense, the specific content of Weber's account of Islam again tends towards a residual form in which it is negatively contrasted with the conditions for rationalization found only in the West. As Turner has so ably shown:

> At the centre of Weber's view of Islamic society is a contrast be-
> tween the rational and systematic character of Occidental society,
> particularly in the field of law, science and industry and the arbit-
> rary, unstable political and economic conditions of Oriental civiliza-
> tions, particularly the Islamic. (1974:14)

In its minor key, Weber's argument attributes this difference to the
Islamic ethic and thus stands squarely in the culturalist and essentialist tradition noted above. But its major themes are developed in
a materialist key, seeking to describe the differing character of
the social and material reproduction of society in the West and the
Islamic world. The organizing framework of the materialist strand
of analysis is that of the development of Occidental rationality, and
its major carrier, modern capitalism, as contrasted with the stagnation inherent in Oriental forms of social organization. In other
words, Weber does not explain but describes Oriental forms
and then only in contrast with the West. Subsequent treatments
influenced by Weber have not wholly escaped these tensions.

Ernest Gellner and Muslim society

The coexistence of culturalist and materialist strands of analysis,
which we met in Weber, can be seen most clearly in the bold and
striking attempt to theorize the nature of the Islamic world offered
by Ernest Gellner. Whereas Weber wrote comparatively little on
Islam and was principally concerned with its fate in the settled
agriculture of the Ottoman empire, Gellner has written extensively
on Islam and has focused on the nature of *Muslim Society* (1981)
in the arid zones of the Maghreb. Gellner's account, and indeed
his more general philosophy of history in which it is couched, owes
many of its questions, if not its answers, to Weber. But his more
immediate sources for the study of Islam are Emile Durkheim's
theory of *The Division of Labour in Society* (1893) and *The
Elementary Forms of Religious Life* (1912) and the historical sociology of Ibn Khaldun.

Thus, before we turn to the work of the most formidable expo-
nent and developer of Weber's legacy, let us first sketch the main
ideas of the fourteenth-century Arab thinker Ibn Khaldun. Where
Weber offers an account of the cyclical contradictions of Sultanism
based upon the instability of patrimonial rule and doctrinally based
justice, Ibn Khaldun locates the unstable, circular character of

Islamic history in the coexistence of pastoral tribalism with urban rule. For all his theological obscurantism, Ibn Khaldun offers an account of history understood as 'information about human social organization . . . [whose guiding principle is] that differences of condition among people are the result of the different ways in which they make their living' (1967:35, 91).

In the world of medieval North African states of which Ibn Khaldun writes in his introduction to history, *The Muqaddimah* (1377), the polity was not territorially fixed but was rather an urban centre based on trading routes, around which a degree of control over the surrounding tribes might be exercised. While the urban merchants possessed estates, these were not large, as their ability to appropriate land was limited by the power of the tribes and the rights of the sovereign. The customary powers of the tribes gave them usufructory rights over the land, which was granted as a charter of *iqta'* to overlords who could raise taxes, but could neither control labour nor administer justice. As Ibn Khaldun pointed out, the dominance of a pastoral economy lay behind the persistence of the tribes. Pastoral life involves the regular movement of herders, and hence co-operation between families; the carrying of arms, and hence the need for self-defence groups; and thus the need for tribal federation.

Because the *iqta'* system did not devolve into a structure of seigneurial privilege, tribal leaders were simply *primus inter pares* with no *de jure* rights. Ibn Khaldun distinguished between 'the rural population, the people of the *bled* – a category which includes both nomads and sedentary farmers – and the townspeople and farmers who live near the towns' (Lacoste 1984:67). Where a temporary acquisition of authority or power, and with it a tribal federation, occurs, a tribe may develop *'asabiya*, or solidarity, 'in which the chieftain has succeeded in asserting his dominance. Only tribes which are no longer egalitarian and which have developed *'asabiya* constitute a political force capable of making their chieftains heads of states' (Lacoste 1984:106). With rulers denounced for impiety by the *ulema*, such a chieftain can overthrow a weakened regime and institute a new one. However, the pacific, trade-based nature of urban life inevitably leads in time to a weakening of the tribal-supported polity and a growing independence of the surrounding tribes. The dynastic cycle may then be repeated by the emergence of a new challenger.

Gellner's own argument begins in familiar culturalist style:

Islam is the blueprint of a social order. It holds that a set of rules exists, eternal, divinely ordained, and independent of the will of men, which defines the proper ordering of society. This model is available in writing; it is equally and symmetrically available to all literate men, and to all those willing to heed literate men. These rules are to be implemented throughout social life. Thus there is in principle no call or justification for an internal separation of society into two parts, of which one would be closer to the deity than the other. . . . [The specific character of this blueprint identified by Crone and Cook above derives from the fact that] the relatively mundane and secular Jewish preoccupation with the regulation of social life, based on human legal wisdom rather than divine authority, when fused with the God-centred, unificatory theology-mindedness of Christianity, produced the characteristically Muslim divinely sanctioned and God-centred legalism. (1981:1, 2)

What, then, is the social significance of Islam? For Gellner the answer lies in the fact that 'by firmly closing the door, in principle, to further additions to the Revealed doctrine, [Islam] enormously strengthens the hand of those who have access to the delimited truth through literacy and who use it as a charter of legitimacy' (1981:23). However, in pastoral conditions, this urban, scriptural Islam must needs be coexist with the folk Islam of the tribal world analysed by Ibn Khaldun. The materialist aspect of the account emerges here: for the mobile character of pastoral means of production, together with the armed character of the tribes, means that central authorities cannot 'control or disarm the countryside' (1981:20). In this illiterate, rural environment of warring segmentary groups and tribes, religion 'is highly Durkheimian, concerned with the social punctuation of time and space, with season-making and group-boundary-marking festivals' (1981:52). Yoked together, the result is the near-permanent cyclical course of Islamic history described by Ibn Khaldun, a movement from central authority supported by a tribal federation, through urban impiety and degeneracy to the crisis which renews the impulse of tribal revolt, and thus instantiates a new central authority. For Gellner 'the fusion of scripturalism and pastoralism, the implication of each pushed *a outrance* in one continous system, *is* the classical world of Islam' (1981:24).

Gellner has often been criticized for over-generalizing on the basis of the Maghreb. But in fact he is at pains to stress that he is theorizing the institutional *differentiae* of Islam in the arid zone, and that where the weight of a settled peasantry engaged in agriculture was greater, as in the Ottoman heartlands, the polity could achieve a greater autonomy from the tribes and the *ulema*. (The full implication of this, I will argue, is that talk of a unitary 'Islam', whether High or Low, is extremely problematic. But this is not a conclusion that Gellner is drawn to.)

On the basis of his model of Muslim society, Gellner has advanced a striking and heterodox claim about the fortunes of Islam in modernity. Modernity is understood as industrial society based upon a continuous, cumulative expansion of scientific (and hence technological) knowledge. The course of human history is a (Durkheimian and Weberian) story of the fortuitous but irreversible shift from magic to religion to science, as well as the accompanying transformations in the division of labour (Gellner 1988). Modern society is thus inherently egalitarian, at least in cultural matters, involving the general literacy and mobility of the entire population. In these circumstances, what is so remarkable about Islam is the manner by which its division into High and Low forms has facilitated its renewal within the modern world. As state formation and development have together eroded the social base of folk Islam, so a return to the 'pure' (High) faith acts as a surrogate form of nationalism. For Low Islam is hierarchical and ecstatic, while High Islam is egalitarian and scriptural. The avowal of the latter is thus congruent with the requirements of an industrial society: High Islam's egalitarian and scriptural features are a functional equivalent for Protestantism's worldly and ascetic qualities. Gellner's conclusion is stark:

> Things may yet change in the future. But on the evidence available so far, the world of Islam demonstrates that it is possible to run a modern, or at any rate modernizing, economy, reasonably permeated by the appropriate technological, educational, organization principles, *and* combine it with a strong, pervasive, powerfully internalized Muslim conviction and identification. A puritan and scripturalist world religion does not seem necessarily doomed to erosion by modern conditions. It may on the contrary be favoured by them. (1992:22)

Indeed, Gellner has some fun imagining us admiring Ibn Weber's *The Kharejite Ethic and the Spirit of Capitalism* had the Arabs won at Poitiers. For 'by various obvious criteria – universalism, scripturalism, spiritual egalitarianism, the extension of full participation in the sacred community not to one, or some, but to *all*, and the rational systematisation of social life – Islam is, of the three great Western monotheisms, the one closest to modernity' (1981:7).

Now, the overall explanatory structure of Gellner's argument is rather difficult to untangle. On occasions, his formulations suggest a culturalist account in which 'Islam is a distinctive historical totality which organizes various aspects of social life' (Asad 1986:3). Different worldviews (High/pure and Low/folk) are loosely linked to different forms of life, but the explanatory weight rests primarily at the cultural level. This interpretation is also congruent with his account of the structure of human history in *Plough, Sword and Book* (1988), which can be read as an investigation of the miraculous emergence of the scientific form of cognition and its impact on the transition from agrarian poverty and violence to the relative comforts of an affluent, industrial society. The stress on the character of Muslim belief in the one is matched by the focus on cognition of the other. As evidence in favour of this reading, we might note that in discussing Islam Gellner stresses the God-centred legalism of the faith, the absence of a sphere reserved for Caesar, its separation into High and Low variants and its resistance to secularization.

However, in each of these cases, Gellner also suggests the outlines of a materialist explanation for the phenomenon concerned. For example, having outlined the salient features of Muslim society in the arid zone, Gellner immediately adds that:

> The rotation-within-an-immobile-structure is perhaps inherent in a certain general ecology, or mode of production and reproduction if you prefer. . . . The pattern as such is not necessarily Islamic: it seems inherent in this kind of ecology. It was found in the arid zone before Islam. . . . Islam provided a common language and thus a certain smoothness for a process which, in a more mute and brutalistic form, had been taking place anyway. (1981:31, 32)

Equally, the division of Islam into High and Low forms – its 'really central, and perhaps most important, feature' (1992:9) – is but a particular, if exaggerated, case of the general social function of literacy in agrarian social orders (see, generally, Goody 1986). Agrarian surpluses allow for the formation of a ruling class, but the unified organization of such a class is always precarious, given its limited ability to penetrate and organize society. In situations of conflict, which are of course endemic to agrarian and pastoral society, and given the unpredictability of outcomes, the alignment of loyalties greatly depends on the legitimacy of the contestants. The conclusion is inevitable: 'This in turn gives considerable indirect power to those who, through a mixture of literacy and ritual competence, possess the near-monopoly of legitimacy-ascription' (Gellner 1988:99).

Moreover, Gellner does not argue that all modernization in Muslim societies is *with* Islam. On the contrary, he argues that a return to a purified, High Islam occurs where colonial rule 'tolerated or utilised unregenerate traditional forms' (1981:58). For here the pure faith can act as a form of reactive nationalism. But in those cases where religion had close ties with the old, declining order – classically in the Ottoman case – then modernization is likely to be *against* Islam, as it was in Kemalism. Finally, where a return to the 'pure', literate, egalitarian faith or the development of a secular alternative is blocked, where the world of Ibn Khaldun persists and cannot be disposed of peacefully, and in conditions of uneven development in an industrializing world, then the social tragedy of the contemporary Middle East is the likely result.

Now, in each of these cases, the locus of the explanation seems to have shifted away from the character of the faith to the relation of the modernizing forces to the indigenous centres of power, to the state and to foreign colonists. The specific features of Islam, *qua* belief, are no longer centre-stage. Thus, the *same* faith can issue in three *different* outcomes: Islamic modernism, secular nationalism (Kemalism) or social conflict and violence. These in broad outline are the options for Muslim society in modernity sketched for us by Gellner.

In case it needs saying, I am not arguing that the specific characteristics of Islamic belief are irrelevant. Rather, I am arguing the need for a historical and materialist approach to the study of Islamic culture of the kind that Gellner himself sometimes provides. Let us give Gellner the final word here, warning us against:

> a certain kind of culture-talk. Now it is indisputable that what men do and endure generally 'has meaning' for them; that these meanings come as parts of loose systems, which are tied both to languages and to institutions; and that in some way or other, these systems must be sustained by the collectivities of men who share them (or partly share them), and, in turn, that they make their contribution to the perpetuation of the said collective. . . . [But] such culture-talk

tends merely to indicate a problem, not a solution. . . . It is as true
that we manipulate social meanings as that we talk prose, but we
should not let this idea go to our heads, and quite especially ought
not to suppose that we have a theory when we merely possess a
style. (1981:218)

In sum, Gellner's account of Islam differs in a number of important
respects from that of Weber. Weber concentrated on the agrarian
Islamic empires, Gellner has been more interested in the pastoral
world of the Maghreb. Weber stressed that rationalization inevitably spelled disenchantment, Gellner has argued the potential congruence of urban Islam with modernity. Yet in the end, it is perhaps
the similarities which are more important: a similar set of questions
and ambiguities threads both discussions. Both oscillate between
culturalist and materialist forms of argument, and both tend
towards descriptive rather than theoretical treatments of social
order. Thus both have a tendency to define the pre-modern and
the modern in terms of a set of binary oppositions which stand in
for the work of substantive, historical theorization. Weber opposed
the Occident to the Orient, while Gellner counterposes the static,
segmented world of pastoralism and agrarian society to the organic
interdependence and mobility-cum-literacy of industrial society.
Consequently, as with Weber's notion of rationalization, so with
Gellner's theory of industrial society, the actual social content of
such terms as 'segmented' and 'industrial' remains indeterminate
and untheorized.

Historical materialism and the Middle East

We have now seen how the work of both Weber and Gellner
appears to offer the basis for a materialist account of 'Islam' and
'modernity', but then fails to break with the ahistorical use of
culturally specific concepts. To be sure, knowledge in the social
sciences must proceed by way of the search for comparisons, what
Runciman has called 'suggestive contrasts' (1983). But if we are to
avoid building into our explanations that which needs to be explained, or to move beyond historical description, such contrasts
should act as empirical controls on our generalizations, and not be
employed as putatively explanatory concepts. This involves drawing a clear distinction between the commonsense terms we use to

describe the institutional alignments of a social order (e.g. 'economy', 'state', 'religion') and the theoretical concepts by which these are explained.

Furthermore, in any concrete explanation, the generic categories of our theory can only be specified empirically and, therefore, historically. For the *general* concepts of an explanatory framework refer to a particular class of phenomena – say, production relations in the case of Marxism – not, at least until further defined, any empirical particulars. Thus the necessary historicity of our basic theoretical concepts follows from the fact in order to apply them to the actual task of explanation they require further (empirical) definition. Our theory may hypothesize that certain kinds of social relations are primary, but what those relations are in any given instance is a question of fact. Put differently, this amounts to saying that we must apply a *common* theoretical framework, using an empirically open methodology, to *different* societies.

As we have already noted, Marxism offers one candidate methodology for such historical explanation. By focusing on the ways by which the socially organized material interchange with nature is configured, and hence on how a socially produced surplus is appropriated, circulated and utilized within society, historical materialism suggests that we will be able to explain its principal features. It follows from the foregoing that the *only* test of this procedure is whether the explanation arrived at is better than its rivals. Unfortunately, Marx's substantive writings do not always consistently follow these protocols, and his comments on precapitalist societies are not without the markings of their time.

On the one hand, some of what Marx (and Engels) wrote was as much under the sway of Occidental triumphalism as anything penned by Weber. Certainly, the notion of an 'Asiatic' mode of production has precious little theoretical or empirical warrant, offering merely a 'generic residual category for non-European development' (Anderson 1974b:494). In so far as Weber contrasted Occidental rationality with what went before, he shared Marx's sense of the radical gulf separating capitalism off from *all* previous forms of human society. And Marx was certainly capable of rendering this difference in the then dominant European intellectual vernacular.

On the other hand, the implication of Marx's general methodological and theoretical position, as well as the force of most of his concrete analysis, is that such binary oppositions as 'Occidental' versus 'Oriental', 'segmented' versus 'industrial', 'West' versus 'East' and, perhaps above all, 'traditional' versus 'modern' cannot adequately grasp the *historical* character of modernity, since they are silent as to its specific social content. Despite superficial appearances to the contrary, Marx's method therefore remains much more firmly rooted in an investigation of concrete historical questions than that of either Weber or Gellner. For this reason the charge of Orientalism laid at the door of historical materialism, a claim made by Said of Marx's writings on India, is entirely wide of the mark. As Ahmad has again detailed with such exemplary clarity, in Marx's thought:

> The idea of a certain progressive role of colonialism was linked . . . with the idea of a progressive role of capitalism as such, in comparison with what had gone before, within Europe as much as outside it. . . . Marx's statement [on the impact of British rule in India] follows not *anecdotally* from Goethe or German Romanticism, nor discursively from an overarching 'Orientalism', but *logically and necessarily* from positions Marx held on issues of class and mode of production, on the comparative structuration of the different pre-capitalist modes, and on the kind and degree of violence which would inevitably issue from a project that sets out to dissolve such a mode on so wide a scale. . . . [Marx's argument] was designed to carve out a position independent both of the Orientalist-Romantic and the colonial-modernist. (1992:225, 230, 235)

Marx on the character of modernity

Everyone knows that Marx placed his analysis of capitalism at the centre of his understanding of modernity. Yet if the recurrent charges of reductionism and economic determinism are taken at face value, they tend to suggest that this fact is almost as widely misunderstood. For Marx conceived of capitalism not as a type of economy but as a form of *society*, based upon novel forms of social relations and hence of the social itself. Derek Sayer, who has done so much to make plain this theme in Marx's work (1983, 1987 and 1991), notes that:

> These forms of modern sociality include what is, for the first time in human history, conceivable as 'the economy', and its essential counterpart, 'the state'. Both rest on a radical transformation of the character of social relationships and the nature of social power, in brief, from what Marx called relations of personal dependency to

relations which are 'impersonal' and mediated by 'things': money, bureaucracy. (1991:2)

For our purposes, it is important to note two general, systemic features of the social order governed by capitalist relations of production. The first distinctive feature of capitalist society is the mediation of social power by direct control over things rather than over persons. Compared to non-capitalist societies, power takes the form of a generalized subjection of all individuals to such abstract features as the rule of law, money and bureaucracy. In the second place, as Robert Brenner (1986) has cogently argued, it is only under capitalist production relations that producers must sell their output on the market in order to secure their own reproduction, and it is therefore only under capitalism that competition acts as a coercive force to bring about continuous improvements in efficiency.

According to Marx, the 'abstraction of the political state' from particularistic communal forms of regulation comes into being only with the establishment or constitution of a modern civil society based on bourgeois forms of property. In this *burgerliche Gesellschaft* the social forms of both private and public power involve the ordering of society by relations among the impersonal forms of 'money' and 'law', private property and the bureaucratic state. Jurisdiction, administration and coercion become separated from the personal power of a possessing class and centralized in a universal, public power – the 'purely political' state. The social forms of the 'market' and the 'sovereign' state are thus *both* specific to the capitalist mode of production. Marx further emphasizes that it is only the generalized separation of the direct producers from the means of production, together with the constitution of these means as 'private property', which enables the bourgeoisie to constitute its class rule through the possession of 'things'; all earlier ruling classes required some form of 'political' domination over subordinate classes.

The other, more familiar, side of this process is the separating out of a distinct sphere governed by the writ of private property, which itself represents the privatization of customary, public forms of political power (Meiksins Wood 1981). This historical constitution of the 'economic' as a separate, institutionally distinct realm of alienable property, in which commodification has been generalized, and hence through which capital can circulate and expand by directly controlling labour and appropriating the surplus, is the process Marx described as primitive accumulation. And as Marx noted, even if he did not explore it in much detail, the process of capitalist state formation is an integral component of this set of changes.

Thus, as Marx formulated it, the main story of modernity has been the emergence of the distinctive social form of the capitalist state, alongside the unique mobility of capitalist economic development. Marx distinguished the quantitative dynamism of capitalism from all pre-capitalist modes as well as highlighting its qualitative difference from all personalized systems of production and domination. The differentiation of both the 'economy' and the 'state', and with them the world market and the system of states, as distinct institutional orders are accounted for by the emergence and consolidation of capitalist relations of production. It is, therefore, the historical spread of these new types of social relations which form the organizing theme of Marx's account of 'modernity'. The global spread of capitalist society, in turn, set in train a process of uneven development; and the resulting penetration of modern capitalism into backward formations, together with state-sponsored attempts to compete with the most advanced metropoles, gave to subsequent development a combined character.

In sum, these formulations suggest a third way of approaching the questions of 'Islam' and 'modernity'. In the first place, historical materialism offers a working hypothesis and methodology which does not build culturally specific judgements into its explanatory concepts. What 'Islam' or 'modernity' is in any given instance cannot be a matter of ahistorical stipulation. And secondly, Marx's application of historical materialism to the analysis of modernity suggests that the latter is best grasped in terms of the development and uneven consolidation of certain historically specific sets of social relations, as well as the distinct social forms, forces and struggles that these give rise to.

An outline history of the Middle East

'Islamic' society exhibited a number of distinctive features that marked it off from European feudalism, on the one hand, and from the tributary structures of Rome and China, on the other. These differences did not derive from Islam but the latter came to play an important role in articulating their empirical particularities.

While civilization, with its attendant class division, city-states, long-distance trade, literacy and increasingly unified cosmologies, had first emerged in Mesopotamia on the basis of a surplus provided by settled agriculture, the poverty of the basic ecology and material development in Arabia precluded any similar development. The contrast was sharp and has been well summarized by Ira Lapidus:

> Whereas the imperial world was predominantly agricultural, Arabia was primarily pastoral. While the imperial world was citied, Arabia was the home of camps and oases. Whereas the imperial peoples were committed to monotheistic religions, Arabia was largely pagan. While the imperial world was politically organized, Arabia was politically fragmented. . . . From the beginning of camel domestication and the occupation of the central Arabian desert in the twelfth and thirteenth centuries B.C., until the rise of Islam in the seventh century, the balance between parochial, local elements and the unifying forces of religion and empire lay heavily on the side of small, relatively isolated communities. Families and clans, often pastoralists and camel herders, and the confederations built upon them, were the basic units of society. (1988:11–13)

The obverse of this lack of progression was that the Arabs 'enjoyed an ethnic and cultural homogeneity quite without parallel in Central Asia or Europe' (Crone 1980:24). In this environment, what Muhammad did was to appropriate for the Arabs the monotheist primacy claimed by the Jews, thereby effecting an explosive fusion of Islamic monotheism and Arab tribal politics (Cook 1983).

During Muhammad's life, Arab power consisted in little more than a coalition of nomadic conquerors held together by Islam and the tribute of plunder. On the death of the Prophet (632), however, the very existence of an Islamic polity was put in question. Secessionist tribes and rival prophets challenged Muhammad's order. To begin with, *ad hoc* tribal federations organized the military and administrative structures of the early Islamic polity, its internal unity secured by the booty from external expansion. The Umayyad caliphate (a state based on a federation of Arab tribes) set out from Mecca and rapidly conquered much of the Middle East, swept through parts of North Africa to reach Spain and France in the West, and through Persia to arrive at India in the East. Contrary to a common assertion that it was the ideological cohesion of Islam which enabled it to overcome these empires, the evidence strongly supports the view that imperial decay was a precondition for, not an effect of, Islamic expansion (see Hodges and Whitehouse 1983 and Hourani 1991). The collapse of the Roman empire in the West had paved the way for the eventual emergence of feudalism, but in the East the pattern of development was altogether different. The retention of an independent peasantry and more established urban power meant that no feudalism was ever established in Byzantium. The more centralized, militarized Byzantine empire successfully resisted Arab sieges of Constantinople (674–8 and 717–18) and, under the Macedonian dynasty (867–1025), drove the Arabs back.

Thus checked by Byzantium, and also by the Franks under Charles Martel at Tours and Poitiers (732), Umayyad rule (661–750) was displaced by the Abbasid dynasty (750–1258) as the centre of Islamic power moved from Damascus to Baghdad. Though vibrant internally, the Persian rule of the Abbasid caliphate had itself dissolved by the middle of the tenth century. During the Umayyad period, a tribal aristocracy, the *ashraf*, constituted the link between governors and governed. Under the Abbasid reorganization, the polity mutated in two directions. On the one hand, the bureaucracy of the Abbasid period, which was increasingly backed by servile and client forces, 'was hugely expanded, fiscal and military governorships began to be separated, and an elaborate espionage system was set up to facilitate central control' (Crone 1980:62). On the other hand, the local notables withdrew from political influence into landed and commercial wealth and religious learning. Abbasid rule soon broke down as governors competed for control over the caliphate and as slave regiments confronted one another. The distribution of *iqta'* and tax farming further compounded the problem, and by 935 only Baghdad remained under central control.

An era of independent succession states followed (945–c.1220), after which Mongol invasions coursed through the Islamic world for four decades. Now expelled from Europe, Islamic rule was to be confined to the Middle East until the Ottoman advance of the fourteenth century. In the East, there was a succession of nomadic empires as the collapse of Abbasid power opened the frontiers to the Turkish peoples of inner Asia; in the West, the Fatamids ruled in Egypt, and Byzantium, Latin crusaders and the Seljuqs sought to conquer. During this time, the social structure of the Islamic world underwent a series of profound transformations. In conditions of drastic economic regression, the arrival of a political elite of nomadic and slave warlords, allowed the consolidation of the new communal religious notability.

Another Islamic resurgence, which was eventually to issue in the Ottoman empire, had started in the eleventh century when an integration of Arab tribes and Turkish cavalry established Seljuq rule in Iraq, Syria and Iran; it confronted, and successfully contested, a now declining Byzantine power. Internally stagnating and stretched by war, Byzantium suffered a major defeat at the hands of the Seljuq Turks at Manzikert (1071) and called for assistance from the West. However, the counter-offensives launched from Vienna – involving the participation of the Franks, the Normans and the Italian city-states – failed, and the Ottoman armies inflicted crushing defeats on feudal Europe at Nicopolis (1396) and Varna (1444). Following repeated Mongol invasions, and after decades of cavalry warfare, the Osmanli sultanate consolidated its rule as Turkish armies went from strength to strength. Constantinople fell in 1453, much of the Balkans followed, as did large swathes of the Middle East in the sixteenth century. Perhaps the most powerful empire of its time, under the rule of Suleiman the Magnificent (1520–66), the Ottoman empire enjoyed revenues twice those of Charles V in the West.

This writ was soon compromised by the rise of separate Islamic empires: the Mughal empire in India (consolidated 1556–1606) and the Safavid empire in Persia (established 1587–1629). The Ottomans were regularly at war with Europe, only being finally defeated at Vienna in 1683; Shi'ite Persians and Sunni Turks fought repeatedly from the late sixteenth through to the mid-seventeenth century; there were internal risings by the peasantry and local magnates; and the Cossacks continued to make numerous cross-border raids.

The block on further geographical expansion heralded a prolonged decline, occasionally interrupted by movements of internal renewal. But in the long run the Ottoman empire proved unable to match the challenge coming from an increasingly dynamic mercantile expansion based on absolutist Europe. In fact, towards the end of the sixteenth century, an increased resort to tax farming coincided with the disintegration of Ottoman rule in Anatolia. The English ambassador remarked in 1607 that the Empire was 'in great decline, almost ruined', and order was only restored in the second half of the seventeenth century. Continued, regular war with its neighbours, as well as numerous challenges to its authority from within, pressed on the resources of the Porte. In the latter part of the eighteenth century, the erosion of Ottoman power became terminal and the question of the future of the 'East' became a constant feature of European diplomacy.

Tributary empire, nomads and tribal state: the three 'Islams'

If we are to make sense of the social formations of the Middle East we must attend to the particular forms by which the material production of these societies was organized, and thence the ways these structured other social arrangements. And if we do this, we find that, roughly speaking, three types of society can be distinguished: the Ottoman heartlands, the areas dominated by tribal nomadism and the Safavid empire. Across much of Asia, but not only there, it was the case that a state class secured political rights to tax a peasantry that it did not tenurially control. (In feudalism, by contrast, landlord control of the peasantry meant that rent was the primary form of surplus extraction.) As Chris Wickham has pointed out,

> [much of the Islamic world] had one socio-political feature in common . . . unlike in the Roman and Chinese empires, where a roughly homogeneous aristocratic class participated in the profits of both state and landownership, in most of these 'Islamic' states a state class clearly stood in opposition to an aristocratic class of local landowners. There was certainly overlap, but the two were socially and often ethnically distinguishable, and frequently antagonistic in ideology, as well as their economic base.(1985:176)

Indeed, in the Ottoman case, a particularly pure form of tributary society emerged. This was consolidated between *c.* 1280 and 1453, posed a challenge to Europe until the seventeenth century and lingered on down to the end of the First World War. The central and overriding fact of the Ottoman state was its tributary character. With the exception of *waqf* (or religious) lands, all land was the patrimony of the sultan. Both Islamic law and Ottoman practice classed land as belonging to the state (*miri*). Peasant families with rights of access to the land constituted the main units of production and consumption, and these were organized into wider village communities. Peasants farmed the land for tax payments to the state. The sultan's household was staffed by ex-Christian slaves taken as tribute and by the Islamic stratum of *sipahi* cavalry, based on the *timar*s (benefices) granted by the sultan in return for military service.[7] (When the cavalry gave way to a salaried army, so the grants became tax farms.) In marked contrast to the position of the nobility within feudalism, such grants were neither hereditable, nor did they connote any rights of jurisdiction over the direct producers, and the revenues attached to them were set by the sultan's treasury. This state of affairs applied most fully in the empire's Anatolian (Turkish) and Rumelian (Balkan) core. By contrast, in some of the outer regions, such as Egypt, Iraq and Arabia, there were no *timar* lands; instead these were garrisoned by janissary troops and paid taxes to the treasury. Profits from guild regulation of markets and customs dues also went to the urban-based intermediaries of the state. It was this urban location and tributary form of surplus appropriation, together with the high levels of tax levied on the cultivators, that dictated the absence of any long-term interests geared towards agricultural improvement: urban consumption, not productive innovation, was the mission of the ruling class.

Formally speaking, the official corps of Sunni theologians, judges and teachers came to run parallel to this tributary structure. This religious hierarchy performed important administrative functions and filled the leading civil and judicial posts of the state. In the provinces, personnel recruited from the *ulema* formed the basis of administration. At the head of the *ulema* stood the mufti of Istanbul, the *Sheikh-ul-Islam*, the supreme religious leader who interpreted the *shari'a* for the faithful. Not recognizing any distinction between 'Church' and 'State', Islamic doctrine provided the ideology of the Osmanli empire. But what was the precise role of the Sunni *ulema*? Dating from the Abbasid period in Sunni Islam, *madrasa* (theological and legal colleges), endowments and fees constituted the clergy as a major group of surplus takers, and on this basis they extended their functions to charity, education, justice and informal social and political leadership. By contrast, the

7 The use of the term 'slave', used in relation to servile forces, in the Islamic world has often been misunderstood. The term 'was a loose one, denoting dependants with a total and exclusive loyalty; collectively they formed the ruler's "family"' (Kiernan 1980:238); and 'the sultan's slaves . . . commanded armies, governed provinces, and controlled the central administrations. Used of these . . . such words as the Arabic *mamluk* and Turkish *kul*, though technically meaning "slave", carried a connotation not of enslavement or servility but of power and dominance' (Lewis, 1988:65).

Turkish conquerors, of nomadic stock and backed by slave armies, had little or no experience of sedentary agriculture and imperial administration. Thus the *ulema* could organize society but they could not suppress banditry and parasitic disorder, while the new overlords could supply order but could not rule. The happy conjunction has been well summarized by Lapidus:

> Faced with military elites unfamiliar with local traditions, the 'ulama' emerged, on the basis of religious prestige and educational and judicial authority as a new communal notability. The 'ulama' married into established merchant, administrative, and landowning families, and merged with the older local elites to form a new upper class defined by religious qualifications. The 'ulama' assumed the functions as well as the status of the former elites. They took charge of local taxation, irrigation, judicial and police affairs, and often became scribes and officials in the Saljuq succession states. While conquerors and regimes came and went, Islam became ever more firmly and widely entrenched as the basis of the social and political order. (1988:176, 180)

This was the pattern that was reproduced throughout the Ottoman empire, and elsewhere besides. But it is crucial to notice which way around the pattern of social causation ran: it was the social distance between the tributary appropriation of the state class and the locally based notability which allowed the consolidation of the religious classes, rather than any intrinsic features of Islam as such. Understood thus, the degree of institutional continuity of Islamic practices emphasized by Gibb (1949), Esposito (1988), Lapidus and others, where it existed, is not evidence in favour of the notion of a distinctively 'Islamic history' or 'Islamic society', but is instead a contingent feature of the necessary intermediation in tributary forms of rule and appropriation, and hence relates to the use made of Islam by historically specific social forces.

In the Ottoman case, the imperial Turkish overlords, whether state officials or military personnel, lived off the land and resided in the towns, and often did not learn the language of the local notability and peasantry. As Weber pointed out, this meant that tacit co-operation of urban forces, especially the merchants and the *ulema*, was therefore necessary. Merchants required the overlords to maintain order and the networks of trade and finance, and their largest customers were often the central tributary authorities. The *ulema* were even more significant to social control than the merchants, for they provided more general social cohesion and regulation. They too depended on order and became dependent on state finance. The longevity of Turkish rule in the Ottoman case brought with it a high degree of state control over the Sunni clergy.

But beyond the compass of the urban Sunni clergy and Ottoman military power lay the tribal forces that remained outside central control. Here we are in the world of Ibn Khaldun. In these regions the tributary state was unable to control the rural areas, essentially because of the greater weight of pastoral nomadism with its mobile means of production, armed populations and absence of urban growth. Tribal pastoralism permitted neither any significant material development nor any lasting and widespread social stratification or political authority within the community. The tribal nobility was not reproduced by regulated intermarriage and it had no power to tax, control or command. And even if tribal warfare precipitated the temporary emergence of a confederation, the paucity of the available surplus meant that state formation was unthinkable: that is to say, rather than fighting wars, nomads had feuds. Where this tribal cohesion survived it proved to be destructive of development as such, for in so far as nomads accumulated surpluses at all this was by means of parasitic plunder from sedentary agriculture or from the siphoning of tribute from trade routes (see Anderson 1974a and Moghadam 1988).

Under these circumstances popular (Sufi) Islam was called on to play a very different role from the literate practice of justice and administration found in the urban centres of surplus appropriation. What Gellner calls 'folk' Islam, and in particular its array of saints, performed the following roles:

> Supervising the political process in segmentary groups, e.g. election or selection of chiefs. Supervising and sanctioning their legal process, notably by collective oath. Facilitating economic relations by guaranteeing caravans and visits to the markets of neighbouring tribes; trade and pilgrimage routes may converge. Providing spatial markers for frontiers: a saintly settlement may be on the border between lay groups. Providing temporal markers; in a pastoral society, many pasture rights may be bounded by seasons and require rituals for their ratification. What better than a saintly festival for such a purpose? Supplying the means for the Islamic identification of the tribesmen. . . . All these factors clearly conspire to one end: the faith of the tribesmen needs to be mediated by special and distinct holy personnel, rather than to be egalitarian; it needs to be

joyous and festival-worthy, not puritanical and scholarly; it requires
hierarchy and incarnation in persons, not in script. Its ethic is one
of loyalty not of rule-observance. (Gellner 1981:41)

Of course, folk Islam was present among the settled rural peasantry
as well, since they also were illiterate and had need of its ability to
facilitate the interaction – material and symbolic – between otherwise hostile communities. This folk Islam, the religion of the
majority of the population, was independent of the state, and often
the urban tributary power sought to suppress Sufi orders, seeing
them as a threat to its own position.

Finally, there was Shi'i Persia. The theological basis of the Shi'i
ulema, articulated at a time when temporal political power resided
with Sunni Muslims, lies in the notion that they are the collective
deputies of the Occulted Imam (Momen 1989). Twelvers take their
name from following the twelve infallible imams. The line began
with Ali, who was the cousin and son-in-law of the Prophet, and
it ends with Muhammad al-Mahdi who is believed to have gone
into occultation in AD 874. These distinctive features of Shi'i
doctrine reflect its formation in acephalous conditions and in opposition to the Sunni caliphate. After the Safavid conquest of Iran,
however, Shi'ism was proclaimed the religion of the state. The
latter was composed of a tributary structure similar to that of the
Ottoman empire, though the control of the central state was
weaker to the extent that its army was composed of tribal levies.
This reflected the greater presence of pastoral nomadism, and thus
tribal organization, as well as effective landlord control, within
post-Mongol Iran. The peasantry had already flocked to Sufi orders. While the empire lasted, the Shi'i *ulema* supported Safavid
power against the Ottoman adversary and the Safavids deferred to
the *ulema* on a range of issues. Lapidus has noted that by the late
Safavid period, 'Shi'ism had duplicated the whole complex of religious sensibility already found within Sunnism. It thus became a
comprehensive alternative vision of Islam' (1988:299). Shi'i jurists
argued that the canonical alms, the *zakat*, were to be collected and
distributed by the clergy, thereby legitimating one of the material
bases of the clergy (the others being the money paid for legal and
educational services by the merchants, the religious endowments
and the *madrasa*).

Post-Safavid Iran was subject to a series of warring dynasties,
and by 1779 the Qajars had defeated their main rivals, the Zand,

to establish a dynasty that lasted until 1924. In this period, the central authority diminished and the corresponding power of tribal leaders and landowners increased, and the *ulema* were able to develop a further autonomy through establishing their own religious courts, private armies and bodies of students. In addition, the location of the most important Shi'i shrines in Iraq, especially the symbolically central site of Karbala[8], further augmented the social distance of the clergy from the state. Taken together, these features meant that the Shi'i *ulema* constituted a powerful grouping of surplus takers, and were able to establish a much greater degree of independence from the central tributary structures than the Sunni clergy of the Ottoman domains.

Thus, by the time of the consolidation of the Ottoman and Safavid empires in the sixteenth century, it is possible to distinguish a range of different societies within the Middle East, in each of which the articulation of Islam took its own distinctive form. The first of these was the heartlands of the Sunni Ottoman empire in urban areas linked to sedentary agriculture where Islam was geared towards the provision of administration and justice. The second consisted of those regions of the Ottoman domain where the centre's writ was more attenuated, either as a result of stronger tribal organization or because of logistical distance from the Anatolian core, where Islam largely meant Sufi orders or the folk Islam of tribes. And finally, there was Shi'i Persia (Iran), where a form of Islam doctrinally distinct from the Sunni mainstream played a variety of roles in relation to political power and social organization.

Historically, then, 'Islam' has had no unitary nature, and therefore it cannot be understood either as an enduring, recalcitrant tradition, a cultural form operating to block other social and historical determinations, or in terms of the *theological* power of the Islamic clergy based on an unchanging doctrine. As a form of religious identification and a culture of signification, 'Islam' remains rooted in broader sets of social and material practices, and thus its changing forms must also be related to the historically given organization of economy and polity. Sunni Islam equally buttressed Ottoman power and tended to the needs of the rural population. Shi'i doctrine seemed equally compatible with acephalous

8 The martyrdom of the third imam, Husayn, by the Umayyad armies of the caliph Yazid at Karbala (AD 680) is central to the symbolism of Shi'ism.

tribal organization, support for the Safavid tributary state and the independent organization of the clergy in post-Safavid Iran. As a determinate set of institutions – the *ulema*, mosques, the *madrasa*, *shari'a* law and *qadi* justice etc. – the role of Islam also varied with its differential relation to the state and social classes. In the urban centres of the Ottoman lands the Sunni *ulema* were organized in parallel to the tributary structure of the state, for the mass of the population 'folk' Islam, or in the Iranian case the Shi'i clergy, was socially and materially independent from the state. What distinguished these 'Islams' were the different functions they were called upon to play in the regulation of social reproduction and the articulation of relations of authority, as well as the differing social forces which were mobilized under 'Islamic' organizations.

The Middle East and modernity

Given these differences, the impact of the West on the societies of the Middle East could not but be uneven. With the phenomenal growth of the world market and European power during the nineteenth century, it was the global spread and stable consolidation of capitalist property and state forms that became the project of the leading classes and powers. Let us recall that tributary and nomadic forms of appropriation contained no dynamic of long-run improvement to the forces of production of the kind unleashed by the establishment of the capitalist mode. At best, social and material reproduction was more or less static, subject to strict Malthusian constraints, if not actually regressive in the nomadic case. For this reason, when faced with a dynamic competitor capable of generating huge surpluses and thus of amassing considerable military power, these societies had no means of internal renewal. It was thus that declining tributary empires fell prey to European expansion. And it was against this backdrop that projects of modernization were launched.

We have also seen that the transition from such pre-capitalist, Islamic forms to capitalist modernity would have to involve two linked processes. In the first instance, the state apparatus must be able to uphold its authority and monopoly of coercion against other sites of political command, such that the general, public functions of society become the concern of a single body of rule-making and coercive enforcement (the modern, sovereign state). And second, there must be a significant degree of separation between the institutions of rule and the mechanisms by which the surplus labour of the direct producers is appropriated, thus uncoupling the material basis of the power of the ruling class from the formal exercise of state political power (the creation of capitalist property relations). Taken together, the emergence of a sovereign public sphere in conjunction with the privatization of command over surplus labour provide the basis for the liberal-capitalist form of state and economy.

The social transformations behind this involve changes in which the means of public administration – a centralized monopoly of coercion, fiscal basis, monetary order and the sanctioning of state decisions by a unitary legal apparatus – become general, public forms consistent with, indeed providing the presuppositions of, private forms of appropriation set free from major communal functions. Yet in the Middle East societies, whose character we have just reviewed, the means of administration and of appropriation were not so differentiated. It follows that those complexes of social power which organized political command and surplus appropriation in the pre-modern era stood as obstacles to the development of new forms of economy and polity. Thus any account of projects of capitalist state formation and economic development must attend to the precise matrix from which these were launched. Let us now turn to a more detailed exploration of the dependent incorporation of the Middle East into the modern, capitalist world.

2

From Tributary Empires to States System

Introduction

At its greatest extent, in the fifteenth century, the lands of the Ottoman empire comprised most of what is now the Middle East (excepting the interior of the Arabian peninsula and Iran), virtually all of North Africa along the Mediterranean coast, Greece and Turkey, together with most of the Balkans, the Crimea, Georgia and Armenia. It was the long historical decline of this dominion, a decline both slowed and aggravated by the intervention of outside powers anxious to put off the large-scale conflicts which would surely attend any final collapse, which forms the substance of the famous Eastern Question. For a century and a half (1774–1923) this combination of progressive internal enfeeblement and external management was to be the leading feature of the development of the region. It was clear on all sides that without internal reform this could only be a postponement of the inevitable. For, in the words of Tsar Nicholas in 1853, Europe had a 'sick man, seriously ill . . . on its hands'.

In the nineteenth century no serious observer doubted that internal reform was urgent, but would it succeed? The optimism of Stratford Canning, 'whose dearest wish was to see "the Bible . . . go forth with the engine, and every choice assortment of Manchester stuffs . . . [and] have an honest John Bunyan to distribute them" ', was poignantly matched by Lord Clarendon's pessimistic, and as it turned out accurate, view that 'the only way to improve [the Ottomans], is to improve them off the face of the earth' (quoted in Kedourie 1987:15). Quoting the quite modest views of the English traveller, Albert Smith, who on encountering the 'dancing dervishes' of Istanbul found them 'inexpressibly sly and offensive' and longed to 'hit them hard in the face', Victor Kiernan reminds us that in the mid-nineteenth century 'the consensus of opinion was that Islam was hopelessly sterile and stationary, that its devotees had walled themselves up in a mental prison from which they could neither escape nor be rescued' (1969:139, 140). The cartoons of *Punch* bear ample testimony to the truth of this judgement.

Despite such strength of feeling, it remained wholly unclear what could or should replace the Ottoman empire. Clearly, an imperial scramble would ensue, for no educated European would dissent from the judgement that the peoples of the empire were demonstrably unfit for self-government. Indeed, for much of the nineteenth century it was only the prospect of imperialist conflict over the remains that bolstered Ottoman integrity. When the empire finally collapsed, however, towards the end of the First World War, the Western armies finally moved in and occupied the region. Now the question which had been postponed for so long had to be confronted head-on: it was thus during the First World War – the long-feared conflagration of the imperialist powers which was indeed sparked by a sub-plot of the Eastern Question – that the alternatives really began to be elaborated. Looking at the states system of the Middle East today, it is all too easy to forget that before, during and even shortly after the First World War, the idea that Ottoman power should be replaced by a set of independent states was treated with derision in the capitals of the European powers. The idea did not make any more sense to the subject peoples of the empire. In fact, it is only a small exaggeration to say that the victorious European allies in the First World War, the British and the French, stumbled into creating a state system in the Middle East for want of a better alternative, not out of belief or design. And once the state-building strategy had been fixed upon, it was prosecuted with indecent haste and with little or no attention to the realities on the ground.

If we are to understand this process of Ottoman decline, European expansion and state building and the legacy it left for the resulting states of the region, then we must, first, examine the nature of Ottoman disintegration and European penetration. This will enable us to fix some of the salient features of the socio-economic changes that occurred in the later empire. The classes formed by these changes, together with the accompanying political ferment, provided one set of factors affecting subsequent development. Secondly, we need to consider the character of European, and especially, British interests in the region. The competition of rival imperialisms, and the strategies of the major European powers, did much to shape the pattern of the modern Middle East. Thirdly, these investigations will allow us to rethink the Eastern Question itself. Too often, the Eastern Question is portrayed either as a European response to a purely degenerative and internally driven Ottoman decline, or as the safety-valve for the pressures emanating from the European balance of power. In each case, the actual structure and dynamics of Ottoman society are ignored, as are the extra-European dynamics of the problem. Finally, we must look at the period of state building that issued from the First World War. For between 1914 and 1922 the Ottoman empire, which had ruled most of the Middle East (Iran and a few Arabian tribes excepted) for nearly five hundred years, was destroyed and a new, European-inspired states system was put in its place. This truly remarkable exercise in political engineering was the origin of the modern Middle East.

Ottoman disintegration

As we have seen, Ottoman jurisdiction was located athwart the East–West trade routes that stretched from China to Europe, both by land and sea. On the Arabian peninsula, desert nomads and urban merchants had long coexisted, while from the steppes of Central Asia the pastoral, cavalry-based peoples swept across Turkey, Persia and India. Forging these together, Ottoman society came to comprise a structure of agrarian surplus production, linked to an urban, tributary form of appropriation, involving centralized taxation of the peasantry and direct political regulation of urban production and trade, organized by the Osmanli state and a sub-ordinate *ulema*. Because of the tributary character of society, there was little impetus for agricultural or industrial improvement. Any dynamic that this society possessed was based on perpetual military conquest; the Ottoman polity was a 'plunder machine' (Jones 1981). In such a social order, the cessation of territorial expansion implied a gradual disintegration of the state and an increasingly counter-productive form of surplus extraction.

External accumulation was necessary in order to provide revenue for the state and to sustain the *sipahi*. Once its path was blocked by absolutist Europe in the north and the existence of rival empires or desert on its other flanks, surpluses could only be raised by an increased resort to tax farming. This in turn led to growing pressure on the peasantry and the rise of provincial notables who became competing centres of appropriation and political power. At the end of the sixteenth century, tax farming did increase as the state sought revenues for military reorganization, and as merchants attempted to benefit from the expanding trade with Europe. However, this predatory appropriation served to undermine the authority of the state, and with it the productivity of agrarian activity. To begin with, tax farms were civilian and non-hereditary, but by the late seventeenth century they began to develop their own armies and *de facto* control. This commercialization of political power through tax farming inevitably tended to result in local conflicts between warring magnates. The general form of the breakdown of tributary power has been identified by Wickham as follows:

> The nineteenth century proceeded with a continual struggle between state and notables as to how far private property law should be accepted, and whom it should benefit; but even the weakened (and commercially undermined) Ottoman state of the late nineteenth century could at least hold notables to a standoff until World War I. . . . Real local independence was . . . only possible by usurping the powers of *central* government – and, in Muhammad Ali's Egypt, actually using them more effectively. (1985:181)

Riven by this basic contradiction, the internal composition of the empire was further transformed by a number of external changes. The re-routing of trade from the East, as the Portuguese, Dutch, French and English pushed into the Indian Ocean and the Mediterranean during the sixteenth and seventeenth centuries, undermined much of the Ottoman maritime trade. The need to replace lost income had the effect of encouraging the export of primary products in return for European manufactures (especially cloth), further expanding circuits of trade outside centralized, political control. The revenues of the state, already reduced by the retention of rising shares of the surplus by local magnates, were also cut by the diversion of trade routes to the Indian and Atlantic Oceans.

Internal response

Thus the fundamental causes of Ottoman decline derived from the internal, tributary structure of society. As Perry Anderson has observed, 'the natural tendency of the system was always to degenerate into parasitic tax-farming' (1974b:500). This dynamic obtained in all of the Islamic land empires (Ottoman, Safavid and Mughal). In fact, there was what amounted to a 'general crisis' (Bayly 1989) of the Muslim land empires in the eighteenth century. The Mughal and Safavid empires were destroyed by 'tribal breakouts', India falling to outright conquest by the British, and Persia maintaining an uneasy independence in the face of Russian and British encroachments. In Qajar Iran central tributary power was never restored, and formal independence coexisted with informal domination by Britain and Russia. Meanwhile, as we have seen, in the Ottoman domains the authority of the Porte was challenged by the rise of provincial rulers: military pashas in Egypt and Syria, *derebeys* (valley lords) in Anatolia, *ayans* (dynastic notables) in Rumelia and *Wahhabi* tribes in Arabia.

Although the fundamental causes of Ottoman decline were internal, these were supplemented in the eighteenth century by the external pressures of European expansion. The European thrust into the Ottoman realms was accompanied by a formidable deployment of military power, especially after the creation of the 'second' British empire following the Treaty of Paris (1763) and the Napoleonic invasion of Egypt (1798). The Porte was far from idle in the face of this twin threat. On the contrary, beginning with Mahmoud II (1809–33), the nineteenth century witnessed a series of vigorous attempts at internal reform as forces within the Ottoman empire sought to overhaul its military and economic capacities. Despite a number of attempts by the Porte to undertake internal reform – most importantly, during the Tanzimat era (1839–76) – the Ottomans proved unable to resist the centrifugal forces from within and the growing pressure from without. The ambitions of Muhammad Ali in Egypt (1805–48) only compounded the fragmentation of the Ottoman state. Nevertheless, the eventual failure of these (and other) reforms should not detract from their importance. If it is true that the Ottoman regime only lasted as long as it did because of external diplomatic support, it is also the case that the internal projects of development had a considerable impact.

The rulers in Turkey and Egypt sought to modernize their armies by adopting weaponry and tactics from the West and replacing mercenaries by conscripts, and this required increased taxes. The attempt to raise revenue by abolishing tax farming, appointing salaried officials and regularizing legal administration exacerbated conflicts between the central administration and local rulers. Additional resources were also required for educational reform to staff the expanding military and administrative posts. As long as the centre held (in the Ottoman core until the First World War, under Muhammad Ali in Egypt from 1805 to 1848), the resulting loss of localized power – as what had become virtual fiefs were replaced by salaried officials – had the effect of drawing the state into a closer infrastructural role, strengthening rural security and thereby laying the basis for sustained economic progress. In Turkey military reorganization was a result of European pressure, whereas in Egypt it was motivated by a desire for independence from the Ottoman centre. In both cases, however, it was the need of the state for revenues which laid the grounds for the formation of a settled, agrarian capitalist class, rather than pressure from landed and commercial elements. In the Turkish case the central tributary apparatus remained strong and no real landed class emerged, but in Egypt a class of big landowners did develop, and they came to monopolize political power. The onerous loans contracted to finance modernization had the effect, secondly, of leading to growing financial penetration by the West. Before long, the failure of the reforms to generate sufficient growth and revenue resulted in the bankruptcy of the state (1875 in Turkey and 1876 in Egypt), followed by direct European supervision of the public finances. In the case of Egypt, European influence produced revolt and this, combined with its strategic position, led to outright occupation by the British in 1882. Let us now review in a little more detail how this came about and with what consequences.

Trade, finance and bankruptcy

Until the late eighteenth century, Ottoman trade with the East was probably more important than that with Europe, at any rate for regions close to the Red Sea and the Persian Gulf. Certainly, until the nineteenth century, the Middle East had a trade surplus with

Europe and a deficit with India and the Far East. Trade with Russia came across the Black and Caspian Seas, Austrian trade traversed the Balkans and the Mediterranean provided the conduit for western Europe. Ottoman tariff policies reflected the interests of the dominant groups, namely bureaucrats and soldiers, whose main concern was the raising of taxation and the provisioning of the cities: tariffs were aimed at maximizing the surpluses under the state's control, and hence they encouraged imports and discouraged exports. By 1789 France accounted for one half of the region's trade with the West; Britain, the Netherlands and Venice took most of the rest. But after the Napoleonic Wars and the industrial revolution in Britain, French trade in the eastern Mediterranean was rapidly replaced by British dominance; and overall, trade with Europe expanded relative to trade within the region.

Who ran this trade? At first minority, non-Muslim communities – Greeks, Jews, Armenians, Syro-Lebanese Christians – garnered much of the commercial and financial activity within the Ottoman domains. But as imports of precious metals from Europe in exchange for exports of agricultural produce and raw materials increased, so European merchants came to play a more important role. In turn this penetration was backed up by geopolitical pressure from the relevant European states. At the Treaty of Kutchuk Kainardji (1774), the Russians established rights of protection over the Christian Holy Places, the Porte's Orthodox Christian subjects and thus their considerable economic activities. The English had already gained a capitulation from the Porte in the seventeenth century.[1] These new networks were increasingly regulated by commercial tribunals controlled by the Europeans. After Muhammad Ali challenged Ottoman authority, the Porte proved more willing to accommodate British demands which were, in any case, aimed more at Egypt than Turkey. The result was the Anglo-Turkish Commercial Convention of 1838 which imposed virtually free trade on the region. France and Russia both gained similar concessions from the Porte. For some forty years Muhammad Ali imposed monopolistic control over the foreign trade of Egypt, the Sudan and parts of Arabia. But eventually, and after considerable pressure,

---

1 Capitulations, from the Latin *capitula*, take their name from the chapter headings of the texts of commercial agreements between the Porte and foreign merchant. Originally struck at a time of Muslim strength, these agreements allowed foreign merchants a high degree of autonomy within the empire.

the Ottoman tariff was also imposed on Egypt. Once defeated, Muhammad Ali was forced to reduce the size of Egypt's army, thereby diminishing the incentive for industrialization even further. Still later, conventions were signed (1861–2) which opened the Middle East market to penetration by European manufactures almost without hindrance. Yet the significance of this trade was always asymmetrical: the importance of Europe for the trade of the Middle East was not matched by a comparable role of Middle East trade for Europe.

The degree of economic change wrought by these free-trade measures should not be overstated. For example, the Anatolian economy remained dominated by peasant production and, under the control of landlords, industry continued to be confined to foodstuffs and textiles. However, in some regions, pastoralism and communal or tribal forms of land tenure were replaced by settled agriculture and the creation of landed estates. Charles Issawi has summarized the results elsewhere in the empire as follows:

> In Iraq and Syria the settlement of titles was carried out in conditions that transferred huge amounts of tribal and village lands to sheiks and other notables; in Egypt Muhammad Ali laid the basis of a large landlord class; and in North Africa a large proportion of the land was acquired, mainly by expropriation or chicanery, by European settlers. (1982:4)

This steady commercialization of tributary appropriation and rule laid the basis for a rapid expansion of trade with Europe during the nineteenth century, facilitated by falling transport and communication costs arising from steamships and the building of telegraphs, railways and ports. Large amounts of European capital were also invested in building the requisite infrastructure, and a financial system emerged to cope with the foreign trade, much of which was handled by local but minority intermediaries and Europeans. Considerable settlement of Europeans occurred in Palestine, Egypt and North Africa.

Increased connections with Europe drove many indigenous manufacturers out of business and encouraged the expansion of cash crops. As a result, economic activity concentrated on the building of infrastructure and the provision of irrigation. In the case of the former, port cities formed the major points of growth; as to the latter, the bulk of agricultural expansion was extensive in character. In addition, the plague disappeared at the start of the century, and later there were improvements to public health. But most of the increased rural surplus did not feed back into further agricultural improvement. Instead it was either consumed by or channelled into the emerging client-patron political activity of the urban notability.

State finances before the contraction of foreign loans may be judged from Roger Owen's estimate that at the end of the eighteenth century the public revenue of the Ottoman empire was perhaps one-fifth that of the British state. Moreover, in the late 1830s, just prior to the Tanzimat reforms mentioned above, some 70 per cent of revenues were spent on the forces of coercion – and still many soldiers went unpaid (Owen 1981). Most of the disposable income from foreign loans to the government was spent on arms and luxury consumption in the Turkish case and on cotton for export in Egypt. Debt servicing sometimes accounted for one-half of the public revenues of Turkey, Egypt and Tunisia. Private sector investment directed towards utilities, mining and manufacturing was generally more productive. None the less, servicing all debts – both public and private – accounted for as much as a quarter of the exports of Egypt and Turkey at times during the period from the 1850s to the 1870s.

The first Ottoman loan took place in 1854, occasioned by the need for finance during the Crimean War. By 1875 one-third to one-half of *all* public revenues went on servicing the debt and the government was bankrupt. Of the foreign loan finance contracted, Issawi has calculated that in the period 1854–1914, 34 per cent went on commissions and the difference between the nominal and issue price; 45 per cent was used to liquidate past debts; 6 per cent was spent on the military; and 5 per cent was invested productively. Wars against Balkan rebels and the Russians, combined with bankruptcy, resulted in the loss of prosperous regions of the empire at the Congress of Berlin (1878). On the other hand, the repeal of the English Corn Laws and the disruption of the Russian grain trade during the Crimean War greatly increased the demand for Turkish produce, further integrating the most prosperous regions into the European market. The Decree of Muharram (October 1881) established the Ottoman Public Debt Administration, which gave control over finance to Britain and France and, soon, Germany. This signalled the complete failure of Turkish efforts to catch up. None the less, the Hamidian era (1876–1908) continued the Tanzimat reforms, with attention being paid to improving communications infrastructure by means of foreign concessions. The effect of this policy was double-edged. For in addition to further encouraging crops for export, 'the railways were also used as the spearhead of European economic penetration of the interior' (Owen 1981:113).

Egypt followed a similar path to Turkey, attempting to construct the basic institutions of a modern state, with bankruptcy coming in 1876 (see Owen 1972 and Marsot 1984). Muhammad Ali employed monopolies on agriculture and customs on foreign trade, in addition to the seizure of tax farms. By these means, most agricultural produce was bought by the state at a politically determined price, with the central authorities appropriating the difference between this and the market price. Corvée labour was used to build irrigation works and the state sponsored some industrial development, especially in the areas of military equipment, textiles and agricultural processing. In this case, the money borrowed went not on administration and coercion but on cotton. Cotton production in the Delta altered the pattern of land tenure (towards large, privately owned estates), increased Egypt's integration into the world economy and turned Upper Egypt into a source of labour for the Lower (northern) region. Although both the demand for, and the price of cotton rose as a result of the loss of American exports during the Civil War, revenues were still unable to keep pace with the debt servicing. In this case, the weaker position of Egypt, economically and strategically, meant that much harsher terms were imposed. In 1878, British and French officials joined the khedive's Council of Ministers, taking the posts of finance and public works, and the subsequent Law of Liquidation specified the ambit of the Egyptian government acceptable to Britain and France. By these means, Europeans were recruited to the very centre of civil rule. The end result was the Urabist revolt and the British occupation of 1882.

Thus the Europeans dominated the economies of the region by a mixture of: the intrusion of foreign currencies; the development of consular or mixed courts administering European legal codes for their subjects within the Empire; foreign control over public revenue and expenditure, or direct occupation; and foreign merchants who came to control large parts of commerce and finance (and even some cotton production and export). And underpinning these forms of influence were the capitulations that were traded by the

Porte for European diplomatic support. As Issawi comments, 'By 1914, Europeans held all the commanding heights of the economy except for landownership in the Middle East, and the minority groups occupied the middle and some of the lower slopes' (1982:9). Not surprisingly, after 1815 the trade balance with Europe deteriorated and remained in deficit until the First World War. The result was the creation of a dependent economy: 'In the course of the 19th century the Middle East was integrated, as a producer of primary products and market for manufactured goods and colonial produce, in the international network of trade' (Owen 1981:29). In sum, the growth of the Middle East in the nineteenth century was shaped by the expansion of the European market for agricultural products, on the one hand, and the reactive attempt to construct strong, centralizing regimes in Istanbul and Cairo in the face of European (and in the Egyptian case, Turkish) pressure, on the other (see, generally, Owen 1981).

European expansion

The Turkish and Egyptian attempts to reform political and economic affairs in order to withstand the pressure from European merchants and states were of course prompted by the spectacular increase in European dynamism and power that gathered pace in the late eighteenth and early nineteenth centuries. What was the character of this expansion and what course did it take across the globe? During the sixteenth and early seventeenth centuries the speculative activity of merchant capital dominated long-distance trade between Europe and the rest of the world: imports of grain from the Baltic were just under two-thirds the value of spices from the Far East and a little over one-quarter that of precious metals from the Americas. At this time, only the North Sea and the Baltic regions were trading in products of mass consumption, while the Mediterranean remained preoccupied by the traditional spice and luxury trade from the Orient and Spain traded with the Americas. This still essentially feudal mercantile activity declined in the first half of the seventeenth century and was replaced by an aggressively mercantilist new colonial system. It was the latter that was to provide one of the essential preconditions for the industrial revolution, a large market in which to buy and sell without hindrance. The other critical condition was an industry which, by revolutionizing its technical means and thus constantly cheapening its output, could create its own demand. For without these advantages, the effort of technological and organizational innovation that lay at the centre of the industrial revolution could not be justified. In turn, this necessitated an end to the fetters placed on widespread proto-industrialization by the persistence of feudal relations in the rural areas. Put another way, for capitalist growth 'what was needed was not the spice trade, but sugar-plantations . . . [and] a cotton rather than a silk industry' (Hobsbawm 1960:103; see also Hobsbawm 1954; and Kriedte 1983).

Thus in the increasingly capitalist growth that followed the 'general crisis' of the seventeenth century, the locus of trade shifted towards the north and the west. Among the Atlantic economies, the period from the 1730s to the 1820s was one of generally rising output; and after the Treaty of Utrecht (1713), intercontinental trade expanded more rapidly than that within Europe. In the course of the War of the Spanish Succession, England emerged from its alliance with Holland against France as the dominant commercial and naval power. However, Amsterdam sustained its predominant role in finance until the French Revolution and the subsequent British victory in the Napoleonic Wars. Meantime, the Seven Years' War (concluded by the Treaty of Paris, 1763) damaged France's position in the triangular trade of the Atlantic networks and fatally unbalanced the fiscal stability of the *ancien régime*. In marked contrast, the British plunder of India provided the means for the national debt to be bought back from the Dutch.

As far as European trade with the East was concerned, the Portuguese failure to restructure Asian trade, together with the continued expansion of such commerce, meant that some 60–80 per cent of Asian exports to Europe continued to come overland in 1600. With the arrival of the English and Dutch East India Companies in the seventeenth century, however, the overland routes became insignificant. The commodity balance of trade also altered: in the Dutch case, for example, spices fell from three-quarters to one-quarter of purchases, while textiles and raw materials for textiles rose to over one-half. Simultaneously, the Companies sought to reduce the European trade deficit with Asia by entering the inner-Asian trade. And while Europe's trade with Asia remained in deficit throughout the eighteenth century, steadily the latter's markets were opened to European textiles and metal goods. By the end of the seventeenth century, English cloth manufacturers were already exporting some two-fifths of their output, and by 1799 over two-thirds went overseas. Together with the exports of other European producers, these were already undercutting indigenous Ottoman production by the 1780s.

While European manufactures were beginning their conquest of the world's markets, states were attempting to sponsor industrial development. But without a fundamental break in agrarian class relations, this proved all but impossible. In England, however, based on a prior transition to capitalist agriculture, the bounds of proto-industrialization were broken by the mechanization of cotton production from the late 1760s. The cotton boom of the 1770s resulted in England consuming twice as much cotton as France by the time of the Revolution. If the last two decades of the eighteenth century saw over half of Britain's new industrial output exported, the cotton boom itself was based on both the home and the overseas market. Only at the turn of the century did exports completely gain the upper hand. Equally, international exchanges were vital for raw material imports: from the 1780s to the 1790s, the share of British cotton imports coming across the Atlantic rose from 69 to 88 per cent. The industrial breakthrough meant that, notwithstanding the loss of the American colonies in the 1770s, the victory at Waterloo gave Britain global supremacy.

British ascendancy

Externally, the creation of the 'second' British empire delivered Britain a formidable reach across the world. After the Treaty of Paris, Britain constructed a commercial network in the Pacific and Indian Oceans, founded on trading ports and naval bases. With the signal exception of India, this was not based on directly colonial arrangements. However, in response to the loss of the American possessions, French gains in the Mediterranean and, most of all, the international threat to property unleashed by the French Revolution in the core and peasant and slave revolts on the periphery, a revived imperial state organization was constructed between the 1780s and the 1830s. Indeed, during and immediately after the Napoleonic Wars much of the Old Corruption of the state as well as a good deal of state regulation of productive activity was abolished.

Challenges to the state and property, both domestic and imperial, came from all quarters. The European 'Age of Revolution', which followed the progress of the armies of the French Revolution, was accompanied by the decline of the Muslim land empires as well as numerous colonial crises. In response, the patriotic, Christian (and increasingly racist) mobilization against the 'levelling' French, together with the pressures on colonial administration, resulted in a dramatic change in the forms of political rule. This entailed separating law and administration on the one side from agrarian reform, private property and freedom of contract on the other. During this 'imperial revolution in government', the state constructed new fiscal instruments (customs and the first consolidated income tax), developed new forms of administration (concerned with land registration and use), created a permanent officialdom subject to supervisory boards (again focused on the creation of property rights and legal innovation), and rationalized the militias into an imperial army (for use against other states, 'native' enemies and workers and peasants at home).

This kind of reorganization was applied as fully to the colonial possessions as domestically – if not more so. Moreover, the regional projects of renewal within the Islamic land empires were essentially similar. The strategy of Muhammad Ali in Egypt or Tanzimat Turkey – settling the peasantry, forming a landed class, creating monopolies over trade and bolstering territorial integrity and identity – was essentially the same as that of Britain's regional governors in India. Throughout the Asian world, whether colonized or independent, rulers sought to make the means of state administration (transport, currency and public order) serve the ends of commerce. Settlement, private property and production for the market were seen as central to this project; free trade and responsible government could come later. By these means, regions that had long been external to the capitalist world, resistant to commodification and (on the whole) maintaining trade surpluses with the European core were gradually incorporated into its orbit.

The establishment of British dominance, if not hegemony, within the global system was thus both cause and consequence of the incipient generalization of the capitalist market and the initial breakdown of the great Asian empires. World trade quadrupled between 1780 and 1850. Speaking of the role of the East India Company, Bayly has argued persuasively that 'the commercialisation of political power within Islamic empires and the eastern seas, as much as the ruthless drive of European capitalism, was a critical

precondition for European world-empire' (1989:74). Bayly has further outlined some salient features of the resulting British 'Impèrial
Meridian' as follows:

> Long dominant in the northern waters, the Royal Navy had now
> replaced French, Spanish and Venetian paramountcies in the western
> Mediterranean and was soon to destroy Ottoman supremacy, and
> engross the import – export trade of the eastern Mediterranean.
> Dutch and French shipping, once powerful in the Persian Gulf,
> Indian Ocean and Red Sea, had lost its teeth, and Britain ranged over
> the newly explored Pacific Ocean. The significance of naval domin-
> ance was increased by the new prestige of British land forces. . . . By
> 1815 the army had invaded France over the Pyrenees. It had also
> staked out Britain's role as a great Eurasian land power by using the
> new Indian army to intervene in Egypt in 1801 and underwriting the
> independence of Iran in 1809. The balance of power in Europe was
> now to be enforced in both East and West. Through the Indian
> empire, Britain could now challenge Russia on land as her naval
> predominance in the Mediterranean could by sea. (1989:3, 4)

The empire, and critically the position in India, was crucial to
Britain's material capabilities on the world stage: prior to the
mid-Victorian boom in the 1840s, the gross national product of
metropolitan Britain was similar to that of France and Russia; yet
the resources of the British empire may have been two and a half
times that of the French and the Russian empires. In India, Clive's
victories and the subsequent expropriation of the revenues of Bengal allowed the creation of a large army; not only was this 'used
in large measure to hold down the subcontinent itself, but after
1790 it was increasingly employed to forward British interests in
southern and eastern Asia and the Middle East' (Bayly 1988:1; see
also Kiernan 1969 and 1982). On the economic front, in addition
to subsidizing the British exchequer, India became an increasingly
important means of balancing the Asian trade as well as providing
an export market for textiles. In the service of the latter, a massive
de-industrialization of India took place: between 1815 and 1832
the value of Indian cotton exports fell thirteen-fold, while imports
from Britain increased sixteen-fold.

Although the experiments in reform outside Europe were soon
overrun, especially in the period from the 1830s to the 1880s as
the massive expansion of the world market based on the railways, steam ships and coal swept away all but the most resilient

formations, the connections between the European and the Asian experiences should be registered. Above all because, as Bayly concludes, 'the period between the end of the American War and the Western-inspired Tanzimat reforms in Turkey during the 1830s seems to stand as a watershed in the creation and consolidation of new forms of power' (1989:255, 256). Everywhere, the capitalist market and recognizably modern forms of state administration, the latter mightily advanced by mercantilist competition, were seen as the only viable means to economic advance and military power.

The Eastern Question

Thus the context of the Eastern Question was given by the process of Ottoman decline on the one hand and the expansion of European capitalism on the other. But the fortunes of north-western Europe and the lands of the Porte were not simply uneven – capitalist dynamism as contrasted with pre-capitalist stagnation. They were also combined. The dynamic of colonial expansion and aggrandizement was itself critically determined by the 'general crisis' of these land empires, and this expansion complemented the hold capitalism had already established on the Atlantic seaboard. Equally, the reformist impulses and recuperative powers of the periphery played an active role in its own incorporation into the world economy and state system. Through this process of combined and uneven development, then, a systemic antagonism between capitalist nation-states and a tributary empire was worked out in which the former achieved a decisive victory by virtue of their economic vitality and military power.

Malcolm Yapp has noted, appropriately enough, that: 'Most people know the Eastern Question as an affair of diplomacy conducted in the chancelleries of Europe; in the Near East it was a bloody battle for land' (1987:16). At the centre of this struggle was the means by which property relations and forms of rule in the Middle East were to be recomposed by, and then incorporated into, the capitalist market and state system of the West. Yet this long decline and incorporation was precisely the epoch in which, first, the distinction was forged between the advanced and the under-developed world and, secondly, the capitalist world market and a small number of rapidly industrializing states established their global dominance. Thereafter, all development was to be dependent development.[2]

Empire to states system

Broadly speaking, the diplomatic manoeuvring of the Eastern Question itself may be divided into four stages. The first period concerned the expansion of Russia into the regions bordering the northern shores of the Black Sea, coupled with the Anglo-French rivalries over the route to India and influence in the eastern Mediterranean. After the end of the Russo-Turkish War (1768–74), Russia reached the Black Sea and at the Treaty of Kutchuk Kainardji gained ill-defined rights over the Orthodox Christian subjects of the Ottoman empire and rights of passage for its merchant shipping through both the Bosporus and the Dardanelles. With the Napoleonic invasion of Egypt (1798), the French Directory sought to challenge the British in the East, prompting a closer engagement on the part of the latter. The British supported the Ottomans against the French, as did the Russians. Britain invaded, and briefly occupied, Egypt in 1801. After the eclipse of France's maritime power following the Battle of Trafalgar (1805), Napoleon's attempt to impose the Continental System against Britain, together with Russian and French antagonism over the Ottoman empire, resulted in war between France and Russia. Just as the prospect of French expansion into the Middle East threatened the overland routes to India for the British, so the danger of expansion in the Balkans and the straits of the Dardanelles and Bosporus worried the Russians. Indeed, both Britain and Russia came to see that the preservation of the territorial integrity of the empire, if feasible, was the best long-term strategy for the safeguarding of their otherwise divergent interests in the region. Equally, as powers concerned with counter-revolution on the European continent, Russia and Britain also sought to discourage challenges to Ottoman authority, lest they provoke instability elsewhere.

2 By this I do not mean to signal agreement with the specific claims of dependency theory, but rather to indicate that late and late – late industrialization faced an environment significantly different from that of the original development of industrial capitalism. The new environment contained both constraints and opportunities, but it was now dominated by a few essentially European powers and witnessed an accelerating progression of the economic and military leading edge. This meant that things had to be done differently in those regions that were in a relation of economic and military subordination to the European world and its offshoots.

A second phase was opened with the Greek War of Independence in the 1820s, representing the spread of 'nationalist' ideas into the European parts of the empire and the entry of public opinion (in the form of the Romantic nationalism of revolutionary Europe) into Western decision-making.[3] At first the powers adopted a policy of non-intervention, but the refusal of the Porte to accept their mediation brought about the sinking of the Ottoman and Egyptian fleets at Navarino (1827). The Ottomans then declared a jihad against Russia and after facing effectively total defeat signed the Treaty of Adrianople in 1829. The Russians continued their traditional policy of favouring the integrity of the empire over plans for partition. Similar threats to the empire were raised by Muhammad Ali's attempt to strengthen the position of Egypt in the 1830s, including the invasion and occupation of the Syrian provinces in 1831. In 1840, the Egyptians were defeated by a contingent of British and Turkish forces, and Muhammad Ali was forced to withdraw from Syria. A loss of central control in Egypt marked the last decade of Muhammad Ali's rule.

During the 1850s, growing capitalist penetration of the empire, fissiparous forces from within and continued Russian encroachments from without, resulted in further crises. Russian attempts to gain further influence over the Porte and especially to strengthen its position in the Black Sea and the straits prompted French and British military intervention. Russian defeat in the Crimean War (1853/4–6) enabled the Western powers to secure the demilitarization of the straits (Treaty of Paris 1856), and Britain, France and Austria soon declared that any breach of the Treaty would constitute a *casus belli*. These provisions did not last. With the French preoccupied by war against Prussia, in October 1870 the Russians repudiated the military clauses of the Paris treaty.

Meantime, the pressures behind Balkan separatism were increasing. On the one side, Balkan claims against the Ottomans were strengthened by the increased wealth that the Christian commercial

---

3 In this context we must recall Eric Hobsbawm's comment on Greek 'nationalism': 'The literate champions and organizers of Greek nationalism in the early nineteenth century were undoubtedly inspired by the thought of ancient Hellenic glories ... Yet the real Greeks who took up arms for what turned out to be the formation of a new independent nation-state, did not talk ancient Greek ... Paradoxically, they stood for Rome rather than Greece (*romaiosyne*), that is to say they saw themselves as heirs of the Christianized Roman Empire (i.e. Byzantium). They fought as Christians against Muslim unbelievers, as Romans against the Turkish dogs' (1990:76, 77).

class derived from a shift away from subsistence to capitalist farming and increased trade with Europe; among the nobility, struggles over access to state power emerged, fought out through local armed conflicts and aggravated by the onerous demands of Muslim landlords; and the spread of literacy, in conjunction with Ottoman resistance to employing Greeks for official posts, further exacerbated a tense situation. On the other side, Ottoman attempts to maintain the integrity of the empire meant that Russian intervention on behalf of the Balkan Christians led to another Russo-Turkish War (1877–8). Throughout the Eastern Crisis (1875–8), the British cabinet was divided as to how to respond to Russia. No direct action was taken, but the Russians were warned that any action against British interests – in the straits and on the routes to the East – would lead to war. At the Congress of Berlin (1878) Russian aims were checked and Britain was satisfied, despite Russia's acquisition of bases in eastern Anatolia. Austria gained some of the empire's European territories.

In the course of these events, however, a subtle alteration in the underlying issues occurred: the strategies of the powers changed, and above all the interests favouring the integrity of the empire were weakened. In addition, German interest in the future of the Eastern Question came to centre-stage as its trade and investments increased, rapidly taking second place in trade to Britain and to France in finance. German financial imperialism was focused above all on the proposed Berlin-Baghdad railway. Both Russia and Britain were concerned lest German influence spread to the straits: Russia feared that a German alliance with the Ottomans could threaten the Caucasus; Britain felt that her dominance in Egypt, Iraq and the Gulf could be compromised. Secret agreements between the Entente powers and the Germans did little to resolve the growing rivalries. This increasingly *capitalist* rivalry effectively opened a third stage, one that only came into its own during the general crisis of European imperialism, leading to the First World War and the Ottoman entry on the side of the Central Powers. Of course, the inevitable consequence of this was the final disintegration of the empire. But the ground for the latter had already been laid by the accelerating annexation of Ottoman lands following the settlement of the Congress of Berlin (1878): France occupied Tunisia in 1881, Britain took Cyprus in 1878 and Egypt in 1882, Austria-Hungary having occupied Herzegovina and Bosnia in 1878 formally annexed them in 1908, Italy took Libya in 1911 and the Balkan

Wars of 1912–13 severed many of the remaining European provinces from Ottoman jurisdiction.

The fourth and final phase concerned the conduct of the First World War and, in particular, the wartime diplomacy of the leading powers, a phase which extended into the 'peace', eventually reaching a conclusion at the Treaty of Lausanne in 1923. In this period a number of schemes for the future of the Ottoman domains were canvassed as the contending parties tried to clarify their long-term interests and as the peoples of the region struggled to assert their claims. At the core of the empire a new state, Turkey, emerged, while in the former Arab regions a number of dependent states were created: in Lebanon and Syria by France, and in Iraq, Jordan and Palestine by Britain. The Gulf sheikhdoms remained, in effect, British protectorates, and in Saudi Arabia and North Yemen new states developed. In Iran also a new state was forged. Egypt remained under British control and in North Africa French influence persisted. Despite this continued European predominance, the terms of imperialist rivalry in the region were altered by the growing importance of the region's oil, together with the entry of the United States into the picture. At the same time, the balance of social conflict was changed by the spread of nationalist movements, as well as the existence of a state socialist regime in the Soviet Union. Finally, with the Balfour Declaration (1917), and more importantly the incorporation of the Zionist programme into the British mandate for Palestine (1920), the seeds of future Arab-Israeli antagonism were sown by the consolidation of Jewish settler colonialism.

Britain, India and the Middle East

In order to grasp the principal war aims of and the changing claims made by the powers, especially the role of Britain as the dominant power in the region, it is necessary to sketch in something of the interests and strategies of the central players. British interests in the East centred on a number of concerns. The most important of these was the security of the overland routes to India. Related to this was a growing unease about Russian imperial designs in inner and central Asia. Expanding trade, especially Egyptian cotton, and financial links provided a final motive for involvement. By contrast, the adjacent landpowers – Russia and Austria (-Hungary) – were primarily interested in the future of the European regions of the Ottoman empire and their rights of access to the Mediterranean. What made this mix so explosive, however, was the fact that as capitalist industrialization accelerated in the second half of the nineteenth century, the expansion of European economic interests served further to entangle the region in the deepening inter-imperialist rivalries of the major powers.

In the eighteenth century, Mughal power and authority were declining as India underwent a commercialization of political power. Whether from Asia or Europe, traders were interested in India for its cloth, silk, indigo, pepper, cardamom and other spices. In return, the Europeans exchanged silver from the Americas, copper from Japan and (some) gold. These precious metals expanded the monetary base of the Indian economy and further extended the scope for commercial networks (precious metals were in short supply from indigenous sources). Trade with China expanded after the Opium Wars (1839–42). British hegemony on the subcontinent, based on its naval supremacy in the Indian Ocean and the Arab seas, had been assured by the time the Seven Years' War ended. At this point, Clive determined that the East India Company should use the revenues from Bengal to finance its trade, to maintain its dividend in London and to pay its army. (The opium trade alone provided some 15 per cent of the Company's revenue and 30 per cent of India's trade down to the Mutiny.)

Thus the lure of profits from tribute and trade in India, combined with the energizing threat from the French in the Revolutionary and Napoleonic Wars, provided a fertile terrain for mercantilist expansion on the subcontinent. Already in 1784 duties on the import of tea from China into Britain had been slashed and the Company needed a major increase of Indian cotton exports to finance this lucrative trade. After 1834 the Company lost its monopoly over the China trade, and the attractions of further commercial advantage, together with concerns to check the Russians in central Asia, stood behind British expansion in north-west India. It was the collapse of a regional power, that of Ranjit Singh's polity in the Punjab, which provided the immediate context for action: the invasion and occupation of Sindh (1838–43), the defeat of Punjab (1845) and the push to Afghanistan. Throughout India, this pattern of collapsing regional authority and expanding networks of trade and plunder drove British expansion ever forward.

It was only after the reorganization of rule following the Mutiny (1857) that British penetration of India accelerated, and commercial and agrarian elites were stablized. Several developments were of great importance in this context, helping to integrate the Indian economy into a wider international network of exchanges and production: between 1857 and 1880 the railway mileage in India increased from 570 to 4,300; in 1869 the Suez Canal was opened; and between 1856 and 1864 demand for Indian cotton almost trebled as a result of the Civil War in America. On this economic and military basis, the British position in India became central to its world-wide empire: as Eric Wolf has remarked, 'Indian surpluses enabled England to create and maintain a global system of free trade' (1982:261; see also Ingham 1984). Consequently, the need to protect the passages to India, and with this the desire to prevent other powers gaining substantial influence in the Middle East, increased. In turn, these aims could be best accomplished by preserving the territorial integrity of the Ottoman empire while promoting the expansion of British economic interests in the region.

In addition, creation of a naval hegemony in the Gulf was regarded as vital to protect the position of India. Yet during the course of the Revolutionary and Napoleonic Wars, neutral nations and regional trading empires, such as the Muscat Arabs, the Beys of Tunis or the Bugis of Indonesia, engrossed much of the eastern trade. In a bid to restore the capital and credit position of the Company, as well as ensure trading stability, the British destroyed local traders and imposed a new law of the sea – British paramountcy.

Throughout the eighteenth century the British had clashed with local traders in the Gulf, especially with the Qasimi tribal confederacy which commanded a fleet of some 900 vessels and a naval force of 8,000 men. Moreover, the power of the Qawasim was strengthened by forging links with the Wahhabi movement on the Arabian peninsula. For inland, the rise of the puritanical Islamic movement, Wahhabism, based on the tribal and pastoral peoples of eastern and central Arabia, had all but undermined Ottoman authority by 1800. In effect, the Qawasim became the naval arm of Wahhabism. In 1809 and 1820 the British destroyed the entire Qasimi fleet, and henceforth 'the trucial system was set in motion. The Qawasim and the shaikhs of Ajman, Umm al-Qaiwain, Abu Dhabi, Dubai and Bahrain capitulated and signed separate agreements with the British government' (Said Zahlan 1989:7).

The tribal leaders of the Arab littoral also established arrangements to prevent maritime warfare in 1835, and in 1853 signed the Perpetual Maritime Truce. The resulting Trucial system (the *sahel Oman*) guaranteed British control over the external affairs of the United Arab Emirates (1820s), and was later extended to Bahrain (1861), Kuwait (1899), Oman (where French influence was thwarted by an agreement with the sultanate in 1891 and with the imamate in 1920) and Qatar (1916). At the junction of the Red and Arabian seas, the British seized Aden in 1839, as a coaling station on the route to India and as a counter to the threat posed by the power of Muhammad Ali in Egypt and the Sudan. At this time, and until the First World War, 'British control was based upon cheap sea power and hardly extended more than a gunshot from the coast. Further inland Britain attempted to do no more than exclude foreign influence' (Yapp 1987:177).

If to begin with the British strategy involved support for the integrity of the empire as the means to keeping Russia at bay and protecting the routes to India, then during the Eastern Crisis (1875–8) an alternative strategy became increasingly attractive. In this rethink, the Suez Canal and hence Egypt played a central role. Initially, having control over the two entrances to the Indian Ocean (the Cape and the Straits of Malacca), the British government opposed the creation of a third in the Canal. As Palmerston memorably put it, sensing that control would require occupation:

> We do not want Egypt or wish it for ourselves, any more than any rational man with an estate in the north of England and a residence in the south would have wished to possess the inns on the road. All he could want would have been that the inns should be well-kept, always accessible, and furnishing him, when he came, with mutton-chops and post-horses. (quoted in Mansfield 1991:87)

Less mindful of such strategic concerns, British shippers and merchants were strongly in favour. None the less, *The Economist* had the measure of the situation when it noted that the Suez Canal had been 'cut by French energy and Egyptian money for British advantage'. Indeed, according to Issawi:

> By 1881, Britain accounted for over 80 percent of Canal traffic (declining slowly to 50 by 1938), and nearly two-thirds of its trade east of Suez passed through the Canal, as did half of India's *total* trade and a substantial and increasing share of that of Australia and New Zealand. Moreover, as holder of 44 percent of the Canal stock after the purchase, in 1875, of the Khedive of Egypt's shares, the British government drew a substantial income. (1982:51)

Together with the huge seapower at Britain's disposal, this meant that the position of India might be best assured by naval hegemony in the Gulf and influence in Arabia and Mesopotamia. For the Iraqi provinces of Mosul, Baghdad and Basra, the opening of the Suez Canal had the effect of rapidly expanding their regional trade and their international commerce with Europe. The provinces were drawn together, agricultural production increased and Britain displaced India as the main trading partner. As the First World War approached, then, the British were reconsidering their overall strategy in the region. The outcome of this was to play a crucial role in the post-war shaping of the Middle East state system.

Let us turn briefly to the question of Russian expansion in central Asia and, in particular, the pressure this imposed on the Ottomans. The growth of grain exports from the Ukraine and the strategic importance of the passage from the Black Sea to the Mediterranean meant that Russia had vital interests in the future of the empire. In addition, the large Orthodox Christian population under the authority of the Porte provided another legitimation for Russian designs. This was further compounded by the rise of demands for autonomy and independence in the Balkans and the competition between Austria and Russia for influence here. Several times the Russians contemplated plans for the partition of the Ottoman empire, but in each case the stability, both international and domestic, provided by its continued survival seemed more important. As the leading counter-revolutionary power on the continent between 1815 and 1848, the Russians could ill afford a general war in Europe. Whether directly or otherwise, the French Revolution had abolished serfdom over most of west and central Europe, but Napoleon's defeat in 1812 ended the immediate threat to Russian autocracy. However, any attempt to break up the empire in Russia's favour was certain to involve conflict with Austria and Britain. Defeat at the hands of the Western, capitalist powers would only increase the pressure for internal reform – as was amply shown by the defeat in the Crimea and the subsequent abolition of serfdom (1861). In fact, the only potentially dissatisfied power in relation to the Eastern Question was France, a result of its eclipse in the eastern Mediterranean under the shadow of British power. Yet here too, and again primarily for domestic reasons, no French government between 1815 and 1848 was prepared to attempt to mobilize 'the revolutionary energies of Jacobinism at home and of liberalism and nationalism abroad' (Hobsbawm 1962:135).

The First World War and peace-making

For these reasons, it was always unlikely that any localized conflict would bring about a complete collapse of Ottoman rule. Rather it was to take the general crisis of European imperialism to restructure the state system in the Middle East. (Thus while it may be accurate to say that the Balkans provided the fuse for the First World War, it was the more general crisis of imperialism that was at the heart of the conflict.) Prior to the imperialist epoch, the overseas expansion of the European capitalist powers into their periphery did not involve the formal annexation of territory 'so long as their citizens were given total freedom to do what they wanted, including extra-territorial privileges' (Hobsbawm 1975:160) – as was provided for under the Ottoman capitulations and commercial treaties. But with the rise of protectionism (at least outside Britain) during the Great Depression of 1873–95 and the growing concentration and centralization of capital in the core associated with the rise of finance capital, new relations began to form as these economies sought out markets and raw materials (minerals, foodstuffs and soon oil) in the periphery.

The determining process here, as Lenin and many others implicitly grasped at the time, was at once political and economic, a new conjuncture in the development of the capitalist world economy – imperialism. Combined with the extraordinary material advance of Europe during the imperialist boom of 1895–1914, the 'New Imperialism' both undermined the socio-economic stability of the periphery and destroyed its archaic polities (ancient empires, multinational autocracies and stateless orders), thereby prompting the onset of formal colonialism as well as preparing the ground for a wave of revolutionary developments of which the Russian revolution of 1905 was the first. The fact that there was a strategic dimension to this rivalry does not undermine the accuracy of this judgment, for as Hobsbawm explains in the British case:

> speaking globally, India was the core of British strategy, and ... this strategy required control not only over the short-sea routes to the subcontinent (Egypt, the Middle East, the Red Sea, Persian Gulf and South Arabia) and the long-sea routes (the Cape of Good Hope and Singapore), but over the entire Indian Ocean, including crucial sectors of the African coast and its hinterland. ... [But] India was

the 'brightest jewel in the imperial crown' and the core of British global strategic thinking precisely because of her very real importance to the British economy. This was never greater than at this time, when anything up to 60 per cent of British cotton exports went to India and the Far East, to which India was the key – 40–45 per cent went to India alone – and when the international balance of payments of Britain hinged on the payments surplus which India provided.[4] (1987:68, 69)

As the new stage of capitalism consolidated itself, the attendant national rivalries underlay the formal colonization of 1880–1914, for they were now intertwined with the inevitable collapse or revolt of peripheral formations. In turn, colonial disputes between the rival powers, and specifically the attempts to avoid unnecessary colonial conflicts, assisted the formation of military alliances. Meantime, on the European continent the formation of the German empire (1864–71) challenged the continental balance struck at the Congress of Vienna (1815), while the precocious German economic advance gave it global ambitions requiring an ability to project power and to trade. The pursuit of a global navy was increasingly seen as a necessity. Given the conjuncture just defined, and given also the economic and strategic position of Britain, this could not but challenge Britain's global position. In the context of this incipient global rivalry, what Hobsbawm has termed the 'combustible material' of the periphery provided the fuse to the First World War, which in turn provided the context for the most significant revolution of the epoch, the Bolshevik Revolution of 1917.

The countdown to war itself was simple enough: the large-scale industrial development of Germany, in conjunction with the imperial compromises made possible between France, Russia and Britain, meant that imperial rivalries would hinge on Anglo-German competition. Although Britain and Germany were able to resolve their differences over the Portuguese colonies and the Berlin – Baghdad railway, the shift from purely colonial entanglements to a more generalized European and global rivalry could not be accommodated by agreements alone. After the demonstration of tsarist weakness in the war against Japan, the French and the

---

4 The significance of cotton can be seen in the fact that: 'In 1880, textiles and clothing were 55.7 per cent of world trade in manufactures by value. In that sector Britain was still in 1880 responsible for 46.3 per cent of world exports: in cotton alone perhaps 80 per cent' (Crafts 1985:144).

British forged the Entente Cordiale based upon reciprocal support in Morocco and Egypt, respectively. In 1907, Russia and Britain came to a similar deal over Iran, Afghanistan and the Far East (this formed the Triple Entente), securing British interests in the Gulf. Once struck, these alliances set the framework for war. The crumbling authority of the Ottoman empire and the tensions thereby created in the Balkans provided the fuse: the Russians supported the Balkan League against Turkey and contested the role of Austria-Hungary; only Germany could guarantee the position of Austria-Hungary; the Franco-Russian alliance strengthened as German power increased; and Britain was threatened by German expansion. The fact that the Entente powers (above all Russia) constituted the greatest threat to the Ottomans and refused the empire an entente made it all but certain that the Turks would enter the conflict on the side of the Central Powers.

British war aims, the peace and state-building

The entry of the Ottoman empire into the war on the side of the Central Powers sealed its fate. The conduct of the conflict itself brought economic ruin to large parts of the empire, and military attrition further eroded central control. But for the duration of the war the influence of the imperialist powers over the economy was reduced. In British planning circles, political and military opinion was divided as to what role operations in the east might play in the War. Clearly, Germany was the main enemy and, by itself, Ottoman power posed no serious threat to the Allies. (Indeed, prior to the outbreak of the war a German military mission to Istanbul had concluded that there would be little or no benefit from an alliance with the Ottomans.) But the war was fought not merely to block German dominance of the European continent but also to defend the British empire. This meant that while Germany was the adversary in Europe, Russia was a potential challenger in Asia. Yet Russia was for the moment an ally against Germany. How, then, could Germany be defeated without also bringing about an expansion of Russian power? It was originally in answer to this question that the importance of military operations in the Middle East was recognized.

At the beginning of the war, British liberals such as Asquith, Grey and Churchill had no territorial designs on Ottoman lands, but the minister for war, Kitchener, saw things differently. Kitchener, whose entire career had been devoted to the military administration of the British empire and who had served in the Sudan, India and Egypt, argued that Russia had to be kept in the war until Germany was vanquished, and that afterwards the Muslim caliphate should be transferred to Arabia which Britain could then control with its naval power. Extraordinary though this now seems, Kitchener and others believed that the Middle East and much of Asia beyond was ruled by Islam; that Islam was something like an extreme form of Catholicism, or at least that the institution of the caliphate was like that of the papacy; that a Muslim holy war against Britain was a real and frightening possibility, especially given the position of the Muslim population in India; and that Britain should therefore seek future control over the empire's Arab regions through the creation of a new, British-backed, Arab caliphate (a 'Pope' of Islam).

In Damascus in 1898 the Kaiser had proclaimed Germany the protector of the world's 300 million Muslims, and the British feared that the Ottoman alliance with the Central Powers would facilitate German manipulation of the Islamic world.[5] Furthermore, military engagements in the Middle East turned out to be far from negligible. As William Keylor points out: 'The closing of the Turkish straits had sealed Russia off from her European allies; the Anglo-French effort to force Turkey out of the war in the Dardanelles expedition of 1915 was a costly failure. Turkish pressure on Egypt pinned down British forces that might have been deployed elsewhere' (1984:60, 61). Thus, Kitchener's stance was no mere whim, but part of a grand, imperial, strategic vision to combat German (and Russian) influence and to secure the Middle East for India and the British empire. The logic of Kitchener's approach has been emphasized by David Fromkin:

The War Minister's plan was for Britain to take possession of Alexandretta [now Iskenderum in Turkey], the great natural port on the Asian mainland opposite Cyprus, and to construct a railroad from it to the Mesopotamian provinces (now in Iraq), of which Britain would also take possession. It was generally believed (though not yet proven) that the Mesopotamian provinces contained large oil reserves which were deemed important by Churchill and the Admiralty. It was believed, too, by Kitchener and others, that

5 John Buchan's novel *Greenmantle* (1916) dramatizes just such a scenario.

the ancient Mesopotamian lands watered by the Tigris and the Euphrates rivers could be developed so as to produce agricultural riches; but in Kitchener's view the principal advantages of his proposal were strategic. The British railroad from the Mediterranean to the head of the Persian Gulf would enable troops to move to and from India rapidly. The broad swath of British-owned territory it would traverse would provide a shield for the Persian Gulf, as well as a road to India. (1991:140, 141)

In view of these developments, Britain's aims came to include the removal of Ottoman claims to sovereignty over Cyprus and Egypt, an extension of its position in the south of Iran to include the neutral zone, and Iraq, together with support of it to the west, namely Palestine. France's main territorial claim was for Syria and Lebanon where French colonialists saw themselves as the protectors of the Maronite community. In the Constantinople Agreement of March 1915, the French and the British promised to Russia the straits and Istanbul if the Allies won the war, thereby attempting to prevent Russia from signing a separate peace with Germany. But with the advent of the Bolshevik Revolution and the withdrawal of Russia from the war (and its separate peace with Germany), the British occupied Palestine, Syria and Iraq. The Allies also proposed to occupy Turkey.

In pursuit of its strategy, Britain thus came to favour the dismemberment of the Ottoman empire and the independence of the Arab provinces. Of course, by this British officials meant 'independence' from Ottoman suzerainty; since the Arabs were unfit for self-government, the Europeans (the British and the French) would have to establish authority and take control. After all, even such a partisan and romantic myth-maker as T. E. Lawrence told his biographer, Liddell Hart, that 'Arab unity is a madman's notion' (see, especially, James 1990). And, on the Arab side, the indigenous resources available for projects of state formation were slender. Certainly, the Arab interlocutors that British officials fastened upon, Hussain the sherif of Mecca and the Hejaz and his sons Faisal and Abdullah, were not nationalists or even proto-nationalists. At the outset of the war, Hussain was an Ottoman governor who had used Turkish troops to quell fractious Arab tribesmen. It was the *policies* of the Ottomans that he opposed, not the Sunni caliphate as such, for the Ottoman proposal to extend the Damascus – Medina railway to Mecca would have threatened the basis of his power which was located in control over the trade and pilgrim routes in Arabia.

The Arab Revolt of June 1916 was itself a relatively trivial affair, 'a side-show within a side-show' as one official described Colonel Lawrence's operations more generally. Although the subject of much later nationalist myth-making, the 'Arab Revolt' is symptomatically misnamed. In the first place, the scale of the revolt was pitiful; at most a few thousand tribesmen took part, attracted by the gold paid as a subsidy by the British. No Arab sections of the Ottoman army defected, and the supposed secret, military organizations of Arab patriots failed to materialize. The Mecca revolt could not even take Medina. Later, it was Allenby's forces that conquered Syria and Palestine, with the Northern Arab Army playing but a minor role. Most importantly, on neither side was there any thought of establishing a pan-Arab state (see, especially, Kedourie 1987 and Fromkin 1991). On the British side, Lawrence, for example, had nothing but contempt for urban, proto-nationalist Arabs. As for the Hashemite cause, Hussain and his sons were primarily concerned to break with Ottoman control, to augment their position in the tribal politics of Arabia and to extract booty from the British.

However, the activities of Lawrence and the Arab Bureau (established in Cairo in 1916) did have the effect of raising the salience of 'Arab' questions in British foreign policy. London's interest in the Middle Eastern dimension of imperial strategy was further increased by the accession of Lloyd George to the position of prime minister in December 1916, with his keen support for the Zionist cause and dreams of creating a pan-Hellenic empire in Asia Minor. At the same time, and fortunately for Britain, the presidency of Clemenceau in France had the opposite effect, bringing to power a less colonialist faction whose single-minded concern was the defeat of Germany in Europe.

After hostilities ended, it was Churchill who recognized most clearly that domestic pressure for economic retrenchment and demobilization might deny Britain the fruits of victory. At home, the economic constraints on overseas expenditures were powerful, especially as the economy went into slump in 1920–1. Thus, on 18 July 1921 *The Times* condemned the government in the following terms: 'while they have spent nearly £150,000,000 since the Armistice upon semi-nomads in Mesopotamia they can find only £200,000 a year for the regeneration of our slums, and have had to forbid all expenditure under the Education Act of 1918.' Coming from a source not known for its social concern, such comment was a clear indication that unless a low-cost solution to the problems of imposing imperialist control could be found, then British gains might be lost altogether. In the Middle East, popular pressure throughout the region soon threatened the British position. Uprisings took place in Egypt during the winter of 1918–19; Afghanistan revolted in the spring of 1919; Ibn Saud and Hussain crossed swords in Arabia from the spring of 1919; the Kemalist revolt began in early 1920 and in the summer Greek forces invaded Turkey with British backing; Arab nationalists confronted French power in Syria in the spring and summer of 1920; and in the summer of 1920 there were tribal revolts in Iraq, which were only put down in early 1921.

During the war Anglo-French competition over territory and oil had been partly resolved through the Sykes-Picot agreement of 1916 to divide the Arab provinces. Britain's positions in Iraq, Egypt, the Gulf, Arabia and Iran were kept off the Versailles agenda, and Clemenceau and Lloyd George agreed that Palestine should come under British control. This left only the fate of Lebanon and Syria to be determined. A final settlement of Allied conflicts was made at the San Remo Conference in 1920, where it was agreed that France would take Syria and Lebanon, that Britain would control Iraq, Transjordan and Palestine, and that Iraqi oil would be shared.

The other major Allied power, the United States, had only limited interests in the Middle East before the First World War. But in 1919 the State Department began to prosecute US interests with vigour, essentially because of oil. As William Stivers has cogently demonstrated, the US oil companies 'were in the vanguard of U.S. penetration into the Middle East' (1982:110). However, the United States did not seek to supplant Anglo-French power. On the contrary, US 'jackal diplomacy' favoured the retention of European hegemony over the region. As Fromkin explains:

> both the Department of State and the oil companies were in favor
> of British hegemony in the area. The oil companies were prepared
> to engage in exploration, development, and production only in areas
> governed by what they regarded as stable and responsible regimes.
> . . . many officials . . . expressed dismay at the thought that Britain
> and France might relinquish control of their Middle Eastern con-

quests, and . . . expressed fear for the fate of American interests should they do so. (1991:535)

Meantime, even with the solution of inter-Allied rivalries, the development of new forms of influence in the region was complicated by the support given to anti-colonial movements by the Soviet Union. No longer was it the threat of pan-Islamic revolt that worried British officials, but rather the dangers of Bolshevism: they blamed 'the supposedly Jewish-controlled, German-influenced Young Turk leadership and now its international ramifications, chief among which were Islam and now Bolshevism in a line that ran from Enver through Alexander Helphand to Lenin' (Fromkin 1991:468).

More seriously, after the defeat of the Central Powers, the Allies, and in particular Britain, had turned towards a campaign against the Bolshevik Revolution. This meant that the Soviet Union 'soon found itself committed, in default of other means of defence, to a general diplomatic offensive against Great Britain in Asia' (Carr 1966:244). Contestation occurred in Turkey as well as Afghanistan and Iran, as the Soviet Union signed treaties with Afghanistan and Iran and provided support to Kemal in Turkey. The importance of Soviet involvement in this new situation was that it made the reimposition of European colonial forms of control all the more difficult. And whether or not Bolshevik activity provided significant levels of material support, the demonstration effect of the Revolution and its corrosive effects on European control were real enough.

To begin with there was considerable uncertainty as to how to resolve these questions; and, given that Egypt was already a British protectorate, the central remaining question was the future position of Iraq. Iraq played an important role in the British strategy for the Middle East because (together with Transjordan, Palestine and Egypt) it connected the eastern Mediterranean to the Gulf and hence to India. As well as being a key crossing for transport routes and having considerable capacity for crop and cotton production, the control of northern Iraq was seen as essential for the control of the south, which in turn was necessary for the military defence of Anglo-Persian's oil fields in Iran. In addition, in time of war the Iraqi oil fields would be vital to naval power in the region. It was considerations such as these that led the secretary to the cabinet, Maurice Hankey, to note that 'the retention of the oil-bearing regions in Mesopotamia and Persia in British hands, as well as a proper strategic boundary to cover them, would appear to be a first class British war aim.' Accordingly, Britain wanted the oil-bearing region of Mosul to be incorporated into Iraq so that its revenues could finance the proposed Iraqi administration. France and the United States were prepared to accept this arrangement in return for shares in the new oil concession.

But how was British power to be maintained at low cost? The British faced a dilemma. Could control of Iraq be maintained by the usual recipe for dealing with tribal magnates, the mixture of fraud and force, gold and silver for bribery and RAF bombs for coercion, as proposed by the colonial government of British India (otherwise known as Simla)? Or was the Arab Bureau of the Foreign Office correct to suggest that the wartime mobilization of the region made 'nation-state building the wave of the future' (Brown 1984:114). Against the arguments of the latter, Simla had opposed the arming of tribal forces during the war as this would inevitably bring with it problems of pacification when hostilities ceased. More importantly, such overtures might have the effect of undermining the low-cost mechanisms of informal control that the security of the routes to India relied upon. Any talk of statehood and independence could only weaken the British position in India in the long run.

To begin with, when the French ousted Faisal from Syria (July 1920), and as conflict raged between Ibn Saud (a client of Simla) and Hussain in Arabia, the Arab Bureau's strategy of backing the Hashemites did indeed seem dangerous. But the spread of revolt in Iraq (September 1920) cast doubts on the methods of the British India official Sir Arnold Wilson. On a wider canvas, the era of Lenin and Wilson, together with the costs and uncertainties of direct colonial administration, argued for a new method of European control through the indirect rule of the League's mandate system.

The solution (agreed under Churchill's leadership at the Cairo Conference in March 1921) was to install Faisal as head of an Arab government in Iraq, to deploy air power for the purposes of tribal pacification and to increase the subsidy paid to Ibn Saud. The logic of the solution was simple. Having failed to involve American power directly in support of their designs (the Senate refused to ratify US membership of the League of Nations), the British decided to follow the tried and tested policy of getting the colonized to pay for their own subordination. If the Americans would not follow

Kipling's injunction to take up the white man's burden, then the 'natives' must be forced to do the job instead. In Iraq a client government was established in which the British maintained effective control over military, fiscal and judicial administration. The revitalized Turkish Petroleum Company operated the Mosul and Basra fields, now with US and French participation. Mosul oil and its revenues financed the state, thereby relieving the British taxpayer of the expense. Revolts were pacified through the vicious use of (low-cost) air power. In October 1922 the Anglo-Iraqi Treaty largely replaced the mandate, but these new arrangements still maintained British control over finance, administration and defence and foreign policy.

Something similar occurred in Egypt. This time a nationalist revolt in 1919 resulted in a reassessment of imperial strategy by the British. In February 1922 the protectorate was renounced, but control over defence and foreign policy, the security of the Suez Canal, the government of the Sudan and the future of the capitulations remained in British hands.

The emergence of the Turkish Republic

In addition to resolving Anglo-French rivalry, the San Remo Conference saw the development of a proposal to bring the Dardanelles under international control, to grant independence and autonomy to Armenia and Kurdistan and to award eastern Thrace to Greece. The sultan's government, no longer fully in control of Turkey, reluctantly signed at Sèvres (August 1920). At this juncture, Allied forces were in control of Istanbul. The situation remained unstable and many of the San Remo proposals proved otiose. Kemal's nationalist forces contested the authority of the sultan; the Greeks claimed territory in Turkey but were thrown out; a proposal that the United States take up the mandate for Armenia came to nothing; Kurdish aspirations fell foul of Iraq's need for Mosul; British and French policy diverged over the Greek – Turkish war; and the Allies had insufficient forces to garrison Turkey. Yet without a long-term solution to the future of Turkey, British designs in Iraq, and thus its power elsewhere in the Middle East, would be compromised.

Amidst the disintegration of Ottoman authority, the Hamidian regime had been overthrown by the Young Turk revolution of 1908 – a movement composed of junior army officers and minor bureaucrats in which the army was the chief beneficiary. The Committee of Union and Progress finally ended the ensuing uncertainty and seized power in a coup (23 January 1913). The CUP continued the formula of Ottomanist reform for the empire: a secular system of law and education, a liberal constitution, a strengthened army and administration and more emphasis on economic development. But given the reality of secessionist movements in the Balkans under protection from Christian powers and dependent incorporation under the aegis of a non-Muslim bourgeoisie, the Turkish national movement increasingly assumed a dictatorial and Muslim-nationalist form, as Ottoman identity proved incapable of providing a unifying framework for programmes of renewal. (Ottomanism had become simply the formula for disintegration, the Sunni *ulema* a bulwark of reaction.) It was from this matrix that the Turkish Republic was forged by Mustafa Kemal after the war.

As noted, immediately after the war, the Allies determined to maintain control of Turkey, and to this end they occupied Istanbul in March 1920. The Soviets supported Kemal from 1919 and renewed their commitment after deteriorating Anglo-Soviet relations in 1921. By the spring of 1922 the (British-backed) Greek forces fighting in Turkey had been routed. Domestically, the civil war was won by the end of 1920 and Kemal was thereafter free to move against the radicals of the coalition that constituted the Green Army, strengthening the Islamic and nationalist elements against the radical forces around the Turkish Communist Party. Allied designs, then, not only failed, but they also had the effect of compromising both the position of 'moderate' nationalists and the legitimacy of the sultan. None the less, it was to take until January 1921 for Mustafa Kemal to persuade the Grand National Assembly that sovereignty resided in the 'nation'. The climax was reached when the Allies invited both the official Ottoman government *and* the Nationalists to the conference at Lausanne. This slight precipitated the abolition of the sultanate (November 1922) and the subsequent formation of the Turkish Republic.

Having consolidated his position internally and secured Turkish independence internationally, Kemal had no further use for Soviet support. Indeed, Turkey's relations with the West might even be harmed by too close an alignment with the revolutionaries in the East. At the Lausanne Conference the British negotiator, Lord Curzon, was able to separate Turkey and the Soviet Union, secured a regime for the straits which suited British interests and 'walked off with the prize of Mosul' (Stivers 1982:141). In return, plans for Allied suzerainty over Turkey and the continuation of the capitulations were abolished. Finally, Anglo-Turkish relations were consolidated in 1926 when Turkey agreed to comply with the League's award of Mosul to Iraq in return for a 10 per cent share of the royalties for twenty-five years. Thereafter, Turkey supported Britain in the region against Russia.

Arabia, the Gulf and Iran

Further south on the Arabian peninsula, the nineteenth century had witnessed a reassertion of Ottoman authority in the north and west and the British had intervened in the south and east. But after 1900 the Ikhwan recovered some control in eastern Arabia, and Ottoman authority was eclipsed by 1914. Ibn Saud increased his power, aided by British subsidy and weapons. However, the role of Hussain as ruler of the Hejaz and thus controller of the pilgrimage, and as head of the Hashemites (his sons Faisal and Abdullah ruled in Iraq and Transjordan, respectively), constituted a threat to the authority of the Saudis. Fortunately for the latter, Hussain undermined his own position through heavy taxation of merchants and pilgrims. Before long (by 1924), Hussain was defeated militarily by Ibn Saud and the Ikhwan. After this, Ibn Saud signed the Treaty of Jedda with the British in 1927 and then used the provision of mechanized weaponry by the latter to suppress the Ikhwan. Founded on the Wahhabi-Saudi movement, the Kingdom of Saudi Arabia was thus established in 1932.

On the Arab littoral of the Gulf we have already seen that Britain carved out a series of client polities, regulating their external affairs and having a virtual veto over their pattern of development. Of particular importance for subsequent events was the position allocated to Kuwait. Before the outbreak of the war, the British were worried by German proposals for a railroad to run from Berlin to Baghdad, fearing that this might compromise the integrity of communications and transport to India. In 1899 what was to become Kuwait came under British control, and the latter agreed to become the patrons of the locally dominant al-Sabah family. This arrangement was formalized by the 1913 Anglo-Ottoman agreement. After the war, acting on 'behalf' of Kuwait, Sir Percy Cox managed to get Ibn Saud to abandon his claim for much of the Basra vilayet in what was now Iraq in return for a large part of the Kuwaiti territory on the Gulf. Nevertheless, these negotiations were to leave Iraq with only a limited direct access to the Gulf at Umm Qasr.

Finally, on the Iranian side of the Gulf, the structure of society and power had evolved somewhat differently to that of the traditional Ottoman pattern. From the end of the eighteenth century, Iran was ruled by the Qajars, a noble class of Turkish tribal origin which had defeated the Zand dynasty of southern Iran. The central state was much weaker and the power of the nobility greater, even extending to foreign policy. In 1906 a Constitutional Revolution took place. Largely a Tehran affair, the deadlock between the Qajar government and the Majlis was ended by the shah's coup in 1908. Against the liberal movement, Britain went along with Russian support for the shah, placing the dictates of the Triple Entente above the appeasement of liberal sensibilities. Then in July 1909 the constitutional forces were bolstered by the support of two provincial groups: the anti-landlord movement in Gilan, led by Caucassian revolutionaries, and the Bakhtiyari tribal nomads. Still, no real government, let alone state, was consolidated. Finally, Russian troops intervened to end the constitutionalist experiment for good in 1911.

This fragmented society had been reduced to the status of a semi-colony by the incursions of Russia in the north and Britain in the south. An arrangement was formalized by the Anglo-Russian convention of 1907 'which divided Iran up into three respective spheres of influence; Russian in the north, British – with the oil concession area – in the south, and neutral in the middle' (Halliday 1974:467). The British D'Arcy Concession of 1901, which formed the basis of Anglo-Persian's power in Iran, had excluded the five major northern provinces precisely because of Russian claims in the region. Iranian weakness rendered it unable to prevent the flouting of its neutrality by Russia and Britain during the war. Also, the closing of the Dardanelles and the collapse of Russia severely damaged the economy. Finally, the Bolshevik Revolution deprived the shah of his key ally, a revolutionary movement broke out in Gilan and by the spring of 1920 Soviet power was established in neighbouring Azerbaijan. The Soviets gave support and recognition to the Soviet Republic of Gilan founded by the nationalist leader, Kuchik Khan.

Meantime, the British Foreign Office sought to establish a semi-protectorate with the Anglo-Persian Agreement signed by Curzon on 9 August 1919, and this involved the supply of British financial advisers for the Iranian government, the retraining of the army and the provision of engineers for railway construction. However, Britain was not willing to assist in quelling internal revolts, though General Ironside did provide support to Reza Khan through 1921. On 21 February 1921 Reza Khan's coup laid the basis for a process of state formation. This was now supported by various elements of the elite because of the fears of Communism and for Iran's independence. This was recognized by Tehran's repudiation of the Anglo-Persian Agreement and the signing of a Soviet-Iranian Treaty on 26 February. Equally significant was the fortune of the Gilan Republic. Kuchik quarrelled with the Soviets, and 'Persian forces reoccupied Gilan with Soviet approval, and hanged Kuchik as a rebel' (Carr 1966:465). Relations between Britain and Russia improved with the Anglo-Russian Trade Agreement of 16 March. Russian and British forces then left Iran in April. The military nationalist leader, Reza Khan, continued to consolidate his rule and, after abolishing the Qajar dynasty, crowned himself Reza Pahlavi Shah in 1925. None the less, British influence remained extensive by virtue of its position in the Gulf, its oil concession and its links with tribal chiefs in the south.

Conclusion

Fromkin has rightly pointed out that 'having destroyed the old order in the region, and having deployed troops, armoured cars, and military aircraft everywhere from Egypt to Iraq, *British policymakers imposed a settlement upon the Middle East in 1922 in which, for the most part, they themselves no longer believed*' (1991:562). That is to say, the replacement of an empire by the system of mandates was known to be arbitrary and known to be incapable of providing political stability. But the thesis originally advanced by L. Carl Brown (1984) and repeated by Fromkin, that Britain 'while bringing to an end Europe's Middle Eastern Question, gave birth to a Middle Eastern Question in the Middle East itself' (1991:563), is only partly correct.

To begin with, the description of the new Eastern Question – at least as formulated by Brown and Fromkin – relies on an ahistorical picture of the region in which its constitutive social groups are taken to be either substate forms, tribes, or supra-state communities, the

Islamic *umma* or pan-Arabism. In each case, it is assumed that the Middle East is in some primordial sense inherently resistant to the politics of a nation-state system. Now, of course, the post-war process of state-building did not produce stable forms of rule and economic progress. Drawing lines on the map, appointing rulers, elaborating structures of bureaucratic administration and taxation, even training and equipping armies, do not by themselves create durable state forms. However, the closing of the Eastern Question by means of the dismemberment of the Ottoman empire, in conjunction with the nationalist and revolutionary legacy of the First World War, did mark a major turning point in the evolution of the modern Middle East. Thereafter, projects of state-building began. And henceforward the politics of tribe, Islam and Arabism were all shaped by this context, rather than constituting impregnable barriers to modernity. As we have seen, the context itself was defined by the inheritance of tributary formations in decline and the presence of classes whose mission consisted in facilitating dependent incorporation into the world market and the consumption of any accumulated domestic surplus.

Viewed in these terms, on the morrow of (semi-)formal independence, the region could be differentiated roughly as follows: in Turkey the Ottoman bureaucracy dominated surplus appropriation (though with the support of rural notables in the west and Kurdish tribes in the east), while the Sunni clergy was dependent on the state and thus lacked an autonomous base of operation; in Egypt, Syria and Iraq urban-based absentee landlords dominated the land and surplus appropriation, gained support from the relevant foreign powers, and there was a Sunni *ulema* (there were also significant ethnic or religious minorities, especially in Iraq and Syria); in Arabia the elite was tribal (and owed its continuing position to British support), and much of the population was nomadic; and in Iran absentee landlords, tribal peoples and a powerful Shi'ite clergy coexisted with a weak polity.

The second difficulty with the thesis of a Middle Eastern Question *within* the Middle East is that it diverts attention away from the persistence of, and even the continuities in the forms of, imperialist control. Obviously, much had changed in the shift from the original, extra-territorial forms of jurisdiction claimed by Europe's traders and investors, through the policies of formal colonialism and military occupation, to the (semi-)independence granted in the period after the First World War. But throughout these changing strategies and forms of political regulation there was an underlying consistency of purpose, especially in the British case. We can see this most clearly if we recall Gallagher and Robinson's discussion of the imperialism of free trade (1953 and Robinson 1972), in which they defined imperialism as the political moment of the process of integrating new regions into the expanding international capitalist economy. The period up to the 1870s, with the important exception of India, was characterized by the attempt to use naval and diplomatic power both to open up these regions to European trade and investment and to encourage them to reform their domestic institutions along European lines. Progress in this, and in particular the project of fostering an export-oriented, commercial class, was further advanced by the practice of extending lines of credit to the reforming polities. In many cases, however, the strains imposed by separating property from rule in order to facilitate commerce and order broke the stability of the societies concerned. At this point formal colonialism or direct, military occupation was sometimes necessary to safeguard imperialist interests. At root, from the standpoint of the West, the project of post-war state-building is best understood as a further element in the development of the imperialist construction of the capitalist world market and its linked sovereign state system. Of course, not all indigenous forces were prepared to tolerate such a project. Let us now turn to a more detailed examination of the subsequent patterns of state formation and economic development in the Middle East.

3

Rethinking Middle East
Politics

Islam, oil and the Third World

In chapter 1 we reviewed a range of theoretical debates on the character of the societies of the Middle East prior to their encounter with Western capitalism and in chapter 2 we attempted to account for the processes by which these regions were incorporated into the modern international system. Here we turn our attention to the fortunes of the Middle East in the modern world, the system dominated by an increasingly global, capitalist world market and a system of sovereign nation-states. We are thus concerned with exploring the character of social and political development in the modern Middle East, in the period since the end of the First World War.

The problematic and peculiar nature of political development in the Middle East is perhaps the single most prominent theme in commentary on the region. This applies as much to journalistic reports as to the academic literature, as much to impressionistic accounts as to those of well-informed commentators and as much to Western discourses as to the claims of many indigenous voices. The specific nature of the charge is that the modern form of sovereign nation-state has singularly failed to strike deep and lasting roots in the region. Politics in the Middle East is, it is commonly alleged, somehow different from elsewhere, and it is this which accounts for the apparent turbulence and persistence of conflict in the region. The root causes of this phenomenon are commonly located both within and without the region.

The most common internal candidate for the specificity of the Middle East is, of course, Islam, but Arabism and tribal forms have also been cited. Accounts of the peculiarities of the Middle East which focus on its internal patterning typically argue that the significant units of social organization within the region, together with their corresponding forms of loyalty and identification, are either sub- or supra-national in their reach. That is, the social structure of the region takes the form of a *mosaic*. Tribal organization and relatively self-governing ethnic and religious communities either operate on a more restricted level than the typical nation-state or are no respecters of its legal codes and boundaries. On the other hand, pan-Arab and pan-Islamic movements are by definition supra-national in scope, operating beyond state borders and without reference to the claims of any particular, secularly constituted nation-state. The refractory, mosaic-like nature of these forms is taken to account for the instability of politics in the region and the relative failure of a territorially defined national consciousness to develop. The most common version of this argument currently ascribes to Islam the primary role in frustrating the consolidation of secular, national polities, but in the 1950s and 1960s it was Arab nationalism that was seen as the central problem, especially as focused through Palestinian antagonism to the Israeli state. From time to time, the persistence of tribal forms, whether understood as extended kin networks or as types of mentalities, has also been put forward to account for the closed, particularistic nature of Middle Eastern politics.[1]

For those concerned with external determinations, it is the presence of Western imperialism, above all in relation to oil, that is seen as the defining feature of the region. This interpretation of the specific character of the Middle East is offered by those who stress the importance of oil to the advanced sectors of the world economy, and the impact of oil in shaping the region's pattern of socio-economic and political development. Viewed from this perspective, it is primarily the imperialist interests of the West, concerned with securing the flows of oil to the consumers of the advanced capitalist economies, which have underpinned the arbitrary state system of the region. Middle East states are, according to this argument, typically rentier or distributive states, with a

---

1 In what follows I will concentrate on the arguments about Islam, but we will return to the question of Arabism later.

highly specific insertion into the world market. This status brings
with it three further peculiarities. First, the dominance of the region's economy by oil has imposed on it a distorted form of growth
which has sharpened inequalities within and between states and
has strengthened the role of the state in the process of accumulation. The resulting polarization of class structures and emergence
of rentier states have together enabled regimes to consolidate forms
of rule without involving the population in more typical kinds of
representation. Second, because of the premium placed upon the

stability of oil supplies, Western patrons have not encouraged
processes of political reform in the direction of more inclusive
polities, for the latter might adopt policies which seek to direct oil
resources towards domestic considerations at the expense of Western oil companies and consumers. Third, given the potential threat
posed to Western interests by radical regimes and by any expansion
of Soviet influence, the leading Western powers have been strong
supporters of the state of Israel as a counter to such forces. In turn,
the resulting Arab–Israeli/Muslim–Jewish conflict has played a
major role in bolstering the position of military and authoritarian
forces in the Arab/Islamic states.

In contrast to these assertions of peculiarity, others have strenu-
ously denied that any such status exists, and have contested these
attempts to exclude the Middle East from common frameworks of
explanation. For example, Fred Halliday argued that 'neither
the determination of the geological substructure nor those of the
religious-ideological superstructure can establish a Middle East
exempt from analytic universality' (1987:212). One of the main
contentions of Roger Owen's exemplary study of *State, Power and
Politics in the Making of the Modern Middle East* (1992) is that
the character of political development in the region does not
differ markedly from that taking place throughout the Third
World. And Sami Zubaida's fecund essays on *Islam, the People
and the State* (1989) argue strongly that the Islamic features
of Middle East politics are the product of contemporary combinations of forces and events, and that they can best be understood
in terms of particular instances of *general* social and political
processes.

Thus, against attempts to define the specificity of the Middle East
in terms of ideology or geology, these writers have argued that its
development is not essentially different from that of the rest of the
(post-)colonial world. In other words, the most significant fact

about the Middle East is that it has developed as part of the Third World. Its problems of political development, of nation building and of economic growth are no more nor less than those of most of the regions outside Europe and the areas of European settlement. Of course, the pattern of colonial expansion and control was not even, and the impact of the encounter with the West differed from place to place. But these particular variations aside, the state system of the Middle East simply is part of the developing world, situated within a capitalist world economy dominated by its advanced regions. In addition, outside powers have continued to play an extensive role in the region, first the Europeans and then the superpowers, but this too has been a feature of much of the non-European world. Finally, as the contest between capitalist and communist forms of development was fought out on an increasingly global scale in the course of the twentieth century, so also in the Middle East alternative forms of social organization contested for dominance. Here again, though the strength of local communist parties varied as did the depth of Soviet influence, the Middle East fits into a picture that was repeated across the developing world at large.

In my view, while each of these perspectives sheds some light on the nature of political development in the region, these formulations – singly or in combination – do not address the basic theoretical questions involved in giving an adequate account of *dependent state formation*, and hence political change, in the Middle East. Building on the arguments of chapters 1 and 2 above, in what follows I will attempt both to further substantiate these claims and to begin the development of a more adequate theoretical and comparative framework for thinking about the process of state formation in the modern Middle East. Though it will comprise the bulk of what follows, I should stress at the outset the provisional nature of the latter undertaking. General theoretical studies of the development of the modern Middle East are still in their infancy. There are some very good general histories, many outstanding treatments of particular countries, a steadily increasing number of studies both of specific aspects of development and of a comparative kind and a small but growing number of thematic accounts.

As yet, however, the widespread dissatisfaction with earlier culturalist and modernization theory literatures has produced little of a theoretically explicit and genuinely comparative nature. With due recognition that the present eassy may as a result be somewhat premature, it is this gap that I seek to fill. I propose to develop my argument in three stages. In this chapter, I will begin this task by reviewing more closely some of the existing approaches towards understanding the problems of modern Middle Eastern politics. On the basis of this critique, I will develop an alternative framework for posing questions about the process of state formation. This will focus on specifying both the social form of political development in the Middle East as well as situating these processes within their appropriate international contexts. In chapter 4, I will present a series of case studies of state formation in Turkey, Egypt, Iraq, Saudi Arabia and Iran and will attempt to explore both the common features and the different forms taken in each case. In chapter 5, I will draw out a general comparative framework from these case studies and, on this basis, suggest a number of theses about the pattern of political change in the modern Middle East. This will enable us to reformulate questions about the lack of democracy in the region and the place of Arabism and Islam in Middle Eastern societies without recourse to culturalist and essentialist judgements.

Politics in the Middle East

Islam and the state

In line with the culturalist perspectives reviewed in chapter 1, there have been a number of attempts to comprehend the specificity of modern Middle East politics in terms of Islam. In his book on *Islam and the State* (1987), P. J. Vatikiotis argues that Islam rejects the idea of the nation-state and with it modern, secular conceptions of nationalism. Thus he avers that:

> Islam and nationalism are mutually exclusive terms. As a construct-
> ive loyalty to a territorially defined national group, nationalism has
> been incompatible with Islam in which the state is not ethnically
> or territorially defined, but is itself ideological and religious. . . .
> Nationality among the majority of their populations is still over-
> shadowed by the religious community; national frontiers are still
> measured by religion. Cultural oneness, especially among the Arabs,
> is still supreme, since Islam is their greatest cultural achievement. . . .
> The loyalties of the masses, as we can witness today from Iran to
> North Africa and from Central Asia to the Sudan, remain religious
> and local. (1987:42, 43, 44)

Confrontation, not co-operation, has marked the Islamic world's response to the modern. Passive obedience to *de facto* authority is the political theory of Islam, government by consent is unknown and autocracy is the only real form of government. This is a result of the fact that in 'Islamic history', religious authority rested with the *ulema* and, in consequence, much of society became non-political, and the state became separated from society. Accordingly, Muslims reject temporal political power.

Another rehearsal of these themes can be found in the last testament of a noted Middle East historian and political scientist, Elie Kedourie's astringent and amusing treatment of *Politics in the Middle East* (1992). Applying the standard formula, Kedourie opens his account as follows:

> Whether it is defined in geographical or cultural terms, and whatever its exact boundaries are held to be, there can be no disputing the fact that the Middle East is predominantly Muslim. . . . [the early Arab Muslim rulers] speedily transformed an unsophisticated tribal polity into one of the most sophisticated and most durable kinds of rule, that of oriental despotism, the methods and traditions of which have survived in the Muslim world to the present day. What the Muslim jurists did was to articulate and theorize the conditions of political life in oriental despotism, and to teach that it was compatible with a Muslim way of life. (1992:1, 12)

For Islam is a religion that does not recognize a separation of temporal and spiritual power, that permits of no intermediate institutions between the religio-political ruler and the individual, and that is only saved from the worst excesses of oriental despotism by the segmented nature of agrarian and pastoral society. With the resources of an industrial society at its disposal, and thus the ability to break down the segmented character of traditional society, Islam can only wreak havoc. So, from the collapse of the Ottoman empire to the present day, the history of the Middle East has been a 'tormented endeavour to discard the old ways' (1992:346). Kedourie's general conclusion is that this endeavour has been unsuccessful, and therefore that the tension between religion and politics in the Middle East is far from resolved. Like Vatikiotis, he argues that Islam is incompatible both with secular nationalism and with representative government. However, unlike Vatikiotis, Kedourie does hold out the possibility (in the Turkish case) that Dankwart Rustow's more optimistic thesis about Islamic modernization might be correct.

Rustow held that the development of an increasingly literate, educated, mobile and urbanized society will bring with it a secular, democratic form of politics. But Kedourie can offer no way of understanding in what way, if this is the case, such an evolution might occur in *this* region. In other words, if an 'Islamic society' can be transformed into a modern, secular nation-state, what are the preconditions for this path to be taken? And surely if it can occur in one Muslim country, then why not in all, and what then of the alleged incompatibility of Islam and modernity? Kedourie has no answer to these questions, concluding instead that 'only time, of course, will show if this optimism is warranted' (1992:154).

A still more optimistic assessment of the fortunes of Islam in the modern world has been offered by John Esposito in his valuable survey of *Islam and Politics* (1991). Substantively, Esposito shows the great diversity of views and practices amongst groups defining their goals in Islamic terms, and he is at pains to stress that in practice there has been a degree of accommodation to the nation-state and even to elements of liberal notions of representative government. However, the basis of this optimism is not clear, given Esposito's understanding of Islam. Adopting a model of 'Islamic society' similar to that outlined by Lapidus (1988), Esposito argues that Islamic history has been marked by a number of enduring continuities which have both given it a determinate form and have set the terms for its encounter with modernity. Central to this tradition has been the role of Islamic law, the *shari'a*. Esposito summarizes the influence of this as follows:

> Islam continued to be operative in political notions of society and citizenship, law and judiciary, education and taxation, war and peace. State institutions concerned with law, the judiciary, education, and social welfare services were administered in large part by the *ulama*. The state was often a major patron of Islam and Muslim institutions ... Moreover, Islam has remained a primary principle of social cohesion and identity in spite of its loss of power and autonomy occasioned by colonialism and the Western secular path followed by most Muslim governments. Its continued presence among the vast majority of Muslims explains the continued appeal to and acceptance by many Muslims of 'Islamic' politics. (1991:280)

Now it is certainly true that from the time of the Abbasids the *shari'a* operated as the framework for judgement by *qadi*s appointed by the ruler. But the *shari'a* was considerably less than law in any modern sense of the term. Some of its provisions were not implemented and it was subject to considerable interpretation. Indeed, *ijtihad* (literally, 'exerting oneself', or reasoning by analogy free from orthodoxy in order to interpret Islamic law) provided a means of adaptation to new circumstances. In any case, the *shari'a* was both unevenly applied (*qadi* justice did not operate everywhere) and uneven in its coverage. According to Albert Hourani, Islamic law 'was most precise in regard to matters of personal status – marriage and divorce, bequests and inheritance; less so in regard to contracts and obligations, and all that concerned economic activity . . . and it said virtually nothing about 'constitutional' or administrative law' (1991:161). The existence of Islamic law, then, cannot provide the basis for a claim about Islamic 'society'. As we saw in chapter 1, to the extent that they existed at all, the institutional continuity of Islamic practices noted by Esposito and others depended on their insertion within the process of production and rule in pre-capitalist societies.

Moreover, what of the influence of Islam once secular legal systems have developed? Here Esposito speaks of the social cohesion and identity provided by Islam. But what does this refer to? Once again, it remains obscure just what this 'continued presence' of Islam among Muslims consists in, save an appeal to the widespread existence of Muslim belief. Equally, the mere existence of Muslim forms of identification in a society tells us very little about the causes of political mobilization, for the same people also identify themselves in terms of a variety of social roles and a range of political ideologies. Which of these aspects of their social position, singly or together, determines their (varied) political behaviour needs to be explained. It cannot be inferred from their religious identification, since that is precisely what they are supposed to have in common. Finally, Islamic teachings do not and cannot prescribe a unitary set of goals, forms of organization and tactics for those groups which do define themselves in religious terms. The doctrines of Islamic forces, as of all other forms of political mobilization and organization, are socially contingent (see, especially, Zubaida 1989a).

In sum, accounts which stress the mosaic character of Middle East societies generally fall back on essentialist definitions of Islam (or Arabism or tribalism), depicting these as unchanging entities which are mysteriously resistant to transformation. But in no region of the modern world did the process of modern state formation begin *ab initio*. On the contrary, everywhere it had to work with a mixed inheritance of particularistic communities and diverse forms of religious and metaphysical identification. These 'Orientalist,' or culturalist, formulations are thus logically driven to argue that political culture in the region is *sui generis*, and unlike that in other parts of the world. In truth, as we saw in chapter 1, there is no such thing as 'Islam' (or, by implication, 'Arabism'[2]), understood as a preconstituted quality, that could in principle constitute such an obstacle to modernity. Any continuing presence of Islam – whether understood in cultural or institutional terms – has to be explained, not by an appeal to the character of belief, but by an account of its active reproduction in the present, in terms of the concrete social and material relations and practices in which it is imbricated. It is only thus that we will be able to explain both the *contemporaneity* and the *variation* in Islamic politics.

The rentier state and oil

The thesis that politics in the Middle East is above all shaped by oil and its associated Western interests is linked to debates about the rentier character of the state and the economy. A rentier economy is defined as an economy in which income from rent dominates the distribution of national income, and thus where rentiers wield considerable political influence. In a rentier state the bulk of the externally derived rent is received, at least in the first instance, by the government, and rent provides the greater part of the state's income. In the case of oil states, income from rent may well dominate the revenue side of the state's budget, and even the generation of foreign exchange, without dominating the distribution of national income as a whole. But whether this is so or not, where rent dominates the state budget, then the primary economic function of the state is concerned with the allocation of these resources. The essence of state activity is simply an expenditure policy. And since the bulk of the surplus available to the state is not generated by the majority of the population, indeed is not in any real sense even generated within the territory of the state, the resulting patterns of representation and legitimacy are likely to diverge strongly from those states that depend either on taxing a domestic productive

2 Culturally speaking, the heart of Arabism is often taken to lie in the unity of Arabic civilization given by linguistic continuity and the central place of Islam in this world.

base, or on managing a large state-owned sector. Whether this form of autonomy for the state contributes to its strength or weakness in relation to its domestic society is itself much debated.

In the case of those Arab oil states with relatively small populations, these features are of course particularly marked. In this context, Giacomo Luciani has argued that the linked developments of colonial expansion and the exploitation of oil resources have consolidated the process of state formation in the Arab world. Moreover, he claims that 'oil production appears to have a strong and decisive influence on the nature of the state. It does so through its effects on the structure of state revenues and the ratio between revenues that are obtained domestically and revenues that are obtained from abroad' (1990:70). However, the rentier effects are not confined to the oil states alone. This is so for two reasons. First, to a limited but still significant extent the rents of the oil states have been recycled to the non-oil Arab states through migrant workers' remittances, through transit fees and through aid. Second, because of oil the Arab world has assumed a wider geopolitical significance in international politics and is thus the recipient of very large location, or strategic, rents in the form of economic aid and military assistance. Hazem Beblawi thus concluded that:

> the oil phenomenon has cut across the whole of the Arab world, oil rich and oil poor. Arab oil states have played a major role in propagating a new pattern of behaviour, i.e. the rentier pattern. . . . The impact of oil has been so pre-eminent that it is not unrealistic to refer to the present era of Arab history as the oil era, where the oil disease has contaminated all of the Arab world. (1990:98)

Similar arguments have also been advanced in relation to Pahlavi Iran during the 1960s and 1970s.

In addition to these specific features of rentier states, the presence of oil in the Middle East has had two further effects. As already noted, oil has attracted the interest of outside powers, and with them the dispensing of strategic rents. But the presence of the Western powers, especially the United States in the post-Second World War era, is also argued to have frustrated reform movements within the region in order to protect the West's access to oil. Defence of the *status quo*, in which the distribution of oil reserves in relation to population (particularly marked in Saudi Arabia and the Arabian Gulf states) favours the West, has been the principal aim of US foreign policy in the region. At the same time, the threat to these arrangements posed by radical nationalist forces (with or without Soviet assistance) has resulted in solid support for the Jewish state of Israel. In turn, the continued reproduction of the Arab-Israeli conflict has conspired to make the Middle East the most armed region of the world, and has thereby bolstered the presence of military and authoritarian forces in the region's polities.

Theories which stress the impact of oil and Western imperialism have a firmer purchase on the patterns of social and material reproduction in the Middle East than essentialist claims about Islam. However, they tend to neglect the internal organization of these societies before the discovery of oil on the one hand, and to relegate the impact of other forms of surplus extraction in shaping modern political development on the other. More specifically, these oversights carry over into two basic problems faced by any attempt to read the development of the Middle East exclusively in these terms. In the first place, some of the salient features of political development in the Middle East are common to both oil and non-oil states, and these derive from certain aspects of the region's history before the discovery of oil, as well as comprising general features of dependent development. Secondly, the variation of political forms between oil-producing states is itself considerable, indicating that other factors are at work in shaping state formation. Therefore, though the rentier character of a number of Middle East states is undoubtedly important, too much emphasis should not be placed upon the role of oil.

The Middle East in the Third World

As indicated above, accounts of the relation between religion and politics and notions of the rentier state do not focus in detail on the *historical process* of state formation in the Middle East. It is here that those approaches which deny the peculiarity of the region are on their strongest ground. Owen, for example, argues that in order to understand political change in the Middle East, as elsewhere in the developing world, we need to take account of a number of common features, among which two in particular stand out. First, these societies underwent a process of development that was shaped by their integration into the capitalist world market, bringing with it a dynamic new relationship between state and society. Second, the establishment of a 'national political field' (Zubaida) with the arrival of the modern state produced determinate effects in the character of political activity. In this regard, Owen suggests that the territorial states inherited from the colonial powers provided the context in which attempts to administer the population were undertaken. This involved both the elaboration of bureaucratic forms, and an emphasis on maintaining internal security through policing. Focusing on timeless categories such as 'tribe' or pan-Islam or pan-Arabism is therefore unhelpful, since 'methods of political organization and styles of political rhetoric are largely defined by the context and . . . from the colonial period on, this context was created by the territorial state' (1992:20). *Owen*

Since creating a nationalist opposition to the colonial power was not the same thing as obtaining domestic legitimacy, and since the structures of the post-colonial state were extremely fragile and fluid once the material and coercive resources of the occupying power were removed, it is not surprising that:

> the difficulties experienced in the first post-independent decades do not seem markedly different from those to be observed elsewhere in the Third World . . . political instability was overcome largely as a result of the general process of the expansion of the power of the central bureaucracy and of the security forces. (1992:26)

Within the context given by this general expansion and centralization of the state apparatus, socio-economic development was frustrated by the power of the urban, notable classes, and thus opposition forces increasingly turned towards the military. During the subsequent period, the post-independence state of an urban-centred, landowning class gave way via military-backed coups to the authoritarian polity common to many post-colonial societies.

This emphasis on the historical process of state formation within the context of integration into the capitalist world market is a salutary antidote to the determinism of culture and oil offered by theorists of Islam and the rentier state, respectively. In contrast to the accounts offered by Vatikiotis and Kedourie, Owen argues that religion neither determined the nature of state power, except in relation to how power was on some occasions legitimated, nor did it provide a significant obstacle to the consolidation of the state's rule: on the contrary, the modernist strand of Sunni Islam was mobilized to legitimate the policies of the state, and political control was extended over the *ulema*. And as against the mono-causal focus on oil, Owen seeks to present a more general framework for understanding Middle East state formation in terms of the consolidation of the state apparatus. Against this background, the development of the oil sector is only one factor to be placed alongside other relevant determinants.

A similar concern with state formation can be found in some other recent studies which seek to bring the study of Middle East politics into the mainstream of social and political theory (see, for example, Davis and Gavrielides 1991 and Sharabi 1990). Eric Davis (1991) has identified a number of different approaches in this field. To begin with, he suggests that much of the work on state formation has been unduly restricted, focusing on the process of formal institution-building in relation to parliaments, bureaucracies, the judiciary, armies and police forces, etc. Davis argues that these developments need to be understood within the context provided by the already existing 'organic social formations' of the Middle East: namely, the forms of social organization that existed before the advent of the modern state system. He is also critical both of liberal approaches which focus on the state's search for legitimacy, and of Marxist concerns with the state's ability to extract a surplus (by which Davis means state revenues). In his view, both kinds of analysis ignore the lack of congruence between the nation and the organic social formations, and both minimize the role of consent (as opposed to force) in Third World state formation. Davis believes that in the Arab oil-producing countries, access to oil wealth has meant that the cultural dimension of state formation is particularly important. He illustrates this point and the *variety* of state formation by comparing the experiences in Iraq and Kuwait:

> In Iraq, the main concern of the state has been to erase confessional and tribal loyalties from political consciousness. Under the al-Sabahs, the main effort of the Kuwaiti state was not to eradicate tribal identities but rather to channel them in directions that it saw as serving its own interests in promoting a paternalistic modern welfare state. (Davis and Gavrielides 1991:132)

The same point about the importance of culture in relation to state formation is made more generally in relation to the vexed question of Arab nationalism by Lisa Anderson as follows:

The individual states of the Arab world are not congruent with, and cannot wholly appropriate, the powerful nationalism of Arab identity, yet they are equally unable to fully transcend or replace it by cultivating purely local loyalties. Thus the political elites of the region have vacillated between attempts to portray themselves as the vanguard of Arab unity and to rely on provincial identities and loyalties to engender political support. (1991:72)

These formulations of Davis and Anderson are especially interesting because they show that a concern with state formation may lead in a rather different direction from that suggested by Owen. For the latter it was the new context provided by the national political field which was uppermost and which largely determined the course of political activity. By contrast, the former emphasize the obstacles to stable state formation posed by the pre-existing organic social formations, as well as the variety of ways in which these are incorporated into the new political systems. Clearly, shifting our attention towards the process of state formation does not, in and of itself, solve our substantive problems of explanation.

Nevertheless, treating the Middle East as but part of the Third World does have the signal merit of applying a common explanatory framework to different forms of society. Yet in practice many such accounts note the imposition of Western state forms in the colonial and mandate era, and then proceed to argue that subsequent political activity is patterned largely by this fact. This is to a large extent the position adopted by Owen. As a generalization, this has much to commend it. But in the process, the variation of social forms found in the non-European world prior to the colonial impact tends to be relegated to a relatively minor role. However, as Davis suggests, these forms (often themselves products of an earlier encounter between local pre-capitalist arrangements and European informal imperialism) have been very diverse. One might generalize this point by noting that it is not that the Middle East is peculiar as the Orientalists have claimed, but rather that *all* contexts of state formation are peculiar. And the variant patterns of subsequent state formation in the post-colonial world might, therefore, be in part a reflection of these differences. The pertinence of this point is reinforced by another consideration: namely, the uneven impact of colonialism itself in the Middle East. Some of the states in the region were the direct result of European imposition, but in other cases either the impact of capitalist penetration or the role of the European powers was more indirect. The imposition of a 'Western' type of state was correspondingly uneven. Thus, while respecting the need to maintain an approach of *analytic* universality, this must not be pressed into an assumption of *empirical* homogeneity. And if we are to explain the specificity of the Middle East, then our historical reach needs to be longer than is commonly supposed, and the indigenous matrix of state formation needs to be considered carefully.

Theorizing state formation

State formation and surplus appropriation

How, then, should we proceed? At one level, the differences between Owen, on the one hand, and Davis and Anderson, on the other, appear to rest on relatively simple matters of fact. Surely, it is an empirical question as to whether or not forces (organic social formations) that did not operate in the national political field were, in Owen's words, 'soon marginalized or destroyed'? Unfortunately, things are not so straightforward, as we do not know which forces, under what circumstances, count as significant. In other words, neither Owen nor Davis provides us with any theoretical criteria by which to assess the processes of state formation. This can be seen most clearly in Owen's account of the consolidation of state power through the territorial definition of politics, the urban location of organized political activity, enhanced administration, the growth of resources devoted to the bureaucracy and the expansion of coercive powers. These changes are indeed central to the process of state formation, but for the most part, the picture drawn is one of an essentially quantitative expansion in the capabilities of the state. The specific forms of power, the social form of the state, goes largely unremarked, save being described as 'authoritarian.'[3]

3 Elsewhere, Owen has suggested that an appropriate methodology for studying state formation in the Middle East might involve looking at the impact of a 'general dynamic', the creation of capitalist property relations, in the context of a 'fluid political and administrative environment' (Mitchell and Owen, 1990:181). He also pays attention to the *constitutional* character of the state – monarchical, republican, etc. – and draws some illuminating conclusions from this. In addition, Owen's discussion is very attentive to questions of historical specificity.

In order to make some theoretical progress here, it is necessary to develop some determinate, qualitative criteria concerning the character of modern state formation. In short, we need a theory of state formation. So, let us begin by rendering explicit some of the theoretical assumptions lying behind the recent concern with these questions. What will emerge is that state formation cannot be understood by isolating it from changes going on elsewhere in society, specifically from changes in the dominant forms of surplus appropriation.

A good illustration of taking the state seriously is Michael Mann's influential essay on 'The Autonomous Power of the State' (1984), and this is the kind of framework that has influenced recent writing about state formation in the Middle East as elsewhere. Mann asks what can explain the *sui generis* nature of state power? His answer to this question is simple and elegant. Noting that the means used by states are the same as for any organization seeking to mobilize power – economic, military and ideological – he suggests that the power of the state is none the less

> irreducible in quite a different socio-spatial and organizational sense. Only the state is inherently centralized over a delimited territory over which it has authoritative power. . . . Territorial centralization provides the state with a potentially independent basis of power mobilization, being necessary to social development and uniquely in the possession of the state itself. If we add together the necessity, multiplicity and territorial centrality of the state, we can in principle explain its autonomous power. (1984:123, 124)[4]

As Mann clearly recognizes, this autonomy is only a *potentiality* and, more importantly, the state does not in fact 'possess' an independent basis of power mobilization, for its infrastructural penetration of society comprises a complex web of social *relations* which neither the state nor its elite can be said to *control* in any straightforward sense. The degree of power exercised can only be ascertained historically and empirically. From a similar standpoint, Giddens (1985) also explicitly cautions against both the realist view of the state as a unified geopolitical agent and the neo-Weberian conception of the state elite as radically autonomous. Neither of

---

4 By the 'necessity' of the state Mann is referring to its organizational role in social development, and by 'multiplicity' he means the range of functions performed by the state.

these substantive propositions follow from the arguments of Mann and Giddens. However, there remains none the less a major difficulty with the formulations of Mann and Giddens. For just as Marx (in the *General Introduction* 1857) cautioned against any attempt to derive the forms of capitalist production from the features of 'production in general', so the project of constructing a general theory of the state in terms of its infrastructural (or administrative) power is bound to involve similar kinds of reification.[5] In particular, Marx argued that while it may be possible to fix some features of all production, these 'so-called *general conditions* of all production . . . are nothing but . . . abstract moments, which do not define any of the actual historical stages of production.' Similarly, Mann's theory of state power encourages the view that the process of state formation is primarily one of a quantitative expansion of capabilities, rather than a qualitative shift in the moment of the 'political' within the totality of social relations. To be sure, in the genesis of the modern state system both quantitative and qualitative transformations have taken place. But no amount of historical attention to the bureaucratic expansion of the state will register the structural discontinuity involved in its new social form. What Mann abstracts transhistorically as the 'arena' of the state is actually constituted in fundamentally different ways in different historical instances. And these differences – far from being explicable *sui generis* – can only be understood in terms of their correspondence to the broader variation in the mode of production and reproduction of social life. To adopt Mann's terminology, the *arena* constituted by the state in the social formation as a whole varies with the mode of production concerned (for a historical and comparative treatment, see Therborn 1978).

Accordingly, the establishment of the modern state cannot be properly understood as a process in which the intermittently expanding infrastructural powers of society as a whole were arrogated to the centralized control of territorially bounded state machineries. For this is to confine our analysis to the general features of political power, the moment of 'rule', and it fails to penetrate the necessary changes in the social relations which underpin and make possible the emergence of modern forms of sovereignty. Modern states do not simply do what traditionally states did – only

5 The much-maligned Marxist theorist, Nicos Poulantzas, made this point some time ago (see 1978, part 1).

more effectively. There is rather a qualitative breach between the personalized forms of political domination in the pre-capitalist world and the character of the capitalist state system. For this reason, the state cannot be understood fully in neo-Weberian terms, as a territorially based apparatus of administration and coercion. Of course it is this, for as Marx once said the state is nothing without its apparatus, but it is also a distinct structure of social relations whose character varies systematically with the form of surplus appropriation dominant in any given society. And the establishment of new social relations is itself a historical process, in which prior forms of appropriation are reworked, destroyed or incorporated into the new arrangements.

Where these relations of production take a (liberal) capitalist form a dual redefinition of the political occurs. On the one hand, the customary powers and definition of property are privatized in the form of economic ownership rights. Property is shorn of its social functions, and appropriation becomes 'economic'. In the process, rule becomes separated from appropriation and can be reconstituted in the form of the sovereign state, taking on an abstract form embodied in law and bureaucracy. The latter is now concerned with general public functions rather than the direct political defence of a dominant class. Historically, these processes usually occurred the other way around: the centralization of the location of rule typically went before the narrowing of its content by the privatization of rights of appropriation. In fact, in many cases neither process was fully accomplished. The centralization of rule may face formidable obstacles in the form of unyielding local sites of authority, especially when these have an independent material base. And even where they are destroyed or incorporated, the production and acquisition of the surplus need not take a private, economic form, in which case the state acts as the dominant appropriator. In both cases, either pre-capitalist forms or the state (or both) remain directly involved in organizing the material reproduction of society and the appropriation of surpluses. And in these instances neither liberal forms of sovereign polity nor liberal democratic systems of representation can emerge. Across much of the post-colonial world, this pattern of development has provided one very important social base for authoritarian rule (see chapter 5 below).

Another powerful stimulus to authoritarian rule has been the subordinate position of the state in the world market and the state system. Long before the development of a *national* market, many regions of the Middle East were more or less forcibly integrated into the *world market* by European traders, investors and governments. Indigenous minority groups (Armenians, Greeks, Jews, etc.), precisely because of their relative exclusion from the prevailing tributary apparatus, also played a central role in this pattern of incorporation. Finally, indigenous mercantile interests, as well urban-based, absentee landlords also became part of these networks. The 'nationalist' dispossession of these forces was, therefore, widely seen as necessary for social development. The transformation of agrarian class relations and the development of agriculture was a prelude to state-led models of catch-up, late-industrialization. The only agency with enough power and legitimacy to carry through such a programme was, of course, the post-independence state. And the inevitable result was that the state came to play a central role in many of the most important sectors of the economy (and this often went along with the persecution of minority groups). By these means, then, *dependent* state formation assisted in imbricating the state directly in the appropriation of surpluses.

Nevertheless, such projects varied in their relation to imperialist interests. Where the region had escaped formal colonial control (Turkey and Iran), or where development was based more or less exclusively on a commodity whose value could only be realized by an alignment with the West (oil in Saudia Arabia and the Gulf states), or where there were elements of both (Iran), then dependent state formation need not take an anti-imperialist form. Indeed, domestic projects geared towards state formation and a degree of independent development might be encouraged by the imperialist powers in order to create sub-imperialisms which could then manage the regional system under broad constraints dictated by the West. In these circumstances, nationalist forces were a threat to the project of the pro-Western ruling groups. By contrast, where foreign control of the economy and polity was marked (Egypt and Iraq), then domestic programmes of state formation and industrial development were more likely to take an anti-imperialist, if not anti-capitalist, form. In these cases, political opposition from the dispossessed landed and mercantile classes was portrayed as inspired or assisted by foreign interests.

In both models, however, the process of state formation had the effect of restricting the play of forces in the political field. On the one hand, pre-emptive state formation in a pro-Western fashion necessitated the repression of nationalist and Leftist groups in the domestic sphere, and on the other hand, nationalist mobilization against foreign influence made it difficult to sustain the open competition between domestic forces. Dependent development, whether for or against the grain of the international system, buttressed an authoritarian form of state.

These general considerations suggest three guidelines for investigating the processes of state formation. In the first place, *a satisfactory account of state formation must relate the development of the state apparatus to the changing nature of those social relations which govern the material reproduction of the society concerned.* This means that we must examine the relation of the state to the important social classes and groups: merchants, landlords, peasants and tribes. We also need to consider the role of the state itself as an agency of surplus appropriation, and not see it as solely concerned with the politics of rule. (In chapter 5 we will see how such an approach enables us to reopen the questions of Arabism and Islam in a non-essentialist fashion. For while culturalist accounts of Islam are unsatisfactory, it is nevertheless the case that the path of secular development in the Middle East has not been smooth. This needs to be explained in terms of the varying social locations of Islam, by virtue of its mobilization by contemporary political forces and by the uses to which states have sought to put it.) Secondly, *the pattern of state formation will be shaped by the position of the state in the world market and state system and the nature of the indigenous response to this.* All state formation in the Middle East was dependent development, but the pattern of integration into the world market varied widely, as did the nature of relations with the dominant powers in the system. (Again, it is in this context that questions about oil and imperialism need to be posed. Whether or not the state was a rentier state has had an important bearing on the pattern of political development, and the presence of oil has also affected the particular patterns of integration into the world market and the state system.) Thirdly, *if we are to grasp the process of state formation as history, then we must be attentive to the play of the social forces which struggle to reproduce and to transform the relations of appropriation and command.* These guidelines, brought together in the substantive investigation of Middle East state formation in chapter 4, will enable us to reopen the vexatious questions of Islam and oil in a way that no longer offers essentialist and reductionist answers. Focusing on these aspects of social reproduction will, I hope to show, furnish us with some determinate criteria for analysing and assessing projects of state formation. Those, at any rate, are the hypotheses which the case studies of chapter 4 seek to test.

The international context of development in the Middle East

It is the pressing need to consolidate capitalist forms of production and rule over and against pre-capitalist, fragmented forms and to establish a degree of independent manoeuvre in the international system (whether sub- or anti-imperialist) which together account for the central role of the military in Middle East politics. In addition, as Charles Tilly (1990) has pointed out, the structure of the international system in the post-war period has augmented the power of the military in Third World states. Thus, before we move to a consideration of our case studies – Turkey, Egypt, Iraq, Saudi Arabia and Iran – let us consider briefly the general international environment within which Middle East state formation was accomplished. This will then enable us to fix the role of interstate competition, the scope of military rule, the scale of resources devoted to military ends and hence the role of the military in the process of state formation.

The position of the Middle East in the international system has been widely discussed (see, especially, Lenczowski, 1980, Ismael 1986 and Korany and Dessouki 1991) and I do not propose to add to this literature here. Rather, we shall sketch in some of the main trends in external involvement from the end of the First World War up to the present and attempt to see how these were connected to the pattern of social and political development within the region. We have seen in chapter 2 how British expansion in relation to India, inter-imperialist rivalries before the First World War, the collapse of the Ottoman empire and the Anglo-French machinations during and after the war all transformed the political map of the Middle East. In addition, we suggested that the new strategy adopted by the British was best understood as a continuation, albeit under new circumstances, of a longer project to establish capitalist markets and stable forms of polity that could complement the international position of the British empire.

It was in the pursuit of this strategy that the British reluctantly came to support a qualified form of self-determination, in the era of the mandates, for the reasons given by Lord Curzon in 1918:

> I am inclined to value the argument of self-determination because I believe that most of the people would determine in our favour . . . if we cannot get out of our difficulties in any other way we ought to play self-determination for all it is worth wherever we are in- volved in difficulties with the French, the Arabs, or anybody else, and leave the case to be settled by that final argument knowing in the bottom of our hearts that we are more likely to benefit from it than anybody else. (quoted in Louis 1984:205)

Or, as Stafford Cripps put it in 1939, in the post-mandate era and in relation to the future of Palestine, the mandate territory was 'to continue as an annex of the British Empire, though it will be annexed by treaty and not by conquest' (Louis 1984:210). This was the general logic of British policy in the Middle East during the interwar years. Stable administrations, respecting capitalist property rights and holding foreign policy obligations towards Britain, would contribute both to the integrity of the empire and to the reproduction of the capitalist order. This was so in a number of ways. By safeguarding the key routes of transportation and communication in times of peace and by providing bases and resources in times of war, these new states would enable sover- eignty to be recognized in their domain while formal empire was maintained elsewhere, especially in India. Through the provision of the necessary administrative framework for the exploitation of oil resources, clear boundaries and stable forms of administration and revenue collection facilitated the extraction of resources to support the new states and provided oil on favourable terms to the Western powers. And by encouraging a more general economic development under the control of notable classes and foreign in- termediaries, what was essentially a colonial division of labour – imports of manufactures in exchange for exports of agricultural produce and raw materials – was reproduced.

However, while the various rebellions against and political chal- lenges to the newly constituted states of the region were contained, as was any prospect of Soviet influence, the inter-war years wit- nessed an erosion of British power and a consequent loss of control in the Middle East. On an economic plane, the inter-war depression was associated with falling levels of world trade, a drying up of international capital flows, declining terms of trade for the primary producing regions of the world and a break up of the international gold standard based on sterling and Britain's pre-eminence in world trade and investment. This produced a general shift to economic nationalism as trade, payments and investment shifted away from multilateral, expansive systems towards bilateral, closed and politically regulated forms of exchange. In turn, new centres of economic growth were developing outside of Europe, above all in the Soviet Union and in the United States. These alterations in the character of the international system reduced the economic dependence of the Middle East economies on Europe and encouraged the start of state-led attempts to sponsor economic growth in those regions that had a significant degree of political independence, their own currencies and tariff autonomy (Turkey and Iran). Elsewhere, the persistence of colonial forms of control, including the absence of central banks and currency autonomy as well as the external supervision of the state's finances, blocked such transformations.

Allied intervention in the Middle East during the Second World War was extensive – for example, the British occupied Iraq and Egypt, while British and Russian forces occupied Iran – but the conflict nevertheless marked a significant phase of decline for the European empires. In the first instance, the European powers were economically weakened by the war, and their relative standing *vis-à-vis* the United States and the Soviet Union was further reduced. Secondly, the war gave nationalist movements an opportunity for agitation and organization, thereby raising the costs of colonial control. And thirdly, the dominant powers in the post-war years, the superpowers, were formally opposed to the maintenance of colonial arrangements. At first, in the new strategic environment of the Cold War, the British position:

> rested on two assumptions: that Arab governments would regard their major interests as being identical with those of Britain and the western alliance; and that British and American interests would coincide to the extent that the stronger party would be willing to leave the defence of its interests to the weaker. (Hourani 1991:357, 358)

Neither assumption proved to be well founded. To be sure, some of the early points of conflict in the Cold War centred on Soviet interests in Iran and Turkey, and the Truman Doctrine was formulated in relation to the eastern Mediterranean countries, Turkey and Greece. (An early draft of the Truman Doctrine mentioned Turkey's proximity to the great natural resources of the Middle East, as well as its border with the Soviet Union.) And Anglo-American co-operation on these issues did seem to confirm the British stance.

However, notwithstanding Turkey's membership of NATO in 1952, it soon became clear with the Egyptian revolution (1952) and the rise of Mossadeq in Iran in the early 1950s that nationalist forces in the Middle East were not ready to throw their weight behind the Cold War policy of the West. Unlike Turkey, they had yet to throw off foreign (Western) control, to consolidate their rule internally and to initiate programmes of state-led capitalist industrial development. In these circumstances, the British sought to maintain their vital interests: support for the Hashemite monarchies in Jordan and Iraq; the supplies of oil from the Gulf; and the protection of their clients in the periphery of Arabia. As Pierre Rondot pointed out, 'this policy of "limited commitment" made [the British] the associates of reactionary governments on the wane, and this was the great weakness of the system' (1961:131).

This can be seen most clearly in the fortunes of the Baghdad Pact (1955). The Pact comprised Britain, Turkey, Hashemite Iraq, Iran (with the shah restored to power) and Pakistan, and it was aimed as much against Egypt as against potential Soviet influence in the region. Together with the rivalry between Egypt and Iraq, this inevitably pushed Nasser's Egypt towards a reliance on the Eastern bloc. Similarly, Syria, pressed by Baghdad Pact powers (Iraq and Turkey) on the one hand and by the United States allies of Jordan and Lebanon on the other, also turned to the Soviet Union. Thus, those states which had undergone a degree of anti-imperialist and anti-landlord mobilization aligned with the Soviet Union, while the powers where the landed class or tribal elites remained in control, or as in the Turkish case where relatively stable capitalist development was already under way, joined the western camp. With the Iraqi revolution of 1958 the Baghdad Pact disintegrated.

During the Second World War the United States had, on the basis of pre-war oil concessions to US oil companies, established relations of economic and military assistance with Saudi Arabia. (Elsewhere on the Arabian littoral Britain remained the protecting power.) The restoration of the shah in Iran, together with the recomposition of the Iranian oil concession, also gave the United States significant economic and military relations with Iran. Before long, the United States came to oppose radical anti-imperialist (nationalist) forces contesting British and French colonial power – as in Iran in the era of Mossadeq and in Egypt under Nasser – and began to support both the conservative, monarchical regimes in Jordan and Saudi Arabia and the pliant nationalist regimes such as Iran once the shah was restored to power and Iraq under Hashemite rule. (Although not a member of the Baghdad Pact, the United States joined its sub-committees on anti-subversion, economic matters and military organization.) US support for conservative forces in the region increased after the radical turn taken in Egypt after 1956 and after the revolution in Iraq in 1958. This was matched by Soviet support for the new radical regimes. Thus, the opposition of the United States to the European empires did not necessarily translate into support for nationalist movements because of the overriding need to maintain imperialist influence in the region and because of the overarching context of Cold War.

Whereas the relative isolation of the Soviet Union in the inter-war years had meant that the dominant feature of world politics concerned inter-imperialist rivalry between the leading capitalist powers, after the war the conflict between 'East' and 'West' came to the fore. Fearful of the implications of nationalist regimes for Western interests and their willingness to align with the Soviet Union, the United States often opposed them through a general anti-communist offensive. At the same time, the Soviet Union hoped that its assistance to the independent states of national democracy could bring about their transition from colonial underdevelopment to socialism – without the need for a phase of capitalist development.

In general, Soviet policy involved a profound misreading of the pattern of socio-economic development in the Middle East and indicated the failure of its model of development to provide a long-run, generalizable alternative to integration into the world market. On the one hand, as Samir Amin (1978) has argued, the nationalization of foreign property by radical nationalist regimes or the creation of a public economy based on oil rents produced not aspirant socialist regimes but a series of state capitalisms which, increasingly after 1967 and 1973, became tied to the world market. This fragmented Arab unity, undercut the basis of a socialist path of development and strengthened the Western position. On the other hand, the autarchic pattern of extensive economic growth in the Soviet bloc and the command character of its economy meant that it could provide only short-run competition with the West. The planned nature of development, with its limited alienability of assets and the consequent absence of exchangeability between money and other resources, implied that the rouble could not function as a hard currency in competition with the dollar. This structural disability of Soviet power in the world market, in particular in relation to the United States, was further compounded by the relative backwardness of Soviet technology, especially in strategically crucial sectors such as agriculture and oil.

This basic failure of the radical challenge, with or without its Soviet support, to alter the pattern of social development in the region in an anti-capitalist direction presaged its medium-term reintegration into the world market and the Western orbit. By these means, the informal control of the United States, organized through treaty networks, bilateral military alliances, an increased presence of US oil capital in the region and economic assistance, replaced the more direct semi-colonial arrangements of the British. Above all, US hegemony within the world market, and the difficulty of anything other than short-term development outside it *in the absence of mass social mobilization*, worked to strengthen capitalist forces in the region. (Indeed, US hostility towards the radical regimes may even have delayed their integration with the West by encouraging a detour through a spell of alliance with the Soviet Union.)

The strength of capitalist interests was underlined by the fact that the post-war order was not only characterized by United States hegemony and the politics of Cold War but also by the economics of the long boom. Until the early 1970s, growth rates throughout the advanced capitalist world and some favoured regions of the Third World, including the Middle East, were unprecedented. In contrast to the inter-war years, post-war growth was based on an international system increasingly open to trade and investment and on the spread of advanced technologies to less developed regions by means of direct foreign investment and import-substituting in-dustrialization. (The terms of trade for raw materials remained stable or gradually deteriorated, but the absolute increase in supply meant growing incomes for many primary producers, in particular for the oil producers.)

Thus access to technology and capital, expanding markets and favourable demand conditions meant that the international oppor-tunities for a degree of industrialization in the 1950s and 1960s were good. To a considerable extent, whether or not a given country was able to take advantage of these circumstances depended on the structure of its internal classes and the orientation of its state. Strong, monopolistic landed classes frustrated industrialization, but equally inappropriate forms of state regulation, in particular policies geared to augmenting consumption (at the expense of investment) and excessive protection of monopolistic producers (thereby discouraging low-cost, efficient production), held back the prospects of industrialization. In economies that could none the less earn significant foreign exchange through access to oil or strategic rents, these problems were often exacerbated still further by a reduced pressure to compete in international trade.

Oil also played a major role in fashioning the character of the Middle East's integration into the international system after the Second World War. It is essential to recall that the states of the region were formed to a considerable extent through the agency of British imperialism (with France playing an important secondary role), both to manage its strategic interests and to control access to oil reserves. In the post-war period, as the informal empire of American hegemony came to replace the more direct administration of Britain and France, strategy centred on integrating the oil-rich economies of the southern Gulf as imperialist relays into a metropolitan circuit of capital whilst simultaneously arming Israel and Iran as counters against the more populous nationalist Arab regimes of the north. The Gulf producers (in alliance with Iran prior to the Islamic Revolution) thereby disciplined the price of oil for the West in return for military protection, investing their returns in the core rather than sponsoring pan-Arab growth.

This maintained Western control of the region and its reserves in order to provide a key material base of American hegemony. For Middle East oil primarily fuelled the rapid growth of post-war Western Europe and Japan and the equally dramatic move out of coal. It was only later during the 1970s that oil imports into the United States became significant. The ability of the United States to underwrite this order with its military power proved to be crucial to its wider management of inter-capitalist rivalries.

Within the Middle East itself, the main threat to that order, from Mossadeq, through Nasser and Khomeini, to Saddam, has come not from the Soviet Union but from indigenous social and national movements seeking to direct resources toward domestic ends, sometimes developmental, more often military and state-building.

Strategic management has therefore turned on isolating or containing any challenge from the more populous states. Virtually unqualified support for Israel has been one consistent element of this approach, a fact strengthened but not caused by the powerful pro-Israeli lobby in Congress. In addition, through a steady supply of arms transfers and economic assistance, it was hoped that in time nationalist ambitions could be tamed further by integrating local ruling classes into the capitalist world market and hence the Western orbit – not without some success in the case of Iran between 1953 and 1979 and in Egypt since 1973. Thus, another aspect of the strategy has been the strong support given to the other pro-Western, non-oil states – Turkey and Egypt – after 1973. (A similar strategy pursued in relation to Iraq during and after the Iran–Iraq war failed dramatically as Saddam Hussein refused to be bound by Western interests and invaded Kuwait in 1990.)

Furthermore, while the Soviet Union could arm and aid its allies in the region (Egypt until 1972, Syria, Iraq and the PLO), only the United States could bring direct pressure to bear on Israel in the Palestinian conflict. Together with the Saudi alliance with the United States and Egypt's turn to the West, this implied that the influence of the Soviet Union in the Middle East was limited even in the strictly geo-political sphere. Paradoxically, the rivalry of the superpowers and the Cold War played a stabilizing role in the region. For as long as the Soviet Union retained a significant influence in the Middle East it generally sought to temper any ambitions of its principal allies which might embroil it in a direct conflict with the United States, while taking opportunistic advantages where possible. But the Soviet position was always weak in the economic sphere, and especially in the oil industry: compare the position of either Iraq or Syria with that of the Gulf states and Saudi Arabia. Finally, Soviet relations with its allies began to deteriorate after the mid-1980s, as it turned its attention inwards to concentrate on domestic reform. Once the Soviet Union began to retreat, its main ally, Iraq, also had a freer hand.

Despite this overall weakness of the Soviet position in the Middle East, the Iranian revolution resulted in the collapse of the 'twin pillar' strategy associated with the regional application of the Nixon Doctrine. This had involved arming Iran and Saudi Arabia as regional clients. The West was therefore prepared to arm and (materially) support Iraq's aggression against the new Islamic regime as a means of containing and subduing Iran (and also Syria).

Throughout, support for Israel continued while the PLO's positions were repeatedly rebuffed. However, while Iran was suitably cowed, stability did not return, as was again demonstrated by Iraq's invasion of Kuwait in August 1990 and the subsequent United States – Iraq war of 1991.

Beyond the conjunctural and structural advantages of the West in its rivalry with the East in the Middle East, the long-term position of this post-war structure of Western (and specifically, US) control embodied a number of potentially explosive contradictions. Most obviously, the United States was the economic and military backer of both the conservative Islamic monarchies of the Gulf and the state of Israel. More important, materially speaking, have been three aspects of the socio-economic development of the contemporary Middle East. First, the Gulf states and Saudi Arabia in effect exchanged US military protection in return for managing the region's oil in the interests of Western consuming nations rather than the rest of the Arab world. Second, the class basis of the nationalist regimes, together with the willingness, even enthusiasm, of the superpowers to arm local clients, provided a fertile soil for authoritarian and highly repressive regimes. Third, the growing integration of local ruling classes into the capitalist world, combined with the essentially domestic base of their social and material reproduction, aggravated indigenous ethnic, religious and social tensions. Given these deep social tensions and long-standing hostility to the contrived and unstable political order in the region, conflict was always a possibility – as events since 1979 have violently demonstrated.

Conclusions: state formation, interstate competition and war

According to Elizabeth Picard, 'military intervention in politics had become commonplace in many Arab states, actually with a much higher frequency than in most Third World countries during the 1950s and 1960s' (1990:190). In Turkey also the military played an important role in the political field, as did the shah's repressive apparatus in Iran. From the early 1970s through to the 1980s, the share of military expenditure in GNP in the Middle East was nearly twice that of the next most militarized region (the Warsaw Pact) and over three times the world average. (In Egypt military expenditure currently accounts for nearly one-fifth of total public expenditure, in Saudi Arabia around one-third and in Iraq over one-half.) During the same period, the proportion of states under military control,[6] however, was on a par with Latin America (just below the world average), and much less than in South Asia, the Far East and Africa. As Tilly has pointed out:

> about 40 percent of the world's states now live under military control, and the proportion is slowly rising. Variations from region to region are dramatic: in Latin America 38 percent of all governments are military, and this proportion declining (after a rapid rise in the 1960s and early 1970s); 38 percent in the Middle East, up from 25 percent in the 1970s; a stable 50 percent in South Asia, a mildly fluctuating 60 percent in the Far East, 64 percent and rising in Africa. Military control, of one variety or another, has become the standard form of government in much of the Third World, notably in South Asia, East Asia, and Africa. (1990:212)

Tilly's explanation for this depressing phenomenon turns on the implications of superpower bi-polarity, and the ensuing competition for the allegiance of Third World states, for the relative strength of the Third World military in relation to other domestic social forces. According to Tilly, the *direct* role of the superpowers in sponsoring military control is limited: only rarely do they play a major role either in coups (he suggests that nearly 90 percent of post-war coups in the Third World 'occurred *without* substantial foreign intervention') or in the direct support of military regimes. But the *indirect* effects of bi-polarity are marked: 'alterations in relations of Third World states to great powers and to each other seem to have contributed importantly to changes in the overall rhythms of military control in the world as a whole' (1990:223). The heightened availability of weaponry, training and other kinds of support, alongside the increased willingness to provide these in return for political favours, access to strategic bases and essential resources, have radically changed the relation of the military to the state as compared with the European experience.

Now this is clearly an important feature of the context of state formation in the post-war period, and it undoubtedly strengthens

---

6 Defined by Tilly as one or more of the following: 'key political leadership by military officers, existence of martial law, extrajudicial authority exercised by security forces, lack of political control over the armed forces, or occupation by foreign military forces' (1990:211).

the position of the Third World military in their contests with other local groups. But it is, surely, a mistake, a confusion of permissive and proximate causes, to view this as the primary dynamic of Third World militarization. The proximate causes of military rule derive from the dilemmas of state formation in conditions of dependency. For dependent state formation brings with it great vulnerability and hence insecurity: the exigencies of rapidly consolidating state power, fostering industrialization from a subordinate position in the international division of labour and forging a new social basis for the regime all conspire to augment the power of the military in the state.[7] It is the imperatives stemming from these necessary tasks, the urgent and primary functions of any developing society, that so bolster the power of the military. In short, the strategic importance of the military is determined by its functional role. And it is on the terrain provided by this *central* feature of Third World politics that the new context identified by Tilly, the superpower competition, worked its wretched logic.

Indeed, as the comparative work of Tilly and others (Sivard 1986) has shown, the level of interstate conflict in the Middle East is not as high as the region's reputation might suggest. The Middle East has been a safer place to live than most of South Asia, the Far East and Africa. (The Arab–Israeli wars were all relatively minor in terms of casualties and force deployments.) In fact, until the Iraq–Iran war of 1980–88 and the Iraqi invasion of Kuwait in August 1990, the main source of conflict in the Middle East was *intra*-state, concerned with the internal pacification and repression of domestic populations. Thus, the objective pressures of militarization deriving from interstate competition are not qualitatively higher in the Middle East than elsewhere in the Third World. What differentiates the Middle East, then, is not the scope of military rule, nor even the scale of conflict, but rather the disproportionately large amount of resources devoted to the military in relation to any conceivable measure of objective need. Of course, the context defined by Tilly assisted here, as he has rightly noted elsewhere:

> With fair consistency, the US acted to protect Israel, to crack Arab unity, to foster oil-producing collaborators who would undercut

---

7 For persuasive accounts of some aspects of these processes in the Arab world, see Lawson (1993) and Sayigh (1993).

OPEC unity, to sell American weapons to reliable clients, and in the process to establish the legitimacy of its own military presence in the Middle East. The United States did not act alone.... [Between 1960 and 1986] world-wide military expenditure, in constant dollars, rose about 40 percent, in the Middle East it sextupled; military expenditure rose less rapidly than national income in most of the world, but increased from 5.6 to an exhausting 18.1 percent of GNP in the Middle East. With help and encouragement from the United States, Israel pumped up its military expenditures from 2.9 to 19.2 percent of GNP, Saudi Arabia from 5.7 to 22.7 percent, Iran from 4.5 to 20 percent, Iraq from 8.7 to a debilitating 32 percent. (1991:40)

But as Tilly is well aware, the reason for this is as simple as it is obvious: the availability of oil rents. It is no accident that the biggest military spenders are Iraq and Saudi Arabia, not the so-called frontline states in the Arab-Israeli conflict: Egypt, Jordan and Syria.

The need for rapid political and economic development imposed by dependent state formation is what defines the salience of inter-state competition and war in the Middle East, as it does throughout the Third World. More generally, the statist tradition of analysis represented by Tilly, Mann and others, with its focus on the geopolitical logic of interstate competition as one of the principal motors of state power, mispecifies the character of the state and the process of state formation. This point has been well made by Justin Rosenberg who has pointed out that:

states have not been principally concerned with war. They have been principally concerned with rule as the precondition of regularised relations of surplus extraction. The reproduction of this rule as a set of social relations has of course required the continuous and costly mobilisation of military sanctions against internal and external challenges. . . . But we do not for this reason theorise the role of the state by casting it as a military agent constituted outside the social order which then approaches . . . society armed with a series of demands and incentives in order to further its quite separate military ambitions. (1990)

If we follow Mann and Tilly, then we start with the state as an actor whose main strategy is warfare, and we reify interstate competition into a game whose rules are relatively constant. Alternatively, if we start with the process of consolidating rule and the relations of this to diverse forms of surplus appropriation, then it becomes possible to see the state as first and foremost a set of social and material relations concerned with rule and hence to situate the *changing* role of interstate competition both historically and structurally. For this reason, the case studies which follow do not examine the logically and historically second-order questions posed by statist theorists. In a fuller account they would have their place, but here we are trying to establish the general framework.

4

Comparative State Formation in the Middle East

Comparative and historical analysis

There are a number of different ways in which comparative and historical inquiries can be carried out. One increasingly common approach is to adopt Mill's method of comparison, involving recourse to both the method of agreement (where the outcome to be explained is common to all cases reviewed and where one searches the otherwise diverse antecedents for a common factor) and the method of difference (where the outcome to be explained is absent in one case and where one searches the otherwise shared antecedents for the significant difference).[1] Logically powerful as this procedure is for clarifying causal paths of social development, there is a danger that the method will determine the conclusions reached. For, in effect, any application of Mill's method must make the following assumptions: first, that the instances to be explained are all members of the same class of objects; second, that there is *one* set of causes operating in all cases; and third, that the basic causal patterns leading to the absence of an instance are different from those leading to its presence (see Burawoy 1989). In these ways, a rigorously applied comparative analysis can, by assuming in advance that all the examples studied are of the same kind, have the

1 The *locus classicus* of this kind of approach is Theda Skocpol's structural theory of social revolution developed in her *States and Social Revolutions* (1979).

effect of denying the reality of historical and conjunctural specificity.

As we will see below, both the changing historical context and the diversity of state formation in the Middle East rule out a strictly comparative treatment *à la* Mill. Thus although the following adopts a roughly comparative approach, I have also tried to remain attentive to the uneven nature of change and the combined character of state formation in the region. Methodologically, then, the case studies below recognize that similar factors may combine to produce different outcomes in different historical circumstances and that different starting points may eventuate in similar outcomes under certain conditions. Both historical and conjunctural specificity, of local conditions and of international determinations, must be accorded as much room as comparative generalization. After all, what we are examining are the historical processes by which indigenous social forces sought to refashion class and state in an international environment that was subject to continuous change. It is these aspects of incorporation into and development within an expanding capitalist world, rather than variant combinations of 'factors', which provide the organizing theme for the narratives that follow.

Substantively, this implies (as suggested in chapters 2 and 3) that a focus on the processes and patterns of state formation provides a way of investigating the recomposition of forms of surplus appropriation and rule as societies are integrated into the capitalist world. Put differently, tracing the varied kinds of state formation in the Middle East is a means of illuminating its specific pattern of combined and uneven development in the modern world. Given this context of incorporation into the capitalist world, we saw in chapter 3 that there are two determinate criteria for assessing processes of capitalist state formation.[2] On the one hand, there is a need to relate the processes of state formation to the changing nature of the social relations of material production. On the other hand, the pattern of state formation needs to be located in terms of the position of the state in the international system. (Within this overall framework, we suggested that the vexed questions of 'Islam' and 'oil' could be posed in a non-reductionist and anti-essentialist manner.)

Specifically, we argued that the conditions for stable (liberal) capitalist state formation were the emergence of privatized forms

2 Our third criterion is more strictly a methodological guideline.

of appropriation, such that political domination could be formally uncoupled from class exploitation, and the reconstitution of political power in a generalized form, concerned with the public functions of rule. And it is the generalization of capitalist relations of production throughout society which underpins both of these forms. We have also seen that this process of state formation was the project of *both* the mandate and protectorate powers, especially the British, after the First World War *and* the indigenous anti-imperialist and anti-landlord forces in the post-independence states. The conflict between these two sets of social forces centred on the class basis of the process of state formation and thus the international economic and political alignment of the new states. In short, the former imperialist powers wished to encourage a process of development in which the colonial division of labour would be maintained and the foreign policies of the new states would be aligned with those of the major capitalist powers. Against this, 'nationalist' forces sought to displace the agents of dependent incorporation into the international system (landed and mercantile interests) and attempted to establish a new balance of class forces internally that would lay the basis for state-led projects of industrialization and a degree of independent manoeuvre in the international system.

In the case studies which follow we will review the outcome of these conflicts in Turkey, Egypt, Iraq, Saudi Arabia and Iran in order to ascertain what comparative and historical patterns emerge. In chapter 5 these similarities and differences will be treated in a more systematic and thematic manner, and we shall develop some general theses about the pattern of state formation and development in the Middle East. Let us now turn to the case studies.

Turkey

In some respects the Turkish experience provided a model for the rest of the Middle East, and it can thus serve as a standard against which developments elsewhere may usefully be compared.[3] This is so because by virtue of the positions of the Muslim state-bureaucracy and the Sunni *ulema*, as well as the international context of the birth of the republic, the consolidation of state authority was relatively unproblematic, if extremely violent. Equally significant is the fact that, once a degree of industrial development had been

3 I am happy to note that on this point at least I agree with Elie Kedourie (1992).

launched, a certain separation of the institutions of rule and surplus appropriation developed. Turkey also represents the exemplary instance of secular development in the region. Finally, the international position of Turkey during the formative years of state formation and economic development meant that the constraints of dependency were somewhat weakened. These facts have pushed Turkey further along the road towards the structural conditions for liberal state formation and capitalist development than any other society in the Middle East. Accordingly, the prospects for a consolidation of democratic rule in Turkey are brighter than in any other major state in the Middle East.

The Turkish case is also of more general relevance, as Caglar Keyder has pointed out:

> With the hindsight provided by Third-World nationalist development schemes in the 1960s and 1970s, the Turkish experience emerges as one of the first examples of what was to become a fairly common pattern. Under the guise of a novel social system, a political elite and a nascent bourgeoisie joined forces to isolate a national economic space for themselves in which heavy oppression of the working class and exploitation of the agricultural sector would allow for rapid accumulation. All this was to be achieved under a more or less xenophobic ideology of national solidarity, one denying the existence of conflicting class interests in favour of a corporatist model of society. (Keyder, 1987:107)

No doubt because of this, the Turkish experience has attracted a good deal of debate, and it has provided something of a testing ground for divergent theories of political and economic transformation. We will return to these debates in chapter 5. Let us now turn to the actual character of Turkish state formation.

As we saw in chapter 2, European economic penetration of the Ottoman empire, together with the internally driven decline, resulted in the development of significant mercantile activity outside the apparatus of tributary power. This activity was under the control of both the non-Muslim minorities within the empire and the Europeans without. Against this background, and given also the European-supported secession of many of the Christian territories from the empire, the Young Turk movement sought to restore traditional Ottoman control. The failure of this project led to the coup by the CUP shortly before the outbreak of the First World War. During the course of the war, foreign control over the Turkish state diminished, allowing a state-sponsored attempt to create an indigenous, Muslim bourgeoisie. As a result of conflict between the Muslim population and the Christian Armenians and Greeks, much of the mercantile sector was either killed or expelled. Indeed, out of a total pre-war population of about 15 million in the area of republican Turkey, Keyder (1987) estimates that as many as 2.5 million Greeks and Armenians died or departed, including some 90 per cent of the pre-war bourgeoisie.

Thus Turkey escaped both formal political control in the colonial era and the mandate or protectorate status imposed on much of the rest of the Middle East in the inter-war years. Because of this, the process of consolidating the power of the post-independence state occurred as early as the 1920s and 1930s, as did the launching of a pattern of state-led development. In turn, this timing had two important implications for the character of Turkey's position in the global system: first, as a bulwark against Soviet influence in Central Asia and the straits, after 1926 Turkey became aligned with the leading capitalist power in the area, Britain; and second, Turkey's model of economic development, that of a protected national economy, was congruent with the more general shift towards national economies and the rise of state economic management in the 1930s.

After the nationalist struggle against foreign and minority influence within and Allied and Greek invasions from without, the Kemalist coup was carried through by the Muslim state bureaucracy – the main axis of surplus appropriation within the tributary order. The coincidence of rule and surplus appropriation in Ottoman society, and the failure of a powerful landed class to develop in Anatolia, meant that Kemalism cannot adequately be described as a 'revolution', since the principal possessing class, the state bureaucracy, was not dispossessed. Instead, this class either expelled or exterminated, and hence dispossessed, the minority commercial classes during and shortly after the First World War. As a result, the state stood centre-stage in the economy of what became the Turkish Republic. The continuity of the ruling elite from the Ottoman to the Kemalist era may be seen in the fact that 93 per cent of staff officers and 85 per cent of civil servants retained their positions under the republic. (As late as 1964 one half of senior officials came from bureaucratic and military families.)

Given the destruction of the old mercantile and bourgeois forces, in the first decade of development, during the 1920s, an indigenous bourgeoisie scarcely existed. At this time, there was no attempt to isolate the economy from the world market: inward flows of foreign capital accounted for the bulk of investment in manufacturing, 'the bourgeoisie did not constitute an autonomous political force, and the economy did not emerge as an autonomous sphere with its own institutionalised rules of conduct' (Keyder 1987:83). By the outbreak of the inter-war depression, however, Kemalist forces had been able to fashion a single-party dictatorship, comprising an organizational framework that owed more to Durkheimian models of corporatism and the organizational forms of European fascism than to Islam.[4]

The armed forces were brought under legislative control, serving officers were excluded from the assembly and the army's share of the state budget fell from 40 per cent in 1926 to 28 per cent in the early 1930s. The political system comprised a strong presidential regime, based on the support of the Republican People's Party (RPP), in which indirect and controlled elections provided for a quiescent assembly. By 1930–1 the bureaucratic elite had gained sufficient unity to respond to the economic crisis by inaugurating a protected economy, with a strong element of state direction and the creation of para-state organizations of social control. This apparatus then steered Turkish development until the end of the Second World War. (The corporatist framework did not extend to labour which was rigidly excluded from all forms of collective organization.) The state and party elite merged in the RPP.

Development during the depression saw a spread of state-led production, bringing about an increase in economic self-sufficiency, a rise in the share accounted for by manufacturing, the growth of state expenditure and a fall in real wages. The role of the state in sponsoring economic development can be seen in the following information supplied by Keyder: 'In 74.2 per cent of all firms established between 1931 and 1940 (and still surviving in 1968) the founding entrepreneurs were bureaucrats' (1987:106).

The failure of a strong class of landowners to develop in nineteenth-century Anatolia meant that Kemalism faced little opposition from the countryside. Relatively small-scale private property in land, together with functioning village communities, were the norm, and

4 It should be stressed that the dominance of Turkish society by peasant, agricultural production, together with the complete absence of an organized working class, meant that there was no scope for the counter-revolutionary forms of mobilization characteristic of European fascism. Kemalism was not Turkish fascism.

this practice was endorsed by the new regime. To begin with, co-operation was encouraged with local notables, the *aghas*, where these had a local power base. This was especially the case in eastern Turkey, in the least developed regions. Where they existed, *aghas* regulated access to the land, to money, to the means of production and to the administration for the rural population, thereby deriving a degree of political control over those organizations concerned with agriculture and mosque building. However, as national policies were developed, and as district-level administration was introduced, the reach of these clientelist networks declined. The creation of a more unified national framework was also assisted by the transition to multi-partyism after 1946. The central adminis-tration increasingly controlled the important material resources: roads, wells, schools and mosques, electricity, irrigation, agricul-tural credits and employment.

Thus, as Eisenstadt and Roniger have argued:

> Clientelistic networks became less localised and more linked to wider institutional frames. Thus, existing local factions were trans-formed into local sections of the national party, and the existing clientelistic networks were politicised. . . . In the more developed regions, the clientelistic networks of notables were replaced by party-directed clientelism. (1984:86)

In relation to Islam the Turkish experience was also pioneering. Kemalist opposition to religious intrusion into public life was dra-conian, and its character has been well summarized by Esposito:

> Kemalist reforms effectively controlled and suppressed the tradi-tional religious establishment of the *ulama* and the heads of Sufi organizations. The secularization of law and education and state control of religious endowments struck at the very heart of the power and authority of the *ulama* who had served as judges, legal experts, and as advisers, educators, and administrators of religious endowments with their related social services. Most of these jobs were now abolished and their revenues sharply curtailed. In addi-tion seminaries were closed, the use of religious titles forbidden, the wearing of ecclesiastical clothing prohibited outside mosques, and religious education in state schools was discontinued. (1991:98)

As if this was not enough, the alphabet was changed, Sufi brother-hoods were banned, sacred tombs were closed, the Koran was translated into Turkish, a mythical Turkish history was invented, people were compelled to take European surnames, the fez and turban were banned and European-style hats were made compulsory; indeed, seventy people were executed for opposition to the hat laws!

Thus, Kemalism was the exemplary instance of modernization *against* Islam, a fact arising from the imbrication of Islam with the discredited old order and the extensive dependence of the Sunni *ulema* on the tributary power of the Ottoman state. Though the defence of Islam became a rallying point for those who sought to resist the centralizing political control of Kemalism, the social location of Islam within the Ottoman order rendered it relatively defenceless against this ruthless onslaught. As a material force, Islam was obliterated under Ataturk. This is not gainsaid by the fact that 'the Turkish national movement was essentially a Muslim protest against Christian assertion' (Yapp 1991:15). In fact, the militant secularism of the state amounted to rigid state control over religious life, and a strict laicism in public affairs, rather than the institutional separation of Church and State or the decline in personal belief. After all, Turkey was purged of its non-Muslim population and it was still predominantly a peasant society: in the new state 98 per cent of the population was Muslim (a majority Sunni), 85 per cent spoke Turkish (10 per cent Kurdish) and some 80 per cent were dependent on agriculture.

During the Second World War, although Turkey remained neutral, the economy became increasingly dependent on the Nazi economy, and both manufacturing and agriculture declined, leading to very high inflation. Turkey finally joined the Allied side in February 1945. Cold War tensions and Turkey's strategic location resulted in the massive provision of US economic and military aid after the Second World War. Turkish forces were dispatched to Korea, and Turkey applied to join NATO, entering the organization in 1952. In addition to guaranteeing Turkey's security in case of any Soviet pressure on the straits, membership of NATO served 'to assert and deepen its European identity' and 'to modernize its military' (Johnstone 1989:17). Once again, then, Turkey's position in the state system resulted in support by the dominant international power, as dollar aid flowed into the economy from official loans and grants and military spending. Equally, the post-war regime of accumulation, involving a growing autonomy for the Turkish bourgeoisie and a programme of import-substituting industrialization, fitted well with US attempts to sponsor the economic containment of the Soviet Union.

In part responding to the liberal ideology of the newly hegemonic United States, after the war the Turkish state announced the need for a party of opposition. The rival Democrat Party opposed the statist order on the grounds of freedom of the market and of religion. The continuing weight of the peasantry and the *petit bourgeoisie* meant that a populist ideology of the market had considerable appeal, and the Democrat Party won power in 1950. At this time, the share of agriculture in GNP was 37 per cent, the rural workforce accounted for some 75–80 per cent of the population and perhaps two-thirds of the population was illiterate. However, in the new domestic and international conjuncture, the spread of capitalist relations was rapid. Wider use of market forces, rapid economic development, urban growth and populist mobilization ensued. The ascendancy of the Democrat Party and the growth of the market marked the increasing political differentiation of the bourgeoisie and its growing independence from the bureaucracy. As political power passed to the bourgeoisie, so the 'bureaucracy lost its status as a social class with its own project and became a group of state managers' (Keyder 1987:127).

But the failure of this model to provide stable accumulation led to the military coup of 1960. The new regime initiated a more technocratic and planned form of development, inaugurating a national capitalist programme of import-substituting industrialization through the state allocation of foreign exchange and credit, combined with an expansion of welfare entitlements in pursuit of social and industrial co-operation. The success of the state in sponsoring the development of a more independent bourgeoisie can be seen in the fact that by the mid-1970s 62 per cent of manufacturing output came from the private sector. However, internal contradictions in the model of accumulation, based on shortages of foreign exchange, a decline in the rate of profit and the strengthened bargaining position of the working class, combined with the worldwide recession of the mid-1970s to produce a worsening economic crisis in the late 1970s.

In parallel with the maturing political independence of the industrial bourgeoisie, the working class also gained a significant degree of autonomy in collective organization, and real wages and the social wage rose. Yet unfortunately for the fortunes of Turkish democracy in this period, the transformation of the RPP into a social democratic party was frustrated by the 'limited weight of organised labour within the working class, and the small proportion of the working class within the total population' (Keyder 1988:215). The agrarian social structure, defined by small-scale private property and peasant production, blocked the development of a rural working class and contributed to the considerable social weight of *petit-bourgeois* forces. As long as economic growth, and with it the expansion of the state budget, was maintained, all social strata benefited. But as the strains of increasing inequality and political mobilization mounted in circumstances of acute economic crisis and social breakdown, the military once again intervened (1980). This time the military regime was the occasion for the introduction of a programme of social stabilization and export-led growth, involving structural adjustment and economic liberalization. Real wages and social expenditure fell rapidly.

During the instability of the 1970s an Islamic reaction did begin to emerge. Moreover, the military regime outlawed political parties and encouraged Islam to combat the left. Compulsory religious education was introduced into the school curriculum. But the conservative urban elites, represented after the restoration of civilian rule by President Turgut Ozal's Motherland Party, have been careful to use the state to maintain a firm control over religious forces and to channel them in regime-supporting directions. Religious officials remain employees of the state.

Precarious and largely formal though it may be, Turkish democracy has been the outcome of early and successful consolidation of state authority under Kemal, relatively impressive levels of industrialization, and with it a degree of organizational independence in civil society, and state control over religious forces. On this basis, a 'restricted democracy' has developed on the basis of the 1982 constitution, and given reasonable economic growth and the ambitions of the Turkish ruling class for membership of the European Community a stable parliamentary system has a fair chance of developing.

Egypt

On some measures the situation in Egypt was not dissimilar from that in Turkey. The Sunni clergy was already somewhat subordinated to the state, and there was also a similar degree of ethnic and religious homogeneity. The extent of tribal nomadism was also very limited. However, in comparison with the Turkish case, there were three fundamental differences. First, Muhammad Ali's abolition of tax farming, and his distribution of state lands to new, large landowners in the nineteenth century, resulted in cotton production for the world market by peasant sharecroppers. Thus, some of the peasantry was wrested away from effective control over the land, although many retained effective possession, and the independence of the state apparatus from the landed class was weak. Second, developments under Muhammad Ali also played a role in fostering a degree of 'national' identity in Egypt during the nineteenth century. The introduction of conscription and the creation of a bureaucratic stratum brought people together in the state, a position highlighted by the 'exclusive monopoly over the higher echelons of service by the Turko-Circassian aristocracy' (Zubaida 1989a:128). Third, the importance of Egypt to the strategic control of the British empire meant that financial collapse brought with it British occupation in 1882, whereas the similar Turkish bankruptcy did not produce direct colonial control. For these reasons, the notable classes and imperialist controls were able to persist until after the Second World War, and the ground was in part prepared for a nationalist and secular current of politics. The consolidation of state power by the post-independence state, therefore, occurred in a very different international and domestic conjuncture to that of the Turkish case. Never the less, once the anti-imperialist and anti-landlord revolution began in 1952, in its broad outlines the pattern of state formation and import-substituting industrialization in Egypt replicated some features of the Turkish experience.

A proto-nationalist revolt in 1919 resulted in a reassessment of imperial strategy by the British. The protectorate was renounced, but control over defence and foreign policy, the security of the Suez Canal, the government of the Sudan and the future of the capitulations remained in British hands. As Malcolm Yapp has pointed out:

> After 1922 British influence was maintained through the high commissioner (British ambassador from 1936) and his staff in Cairo, through advisers with the Egyptian government in the departments of justice and finance, through command of the Egyptian army, through the British garrison in Egypt and through the British presence in the Sudan. If necessary British power could be supported by a naval demonstration in the Mediterranean. (1991:57)

The Anglo-Egyptian treaty of 1936 sought to deal with four issues that had not been resolved in 1922: foreign and defence policy was covered by a twenty-year offensive and defensive alliance; judicial and financial advisers were scheduled to leave; Egypt was to join the League of Nations; and the question' of the Sudan was shelved.

Within the restricted field imposed by British control, the constitution enabled the king to keep a government out of, but not in, power. Given the fact that all elections after 1923 were won by opponents of the king, parliament was often dissolved. However, legislative instability was combined with considerable ministerial continuity, as some 60 per cent of ministers were notables. The latter engaged in political activity in pursuit of government patronage.

In 1920, over 90 per cent of the 13 million population was Muslim (nearly all Sunni), and about 70 per cent were based in agriculture. Such Egyptian industry as existed was owned both by foreigners and by local notables. The capacity of these forces to prosecute development can be seen in the fact that per capita income did not increase between 1910 and 1950, while the class distribution of income widened in favour of the notables. During the 1930s the Muslim Brotherhood challenged the secular path of development.

During the Second World War, Egypt proved to be vital to British military and strategic interests, and after the war the colonial power was reluctant to cede influence in the Middle East. Against this background, the Egyptian revolution of 1952 was aimed at establishing full national control over its territory and at gaining room for independent manoeuvre within the international system. After the British left in 1954, and until defeat in the 1967 Arab-Israeli War, Egypt pursued a radical anti-imperialist programme abroad, rejecting the Baghdad Pact, nationalizing the canal, countering the invasion of 1956, intervening in Yemen and supporting dissent within the Saudi royal family.

Related to this was the shift in US policy in the Middle East noted by Owen:

> a key moment was the American decision taken in the mid-1950s to abandon its brief search for alliances with secular nationalist Arab leaders like President Nasser and to base its Middle Eastern position on its support of conservative, or 'moderate', monarchical

regimes like the Saudis, Jordanians and Moroccans, none of which posed any threat to its other ally, Israel. (1992:103)

This did not mean an end to US relations with Egypt, but it did in turn give the Soviet Union an opportunity to seek allies and influence in the region. However, within Egypt itself power resided with the nationalist movement of Free Officers, not with the Egyptian Communist Party, and Nasser maintained a degree of independent manoeuvre in relation to the superpowers.

Domestically, the revolution had two main features:

> The first was the replacement of the old landed urban notables who had dominated the political system of Egypt since the nineteenth century by a new ruling elite, composed initially of military officers and subsequently of a mixed military-civilian class of state functionaries. The second was a major shift of political, economic and social power to the state. (Yapp 1991:211)

Agrarian reform had already been proposed by the United States and the United Nations, and it had some support among the bourgeoisie. The project of state-led, industrial development had long been the aim of the national bourgeoisie. Land reform was instituted, agricultural co-operatives were established and there was an extension of the area of cultivatable land. Prior to the land reform, in 1952, 70 per cent of Egypt's cultivatable land was owned by 4,000 families, some 1 per cent of the population, and less than 3 per cent of all landowners owned just over one-half of all arable land. The land reform programme dispossessed large land owners and thereby destroyed the political dominance of this class; it also created a class of middle-income farmers and resulted in greater state control over the sector. However, in contrast to the Turkish case where large landowners were rare and where a greater proportion of the population was rural, the demands placed on Egyptian agriculture both in terms of feeding the urban population and in supplying surpluses for industrial development were correspondingly greater.

Until 1956 the economy continued to be dominated by the private sector. Thereafter, industrial growth was sponsored by the state and a programme of welfare reforms was initiated. The construction of the High Dam was an aid to irrigation but its main importance was to provide the electricity needed for industrialization. The Suez Canal was nationalized in July 1956, banks, insurance companies and commercial agencies in January 1957. Between 1959 and 1961 state control was extended to Egyptian capital, foreign trade, labour organizations and agricultural co-operatives. In addition, progressive income taxes and confiscatory measures for personal wealth were adopted. The 1962 National Charter did not herald the end of private property in Egypt, recognizing the latter where it was 'free of exploitation and monopoly, and independent of foreign influence'. This private sector of 'national capitalism' was regulated by the state. Table 4.1 shows the Ministry of Planning's figures for the relative shares of the public (state-owned) sector and of national capitalism in 1970–1. Together, these policies were aimed at providing the resources and control necessary to launch a state-capitalist programme of import-substituting industrialization.[5]

Table 4.1 Relative shares of the public sector and national capitalism in the Egyptian economy, 1970–1

	Public sector (%)	National capitalism (%)
Agriculture	20	80
Extractive industries	88	12
Manufacturing industries	60	40
Internal trade	14	86
Transport and communications	52	48

Source: Azim 1989

The degree of social transformation was initially impressive. Between 1952 and 1967 real wages rose by 44 per cent. At the same time, the population expanded rapidly: from 20 million in 1950, through 30 million in 1966 and 37 million in 1976, to 50 million (and rising) in 1986. The public sector expanded from 15 per cent of GNP in 1952 to 48 per cent in 1972. In 1952, agriculture accounted for 40 per cent of GDP, 65 per cent of the labour force and 90 per cent of exports; by 1970 its share of GDP had fallen to 23 per cent with industry accounting for a similar amount and the rest in services.

5 The main newspaper of the regime, *Al-Ahram*, serialized chapters of Walt Rostow's *The Stages of Economic Growth*, with its headline taken from the book's subtitle, 'a non-communist manifesto'.

The new, 'secular' regime also moved against the position of religion, seeking to subordinate it to state control. In 1952 family *waqfs* were abolished, the public ones brought under state control in 1957. The *shari'a* courts were closed in 1956, Sufi brotherhoods were officially outlawed in 1961 and the orthodox *ulema* co-operated with the state. Finally, the political activity of the Muslim Brotherhood was suppressed. State control of al-Azhar University in Cairo as well as those mosques that came under the Ministry of Religious Endowments enabled Nasser to mobilize modernist Islam in defence of his policies *vis-à-vis* the radical regimes of Syria, Iraq and Algeria, the conservative monarchy in Saudi Arabia and domestic critics (Esposito 1991). In 1964 a clause was inserted into the constitution declaring Islam to be the religion of the state.

Defeat in 1967 constituted a profound shock to the army and the regime, and it resulted in a shift in the balance of political and strategic alignments as the financial capital of the oil-producing states was increasingly tied into the international capitalist system. The power of Nasser's arch-rival, the Saudi monarchy, increased accordingly. Thereafter, and especially once the October War (1973) opened up the prospect of substantive negotiations with Israel, the prospects of peace and favourable treatment from the United States in the fields of economic and military aid beckoned. This changing international environment provided one of the conditions in which the Egyptian open-door policy, or *infitah*, was launched. Domestically, there was a push from the right to increase the independence of the national capitalists and the state bourgeoisie. The aims of this shift were to attract foreign investment, to develop the private sector and to restructure the public sector.

However, the seriousness of the economic crisis, and the political resistance to the reform of subsidized basic goods expressed in the January 1977 riots, forced the state to climb down on the proposals of the International Monetary Fund (IMF), and drove it towards a *'rentier* quest' to liquidate state capitalism, supply surplus labour to the oil states, and garner foreign rents from aid, oil, profits on the canal and tourism (Aulas 1988). The *infitah* did raise the share of GNP devoted to investment, and it also increased the share of investment coming from abroad, but much of the latter went into services (especially tourism) and oil and construction. By the end of the 1980s, agriculture accounted for less than one-fifth of GDP, Egypt imported over half of its food requirements and the largest sources of foreign exchange had become oil, remittances from migrant workers, tourism and the fees from the Suez Canal.

As part of this shift away from Nasserist state capitalism, under President Sadat (1970–81) control over Islamic institutions was relaxed in order to counter the power of the secular left. According to Michael Gilsenan, the technocratic and managerial bases of the new regime 'were interested in the prospect of Islamic law being appropriated to the state in a possibly expanded way, but not in a serious extension of influence by the clerical estate who are seen rather as a useful adjunct to the apparatus and ruling strata' (1988:178). The number of private mosques doubled during the 1970s, from roughly 20,000 to 40,000, leaving only 6,000 under state control. At the same time, political liberalization was limited. The Arab Socialist Union was restructured in a nominally more pluralist direction, but the controlled experiment in democracy after 1976 allowed no space for the main political currents – the Nasserists, the Wafd and the Muslim Brotherhood. (The Egyptian polity comprises a strong presidential regime in which parliament has little real power. In 1981, for example, Sadat arrested virtually every critic of the regime.) The final years of Sadat's rule, then, were marked by increasing opposition between the government and militant Islamic groups, culminating in the assassination of the president in 1981. Under President Mubarak (1981-) a degree of political liberalization was combined with the reimposition of government control over mosques in the mid-1980s and again in late 1992.

However, Islamic organizations have increasingly come to play an important role in providing for the social and material welfare of those who have not benefited from the *infitah*. (In the early 1980s, it was estimated that one-third of the adult, male population belonged to Sufi brotherhoods.) Thus, according to Saad Eddin Ibrahim:

> This strand of Islamic activism has therefore set about establishing concrete Islamic alternatives to the socioeconomic institutions of the state and the capitalist sector. Islamic social welfare institutions are better run than their state/public counterparts, less bureaucratic and impersonal ... They are definitely more grass-roots oriented, far less expensive and far less opulent than the institutions created under Sadat's *infitah* ... institutions which mushroomed in the 1970s and which have been providing an exclusive service to the top 5 percent of the country's population. Apolitical Islamic activism has thus developed a substantial socioeconomic muscle through

which it has managed to baffle the state and other secular forces in Egypt. (quoted in Esposito 1991:228)

With the accession of Mubarak, some parties have been allowed to form, the press is freer than at any time since 1952 and the judiciary has increasingly asserted both its independence and the need for constitutional propriety. Yet the elections of 1984, 1987 and 1990 were not free and were conducted under the state of emergency legislation imposed after the assassination of Sadat. Meanwhile, Islamist forces have increasingly penetrated professional organizations and elements of the state apparatus.

As compared with Turkey, a dual problem of reform persists. On the one hand, the depth of economic crisis, together with the relatively short duration of state controls over religion, has produced a corresponding problem of Islamist opposition. And on the other, the very presence of the state in the economy (the public sector still accounts for some 70 per cent of industrial activity) and the continued power of the military and security services frustrate further democratization. The role of Egypt in the recent Gulf War strengthened its position in the Arab world, improved its standing in the West and, perhaps most importantly, facilitated the write-off of tens of billions of dollars of debt (subject to continuing IMF surveillance of the reform programme). Yet, the underlying problems remain largely unresolved.

Iraq

Of all the major states in the Middle East, Iraq faced the most formidable obstacles to state formation. While the presence of a notable class, British control and a Sunni bureaucracy and *ulema* suggests some parallels with Egypt, the sheer arbitrariness of the country's formation, together with the absence of any developed tradition of state stability and the degree of ethnic and religious heterogeneity (both a sharp contrast with Turkey and Egypt), produced an extremely refractory inheritance for state-building. In addition, as a major oil producer during the critical period when the state's authority was finally imposed on society, the rentier aspects of the Iraqi polity further increased its ability to opt for coercion over less brutal forms of mobilization and control. The consequence has been the creation of the most controlled and repressive society in the Middle East.

We saw in chapter 2 how developments in the late nineteenth century brought about a reorientation of economic activity in Iraq, drawing the provinces into closer exchanges with one another, expanding agricultural production and redirecting trade towards Britain. At the same time, after the Ottoman land reform law of 1858, there was a process of large-scale estate formation in Iraq, as tribal sheikhs who had previously held more or less titular power became large landowners and began to displace tribal nomadism. We also saw the specific circumstances of the formation of modern Iraq. The predominantly Shi'ite tribal revolt of 1920–1 was suppressed by the British, and Sunni-based support for Sharifian forces was installed under King Faisal's leadership. But Shi'ite tribesmen had gone along with Sharifian agitation to expel what Kedourie has called the 'disquieting propensity to control and administer' of the British, not to bring about a process of state formation, let alone one dominated by Sunni Arab nationalists. One consequence of this has been summarized by Kedourie as follows:

> The 1921 settlement left no machinery by which differences between ruler and subject, or between group and group could be composed with peace and moderation; it organised a central government, able to use all the modern techniques of administration, and handed it over to [Faisal and the Sharifian forces] to use as they liked; authority was drained from all localities and communities and concentrated in them; a group at odds with them would either be crushed wholly and finally or, if it could, would uphold its cause by the sword. (1987:213)

And in 1933, King Faisal defined the problem of state-building as follows:

> In Iraq there is still . . . no Iraqi people, but unimaginable masses of human beings, devoid of any patriotic ideal, imbued with religious traditions and absurdities, connected by no common tie, giving ear to evil, prone to anarchy, and perpetually ready to rise against any government whatsoever. (quoted in Yapp 1991:70)

If we can excuse the contemptuous tone from one whose own ancestry should surely occasion a greater respect for such people (the qualities listed were after all those of his father, Hussain), then from the point of view of an emergent state power Faisal's depiction is accurate enough. Sunni Arabs made up one-fifth of the population, Shi'ite Arabs about one-half and Kurdish tribes one-seventh. Much of the population was tribal and perhaps 5 per cent were literate.

Sunni and Shi'ite notables and Sunni bureaucrats, installed under Ottoman rule in the second half of the nineteenth century and strengthened by the British, supported the Hashemite monarchy, and tribal sheikhs (often Shi'ite) were an important source of support at provincial level. Commerce and banking were originally dominated by Jews, but after most were airlifted to Palestine by the British in 1950, Persian and Kuwaiti families (largely Shi'ite) took their place. Land ownership was extremely concentrated and the position of the direct producers was wretched. The policy of converting tribal leaders into landowners had continued under British rule and throughout the inter-war period, as such figures became the main pillar of local administration. In fact, most of the private land in Iraq was acquired after the promulgation of the 1932 land law; by 1958, some 60 per cent of the land in Iraq was owned by big landowners. Thus, as Haim Gerber has argued, 'in 1958 tribal chieftains owned a vast proportion of Iraq's arable land, and together with the ruling elite of ex-Sharifian officers they formed a tangible landed upper class that completely controlled Iraq both socially and politically' (1987:91). At first, tribal chiefs maintained private militias to control the peasantry.

The Iraqi army was composed of ex-Ottoman and ex-Sharifian forces, and was therefore almost exclusively Sunni. During the 1930s the army broke the military power of the tribes, except in Kurdistan. (In 1933 the tribes were estimated to have 100,000 rifles as against 15,000 in the army.) Indeed, in the 1930s Faisal had his own version of a two-power military standard: namely, that the Iraqi army needed to be able to put down two *rebellions* at the same time. The weak consolidation of the state was shown by the spate of inconclusive military interventions in politics and the tribal revolts of the period 1936–41.

The Anglo-Iraqi Treaty of 1922 (and the military agreement of 1924) provided for British control over foreign and defence policy and the provision of internal judicial and financial advisers. A new treaty was signed in 1930 and Iraq joined the League of Nations in 1932. These new arrangements gave the British sovereign rights in two bases, at Habbaniyya 50 miles from the capital, Baghdad, and at Sha'iba near Basra and the Gulf, as well as complete rights to Iraqi facilities in time of war. With the outbreak of war, and the ascendancy of a pro-Axis faction in Baghdad, Britain again occupied Iraq by military force, and remained in control for the duration of the war. During and after the Second World War struggles over relations with the imperial power intensified.

As in the Egyptian case, therefore, the revolution of 1958, which overthrew the monarchy and instituted a republic, had both an anti-imperialist and an anti-landlord character. The landed political class was replaced by an elite based in the civil and military bureaucracies of the state. Yet for a decade there was no real consolidation of state authority. The absence of a secure class basis for the regime was itself in part a reflection of the pre-revolutionary religious division of power. As Kiren Aziz Chaudhry has pointed out: 'With the replacement of the Jewish merchant communities, Shi'is dominated the ranks of both the landed and merchant elite, while the civil service and the army remained in control of the Sunni Arab minority' (1991:21). Thus, the overthrow of the landed classes by the state-military elite also represented an assertion of the Sunni bureaucracy over the Shi'ite notables. At first President Qasim relied on the Iraqi Communist Party (ICP) which played a dominant role in the mass organizations of workers and peasants, and controlled the strategically placed workers in the railways, the port of Basra and the oil fields. But the old Shi'ite elite continued to oppose change. In 1963 Arabist and Ba'athist groupings attempted to seize power but the disunited Ba'athists were soon expelled from government. However, in 1964 President Arif 'nationalised all agricultural lands, industry, banking, insurance and services, virtually eliminating the top layer of the largely Shi'i commercial elite' (Chaudhry 1991:21).

Politically, the Ba'ath sought to mobilize and organize radical nationalist, *petit-bourgeois* elements from the urban areas and in state employment, as well as attempting to win over key sections of the military. In 1968 Ba'athist coups were successful and a pattern of mobilization and organization familiar from state-led industrialization in dependent economies was inaugurated. Land and welfare reform followed the Egyptian model, but the former was poorly executed due to political disruption and the absence of trained personnel.

On seizing power, the membership of the Ba'ath party was a mere 400–500. To begin with, an alliance with the Kurds enabled the Ba'ath to move against the left, and then a restoration of relations with the ICP and a treaty and alliance with the Soviet Union facilitated repression of the Kurds. By 1976 the membership of the Ba'ath had risen to one million. Intense levels of repression characterized the post-1968 Ba'ath political order, especially after Saddam Hussain consolidated his power through the security apparatus. The regime found a narrow social base in the (huge) security services and elements of the military. This was combined with a highly centralized and brutally repressive political order, straddling a society of considerable ethnic and religious diversity. In the absence of an indigenous bourgeoisie and also given the physical extermination of most of the left, oil revenues and terror became the mainstays of Ba'ath rule. By the mid-1970s, the combination of oil rents and repression allowed the Ba'ath to consolidate power (see Farouk-Sluglett and Sluglett 1990).

Under Ba'athist rule, far from constituting a general public power, the Iraqi state has seized hold of, manipulated and thereby transformed the pre-existing kinship and ethnic cleavages of the society, physically destroying enemies, uprooting those communities which offer any resistance to the policies of the state and incorporating the regime's clients. This little-analysed aspect of Ba'ath rule has been noted by Isam al-Khafaji, who argues that while 'the present leadership did not invent the ethnic, religious, sectarian, regional and tribal cleavages in Iraqi society', it has never the less:

> perpetuated and exacerbated these cleavages rather than worked to overcome them. The supporting actors (or victims) in Iraqi politics have not been individuals or citizens as such. They have rather been treated as members of this sect or that tribe, as sons of certain towns and regions. This applies to the way some are incorporated within the state system, and to the way others are excluded from it, or assigned subordinate roles. . . . Just as positions of power are reserved for loyal families, the regime holds families of dissidents responsible for their 'crimes'. . . . More than three decades after the 1958 revolution which overthrew the monarchy and the domination of tribal landowners in Iraqi politics, Iraq has relapsed into family rule under a republican guise. (1992:18, 19)

It is this brutal imbrication of personalized forms of pre-capitalist authority and domination with the political power of an extremely coercive and violent state apparatus, resting on the resources of massive oil rents, that makes the Iraqi polity so difficult to characterize. For it is neither the atomized, centrally controlled polity of near-Stalinist terror so harrowingly portrayed by Samir al-Khalil

(1990), nor is it simply a broadly secular, modernizing regime like, say, Turkey or Egypt as is suggested by many others. Both of these views are in danger of taking Ba'athist ideology too seriously. Whether the latter is seen as inherently totalitarian by its critics (most notably al-Khalil), or as a form of secular, Arab nationalism (Marr 1985), it is inherently implausible to attempt an explanation of Iraqi politics in terms of Ba'ath ideology.

The mobilizing ideology of the Ba'ath, Arab nationalism, in fact became little more than an appropriate ideological vehicle of Sunni, later Tikriti, assertion in a state where they were significantly outnumbered, though it is true that many Iraqi Shi'ites also joined the Ba'ath Party. (Something similar could be said of Alawi dominance in Syria.) That the ideology of the Ba'ath modelled itself on pan-German nationalism was simply a reflection of the central importance of *language* to German thinking about nationalism, making it a relevant ideological model for a putative '*Arab(ic)*' nationalism, and of the fact that Britain and France were the colonial powers in the Middle East, making Germany an obvious 'ally' (as some Zionist factions also concluded). Frank Ryan, the Irish republican who fought for the International Brigades in Spain, also ended up attempting to trade terms with the Nazis. Perhaps these instances tell us something about nationalism, or about the conjuncture of international power in the 1930s and 1940s, but they say very little about the affinity between Ba'athism and fascism, any more than between the latter and Zionism or Irish republicanism.

As noted, oil became central to Ba'ath rule by virtue of its dominance of the economy. In 1972 the Iraqi Petroleum Company was nationalized and in 1973–4 the price of oil increased four-fold. By the mid–late-1970s oil accounted for nearly two-thirds of GDP, nearly 90 per cent of state revenue and virtually all of Iraq's foreign exchange. According to Joe Stork, during the 1970s:

> Iraq . . . imported machinery, equipment and capital goods worth over $2 billion a year, more than twice the value of the country's entire manufacturing sector. Consultant and service fees alone each year amount[ed] to hundreds of millions of dollars – more than twice the value of all Iraq's non-oil exports, and more than ten times the total expenditure for local research and development activities. (1989:45)

State control over the economy was considerable. Half of all agricultural land belonged to the state, and the state controlled the inputs into agriculture and agribusiness. By 1987 state-owned factories accounted for 96 per cent of the industrial workforce, 84 per cent of industrial output and the state accounted for 76 per cent of gross fixed capital formation and 77 per cent of GDP. Only the construction sector was predominantly in private-sector hands, although here too the state retained considerable powers of patronage through its control over licences and raw materials. Even when a new industrial and commercial elite did emerge under the privatizations and the deregulation following the Iran–Iraq war, it retained close kinship, financial and political ties to the regime.

Politically, then, the process of state formation in Iraq has failed to consolidate a secular, republican government. Not only has the state been unable successfully to impose its authority *vis-à-vis* competing centres of power, but also the narrow ethnic and religious basis of the regime has frustrated the development of a more inclusive form of legitimacy based on either Arab nationalism or Iraqi patriotism. (As indicated above, however, this should not be read as an inherent communal or religious opposition between Sunni and Shi'i, as both have been mobilized into politics under religious leaders, by the ICP and by the Ba'ath.) At the same time, the rentier aspects of Iraqi society have both given the state immense powers of repression and largesse and prevented the emergence of even relatively independent forms of organization based on modern social classes.

The grip of the Ba'ath was strengthened after the 1975 Algiers Agreement, when Iran ceased support to the Kurds, and in 1976–7 when the Communists were repressed. In 1977 a major Shi'ite rebellion led by the Da'wa Party broke out in the holy cities of Najaf and Karbala. Bloody repression was the response. In 1979 Saddam Hussein became president, and the Iranian revolution toppled the shah and brought the Shi'ite clergy to power. At this juncture Iran appeared to be weakened by revolution, while its support for Shi'ite oppositionists in Iraq posed a political challenge to Saddam's regime. A number of factors may have motivated Saddam Hussein's decision to invade Iran: the attractions of seizing control over the Shatt al-Arab waterway and the oil-rich Iranian province of Khuzestan (which had a large ethnic Arab population); a decision to align Iraqi power as defender of and influence over Saudi Arabia and the Gulf states; and the belief that the unpopularity of the new regime in Tehran in the West would mean that Iraq's aggression would at least not be opposed.

Whatever the reasons, eight years of conflict took a terrible toll on both combatants. In Iraq's case, the massive costs of the war against Iran had resulted in the cancellation or delay of much-needed economic development, and the anticipated post-war reconstruction had proved disappointing. The crisis was clearly spreading into the public sector and even into the state apparatus itself, evidenced by repeated executions of those close to the centre of power. Under these circumstances, Saddam appears to have decided on an aggressive policy of annexation in Kuwait to garner oil assets and bolster support throughout the (non-Gulf) Arab world (Bromley 1991a and al Jabar 1991). While the Gulf War led to the destruction of much of the civilian and military infrastructure of Iraq, Saddam Hussein remains in power and the levels of internal repression have scarcely diminished.

Saudi Arabia

Saudi Arabia provides a striking contrast with the regimes dealt with so far. Seen in comparative perspective, three facts account for this. In the first place, modernization and state formation occurred *with*, rather than against, Islam. Second, the absence of a landed notable class meant that there was no need of a military-based agrarian transformation in order to initiate socio-economic development. Third, the huge abundance of oil in relation to population provided large rents for both the Saudi economy and state, and oil also guaranteed that external protection would be forthcoming from outside the region.

As we saw in chapter 2, the puritan, revivalist Islam of Wahhabism joined forces with the tribal forces of the Saudi clan. The material basis of this alliance lay in the taxes collected and distributed to the bedouins as booty and in the security provided to the settled population. To begin with, the reassertion of Wahhabi-Saudi power came from a form of revivalist movement common in segmentary societies facing external pressure. Other instances include the Sanusi and Madhist movements in Libya and Sudan, respectively. In this context, Ernest Gellner has pointed out that Islam's

> traditional internal differentiation into the folk and scholarly variants was actually helpful in effecting adjustment. The folk variant can be disavowed, blamed for cultural backwardness, or associated with the political machinations of colonial powers, whilst the

'purer' variant can be identified all at once both with pristine origins and with a revived, glorious, modern future. (1981:5)

But, as Zubaida points out, the common features of these movements 'are not the product of a unitary Islamic history but of the common sociology of that form of society in response to external threats' (1989b:39). Moreover, this reassertion of the Wahhabi-Saudi movement did not lead by itself to the consolidation of state power in Saudi Arabia, and Islam did not remain the sole source of legitimacy for the Saudi regime. On the contrary, had other factors not intervened, notably British assistance, there is no reason to believe that it would have been any more durable than the earlier movement of the late eighteenth century. For, as Yapp has noted, 'before 1920 states in Arabia were little more than the assertions by oases of claims to tax their users, by religious dignitaries of claims to recognition, and military alliances among tribes' (1991: 189). As ever, controlling the rapacity of bedouin searches for booty, their continued attacks on other tribes and their hostility to foreign intrusion created problems, and it was only with the financial and military backing of the British that Ibn Saud was able to crush the Ikhwan and solve them.

Most importantly, the process of state formation, in any recognizably modern sense, only gathered pace as oil was discovered and as oil rents began to enter the kingdom. The need of the oil companies for clear property rights was the occasion for the precise settlement of borders in the region; it was only access to oil wealth that enabled material development and with it the augmenting of state resources; it was only these resources which solved the problems of tribal rivalry and permitted the bedouin and the merchants to be paid off; it was only by means of oil that the economy was linked into the world market; and it was only because of the latter that this small and, therefore, relatively defenceless state attracted the support of an outside power, the United States.

In the process, the form of the original Wahhabi-Saudi alliance underwent a fundamental transformation. Indeed, as Ghassan Salame has pointed out, with the formation of the state of Saudi Arabia in 1932:

'Abd al-'Aziz was to trade his imam title for a secular royal one. . . .
The Saudis were . . . to witness a clear concentration of power within the now-royal family, and eventually within one exclusive

'House', that of 'Abd al-'Aziz. Largely similar movements of power concentration took place in Bahrain, Kuwait or Qatar. In these shaykhdoms, however, politics were traditionally dominated by a ruling coalition between the Amir and the leading trading families. But, with oil, the Amirs were able not only to settle the ruling families' debts to the merchants, but also collectively to buy them off. (1990:45)

In general, then, the ecology and pattern of cultivation in Arabia had not given itself to the consolidation of large estates, and the 'wealth and power of traditional notables had derived less from land and more from tribal authority, religious status, and trade. In Arabia the great destructive force of land reform had little on which to work' (Yapp 1991:355). By contrast, Arabia and the Gulf states had oil in abundance, and it was this, together with the outside support which it soon attracted, which enabled tribal elites to hang on to power. In the process, states which were formed to distribute oil rents facilitated the transformation of ruling families into ruling classes. (It was only in South Yemen that a notable class fell with the retreat of the colonial power that had fostered its original formation.)

The organizational development of Saudi Arabia was extremely limited during the lifetime of Ibn Saud (he died in 1953). Some rudimentary structures did emerge: relations with foreign states forced Ibn Saud to create a Ministry of Foreign Affairs, the presence of oil companies resulted in the formation of a Ministry of Finance and the development of the US military base at Dhahran in 1944 was to lead to the emergence of a Ministry of Defence. Much of the material development of the kingdom was initiated by the US oil consortium, ARAMCO, which

> engaged not only in all phases of Saudi oil production, but also built housing, airports, hospitals and schools, laid down roads, founded educational centres, dug for water, launched agricultural research and, above all, encouraged the US government to install a military base near the oil fields that would protect them and the people who worked there. . . . In 1953, at the death of Ibn Saud, the kingdom found itself in an absurd situation: oil, its principal resource, was formally nationalised, but there was no state apparatus capable of administering it. (Salame 1989:73)

In order to cope with this state of affairs, a degree of reorganization was called for. In 1958 a royal decree announced that an appointed council would advise the ruler, but that the king remained responsible for all domestic legislation and external treaties. A US financial mission in 1951–2 restructured the kingdom's finances, resulting in the formation of the Saudi Arabian Monetary Agency; in 1954 a new Ministry of Economy and Finance was established in order to manage the country's revenue and fiscal affairs. Prior to this the state had no budget. The coercive apparatus of the state was also developed. Threats to the regime came from within and without, from the internal fragility of state power and from regional rivals in Iraq, Jordan and Egypt, and resulted in the formation of two separate, if complementary, forces: the army and the national guard. According to Salame, the division of responsibility between these corps is such that 'the armed forces are charged with defending the borders and helping to put down internal rebellion' and that 'the guard is principally charged with the protection of the cities and oil wells' (1989:75).

As oil wealth accumulated in Saudi Arabia, as in the other Gulf states, so rentier economies and states emerged, fostering state-led industrial development, urbanization and the creation of a middle class of welfare workers, military personnel, bureaucrats and professionals. This went along with generous welfare provisions to the indigenous population. And while the principal benefits of these rentier economies have been the nationals, most of the domestic productive labour, both unskilled and skilled, has been undertaken by expatriates. In addition, virtually all the low-grade service-sector work has been carried out by migrant labour from the non-oil Arab states and the Indian subcontinent. Kuwait provides a dramatic example of this pattern of development. In 1989 Kuwait earned more income from its vast overseas investments located in the capitalist metropoles than from its oil production ($8.8 billion as compared with $7.7 billion), invested only some 15 percent of its state reserves in other Arab economies, and had a labour force composed of native Kuwaitis (18 per cent), Asians (42 per cent), Arabs (38 per cent) and Westerners (2 per cent). An extreme example to be sure, but none the less a dramatic illustration of the character of economic integration in the Arab world.

Saudi Arabia and the other Gulf Co-operation Council (GCC) states all have chronic non-oil balance of payments deficits. The share of manufacturing in GDP ranges from 19 per cent in Bahrain to 3 per cent in Oman. In Saudi Arabia, which in 1989 accounted for one-half of GCC manufacturing output, less than 9 per cent of its GDP was in manufacturing. This reflects the absence of a *national* market in these states. The small size and political fragmentation of the GCC market, together with the rentier character of the economies (including the absence of an indigenous industrial labour force) and the state's concentration on infrastructural activities and off-the-shelf military purchases, has meant that manufacturing development has been constrained. (The construction sector still accounts for the bulk of fixed capital investment.) As the oil wealth of the region has accumulated, so ruling families have begun to develop into ruling classes as members have moved into business activities, often in joint ventures with local merchants and with Western capital.

During the 1980s, Saudi planning shifted towards encouraging productive activities, the fall in the real oil price brought about altered financial circumstances, including budget deficits since 1983, and moves were taken to foster the development of the private sector. The manufacturing sector is dominated by petrochemicals and petroleum refining, and most of this output is exported. Current developments involve a big expansion of oil output capacity, as well as gas projects, an increase in domestic refining and further expansion into marketing by joint ventures in the United States, the EC and Japan. By these means, linkages with the consumer markets of the West are being cemented in order to guarantee Saudi Arabia's market share. This also gives the kingdom the same interest in pricing as the West, as it seeks higher value added for its integrated petroleum concerns, rather than higher prices for crude oil.

Together with the scale of Saudi financial investment in the West, and its military dependence on the United States, this new economic orientation has secured Saudi co-operation with the advanced capitalist world. As I have argued at length elsewhere (Bromley 1991b), US hegemony during the post-war era has been and remains materially dependent on a directive role in the international oil industry. Specifically, after the majors lost direct control in the mid-1970s, this role came to depend on the connections established to the Gulf producers and especially to Saudi Arabia. Regional stability and the integrity of the Gulf states is a vital base for US power in the international system. By the same token, despite aid and investment elsewhere in the Arab world, Saudi Arabia and the other GCC states have not sought to integrate their economic fortunes with those of the rest of the region.

Throughout Arabia and the Gulf, the orthodox Sunni *ulema* have by and large backed the rule of tribal families, most obviously in the case of Saudi Arabia where the 1926 constitution stated that 'all administration is in the hands of His Majesty King 'Abd al-'Aziz Ibn Sa'ud. His majesty is bound by the laws of the Shari'a.' In practice, however, this has not proved unduly restrictive. Although the Koran and the *shari'a* officially form the basis of the state, the ruling family is free to make policy in those areas not spoken for in Islamic law. Moreover, the Saudi *ulema* use the Hanbali legal tradition, in which, 'unlike other Sunni law schools, reinterpretation has remained open in principle' (Esposito 1991: 107).

As noted, the Saudi state rests on the rule of the monarchy. This was reaffirmed after the Gulf War of 1991, when in February 1992 King Fahd announced a new basic system of government. This invested the monarchy as the ultimate source of legitimacy. Article five states that rule 'shall be confined to the sons of the kingdom's founder, Abdel-Aziz Ibn Abdulrahman al-Faisal al-Saud and grandsons'. Plans for a sixty-member appointed and advisory Majlis al-Shura were also announced, as was a parallel set of provincial councils to advise the country's governors. Opposition is very difficult to sustain and to organize, though the Gulf War of 1991 did witness the visible emergence of women's opposition to the more blatantly patriarchal aspects of Saudi life. Elsewhere in the Gulf states, where consultative councils or supervisory bodies exist they are extremely limited in their powers; nowhere are they directly elected from the adult population as a whole, and they largely represent mercantile and religious forces. Political democracy is non-existent and the (foreign) labouring classes are excluded from all forms of participation. (In many cases, the expatriate working population outnumbers the native workers.) Thus far, however, while the small beginnings of an indigenous, private-sector, capitalist class can be seen, the prospects for democratic reform are scarcely visible.

Iran

While there are obvious parallels to be drawn between the experiences of Iran and Turkey, Iran differed in a number of ways from the states considered so far. In comparison with the sedentary agriculture of the Ottoman lands, the weight of pastoralism and nomadism was greater and the power of the nobility more extensive, even extending to foreign policy. Accordingly, the central state was much weaker than the Ottoman polity, and centralized state power scarcely existed under Qajar rule in the nineteenth century. As we saw in chapter 1, the Shi'ite *ulema* had also carved out a position of substantial material autonomy from the state. Like Turkey, Iran escaped formal colonial control and was penetrated economically by Russia and Britain. The effective constraints on Iran's room for manoeuvre were never the less very strong. Like Turkey also, the era of state formation under Reza Shah began in the 1920s and 1930s, but the latter's autonomy was much more strongly circumscribed than that of Kemal Ataturk by the power of landed and tribal forces, by the independence of the clergy and by the continued encroachments of the Soviets and the British. Finally, the post-Second World War strengthening of the state apparatus and the programme of import-substituting industrialization was coincident with, indeed was made possible by, the arrival of oil rents. The resulting pattern of development was to lead to an event unique in modern history: a revolution carried out under clerical leadership.

We have seen in chapter 2 the sequence of events which resulted in Reza Shah's accession to power, but let us consider the nature of the society over which he sought to rule. In the nineteenth century, Iran's foreign trade increased rapidly, its composition altered in the direction of a typical colonial pattern (exports of raw products increased as did imports of manufactures), the balance of payments moved into deficit and Russia and Britain came to control the vast majority of imports and exports. Together with the collapse of central authority, this growing integration into the world market altered the internal balance away from peasant-landlord sharecropping to the production of cash crops for export, away from tribal nomadism and away from merchant control over foreign trade to European intermediation. Protest against this dependent incorporation was encouraged by the defeat of Russia in the war against Japan (1904–5) and the Russian revolution of 1905.

In 1906 a constitutional revolution took place. To begin with, the symbiotic relationship between the *ulema* and the bazaar classes – in which education and legal services were exchanged for financial support – supported the artisans and the intelligentsia in a broad populist alliance. These forces were represented in the first

Majlis (1906–8). However, the second Majlis (1909–11), after the shah's coup, signalled a shift in the balance of forces towards tribal and landed interests. As John Foran has pointed out, even if the populist alliance had been more united, 'it still had to work with no control over certain institutions of the state (notably the monarch who still possessed the court, cabinet, and a modicum of legitimacy) and had to face growing foreign pressure without an army or real control over the budget' (1991:816). At the same time, the British acquiesced in Russian intervention in support of the anti-constitutionalist forces, fearing for their oil interests, the spread of such ideas to India and the need of an alliance with Russia against Germany in Europe. Russia supported the coup in 1908 with the Iranian Cossack Brigade and intervened directly in 1911.

The First World War damaged the Iranian economy, led to the transgression of its neutrality by Russia and Britain and, with the outbreak of the Bolshevik Revolution, deprived the shah of his principal ally, the tsar. In the post-war turmoil, Reza Khan used his position in the Cossack Brigade and as minister of war (after 1921) to construct an army that could impose its authority on the state, finally abolishing the Qajar dynasty and declaring himself Reza Shah in 1925. In some respects his project reflected that of Kemal Ataturk, but the power of the landed class and the independence of the Shi'ite *ulema*, together with the absence of a strong central authority from which to launch a project of state formation, forced Reza Shah into a much weaker position. During the 1920s and 1930s, he sought to settle nomadic tribes, to bolster the power of landowners *vis-à-vis* the clergy (while confiscating land and becoming the largest landowner himself) and to strengthen the army. As a result, by 1941 nomadism had declined to no more than 10 per cent of the population (from perhaps 25 per cent at the beginning of the century), after 1928 the Majlis came under landlord rather than clerical control, and in 1925 conscription was introduced and the armed forces increased to 130,000 by 1941.

Again, as in the Turkish case, towards the end of the 1920s declining world trade, a deterioration in the terms of trade for primary producers, the drying up of international financial flows and the regaining of tariff autonomy in 1928 enabled Reza Khan to foster industrial development. However, while state controls over education and law, together with restraints on the material bases of the clergy, were established, development was limited. Agriculture remained dominated by absentee landlords and was ignored, and attention focused on import substitution and infrastructure. The limited internal resources of the state derived from indirect taxes on the one hand, and from state monopolies in tea and sugar on the other. Government revenues from the Anglo-Iranian Oil Company (AIOC) at this time amounted to a mere 10–15 per cent of the value of oil exports.

Allied occupation during the Second World War served to compound the internal struggle for power, and only after the coup of 1953 did stability return. The Tudah Party, with its base in Tehran and among the oil workers in Khuzestan, demanded a national democratic revolution. Under Mossadeq's leadership (1951–3), the Majlis refused to ratify the oil agreement covering Anglo-Iranian's operations and demanded the nationalization of the oil industry. Religious protests also increased. Mossadeq and other nationalist landowners wanted to expel the AIOC and to reduce the powers of the shah, but his reliance on the streets alienated the landowners and the *ulema*. After the coup, the shah smashed the Tudah and the National Front. The army was enlarged and SAVAK founded. Outside the rapidly expanding repressive apparatus of the state, the shah's power depended on the conservative landowners who dominated the Majlis and the clergy who serviced the bazaar.

Economic problems persisted, despite rising oil revenues. Local industry could not provide for the expansion and diversification of domestic demand and the balance of payments moved into deficit in the early 1960s. At the same time, productivity in the relatively backward agricultural sector failed to keep pace with rising consumption levels and food prices rose. Notwithstanding rising oil revenues, the shah needed greater resources to finance military expansion and economic development. In response to these pressures and with support from the United States, in 1963 the shah launched the White Revolution, the centre of which was a programme of land reform. Other elements included an attempt to reduce the power of the clergy and policies to win the support of industrial workers and women. However, as Massoud Karshenas has pointed out:

> The break in the alliance of the regime with the traditional propertied classes did not imply a move away from the clientelist form of representation of the state towards more democratic forms. On the contrary, after the crisis of the early 1960s, there was a tightening in the hold of the state over the society and a growing concentration

of political power in the hands of a small elite, at the centre of which was the Shah and his court. (1990:236, 237)

The uneven character of the oil-backed industrial development, and the scale of the US-backed military aggrandizement, resulted in huge social dislocations. Rapid urban expansion was combined with widening patterns of inequality. As the demand for oil and its real price fell in the late 1970s, so growth was increasingly constrained by the balance of payments and by inflation.

At the same time, the base of the Iranian state in oil rents, together with its politico-military links to Washington, permitted an expansion of its compass without the development of corresponding mobilizing or representative institutions. The centralization of political power under the shah and his circle created a number of problems. The distribution of oil rents through the state bolstered an industrial elite, the repressive apparatus of the state and the wealth of the shah and his court. In response, the traditional economy, represented by the bazaar classes and the clergy, became increasingly resentful. Equally, political centralization of economic decisions resulted in increasing inequalities and administrative incoherence in the planning process. Political control over the army, especially rapid changes at officer level, undermined its autonomy and professionalism, perhaps contributing to its reluctance to intervene to save the regime. And finally and most importantly, to the extent that the state had become a sphere of private decision-making, more or less insulated from social pressures, so institutions outside of the state – especially centred on the bazaar and the clergy – became the sphere of public politics, itself increasingly focused against the shah's regime.

It was these particular characteristics of the polity, ultimately deriving from its rentier nature, in combination with the uneven pattern of state capitalist integration into the world market and the material durability of the Shi'ite *ulema*, that rendered the state vulnerable to overthrow from below. These features also account for the paradoxical character of the Iranian revolution noted by Halliday: namely, that it 'was the first contemporary instance to be religious in orientation, [and] was also the first ever "modern" revolution' (1988:35). The comparative modernity of the Iranian revolution that Halliday refers to consisted in the relatively advanced nature of Iranian socio-economic development, the urban location of revolutionary mobilization, its prosecution through political rather than military conflict and the absence of any significant external weakening of the state prior to the outbreak of the revolutionary crisis.

In view of the 'Islamic' character of the Iranian revolution, the position of the Shi'ite *ulema* needs further consideration. Under Reza Shah, the power of the clergy was undermined as the state extended control over the administration of justice and the provision of education, and passed new laws on Western dress for men and the unveiling of women. Equally, the material basis of the clergy was attacked as government control over *waqfs* diminished the income of the *ulema*. After 1953, with the shah's son restored to power, a degree of reconciliation occurred when the state provided greater funding for schools and mosques. But the shah's land reform and the marginalization of the bazaar implicit in the programme of industrialization was a step too far, striking at the base of the clergy's power. This point has been well made by Yapp:

> Religious opposition was partly the consequence of the direct threat to the income of the ulema through land reform and its application to *waqf* lands ... Shi'i Islam in Iran was a major institution ... a reasonable estimate is that in Iran during the 1960s there were about 100 *mujtahids*, 10,000 *mullas*, 80,000 other religious functionaries, 5,000 major mosques and perhaps another 15,000 minor ones, and 4 major seminaries, in all more than 100 *madrasas* with nearly 10,000 students. ... Apart from their income from *waqfs* and providing services the ulema received payments from the faithful in the form of the religious taxes known as *zakat* and *khums*. It has been suggested that [during the 1950s] taxes paid to the ulema exceeded those paid to the government. ... [And] the traditional bazaar was the main source of the ulema's income. In return for these payments the ulema provided certain services, principally legal, educational, religious and what may be called articulatory – in effect expressing popular grievances to government. (1991:337)

Thus the *ulema* resisted the changes of the White Revolution as it impinged directly on both their material interests and their ability to articulate the wider process of social reproduction, especially the activities of the bazaar. Similarly, it was this social and material location of the Shi'ite clergy in Iran which gave the revolution its Islamic character. This was true in both an organizational and an ideological sense. Organizationally, Farideh Farhi has suggested that 'without Islam's collective ... capacities and the autonomous resources (mostly furnished through the bazaar), the co-ordination among various groups would have been impossible, and popular resistance could not have been sustained' (1989:103, 104). On an ideological plane, the theology of Shi'ite Islam can equally legitimate positions ranging from quietist aloofness from politics, through support for the government, to militant opposition (Momen 1989). There is no inherent opposition to temporal political power in Shi'ite Islam. Rather, the ideology of the revolution, as articulated by Khomeini and other leading clerics, was as much an assertion of Iranian nationalism against a foreign model of development and the social dislocations of dependent development as an assertion of Islam.

As to the revolution itself, despite the mobilization of the urban masses, and commitments to land reform, income redistribution and the nationalization of foreign trade, its socio-economic content has been limited. Before long, conservative forces were able to block radical transformation, especially the land reform and the nationalization of foreign trade. In fact, in many respects the Iranian experience is better compared to examples of Third World populism than to examples of social revolution. In this context, Ervand Abrahamian has drawn attention to the following similarities between the Iranian and Latin American situation:

> economic rather than political dependency on the West; informal rather than formal subjection to imperialism; an upper class that included the comprador big bourgeoisie; an anti-imperialist middle class; an industrial working class unorganized by the Left; and a recent influx of rural migrants into the sprawling shantytowns. (1991:118)

Finally, Khomeini's social and political thought, and especially his reworking of the doctrine of *velayat-e faqih* (legal guardianship) to include the clerical supervision of affairs of state, broke radically with Shi'ite thought, and in other respects the constitution of revolutionary Iran owes more to the French Fifth Republic than to any model of classical Islam. While the 'Islamic Republic' has introduced clerical supervision of the executive and the legislature, and has introduced *shari'a* courts, the principal change has concerned the personnel in charge of the state. The post-revolutionary regime remains as dependent on oil rents as the Pahlavi regime, and 'there are no systematic Islamic principles, such as constitutional or public law to apply to the system of administration or to the organisation of government departments. Islam does not significantly alter the constitution or the administration of the state as such' (Zubaida 1989a:175).

5

Patterns of
Social Development
in the Middle East

Having reviewed the pattern of political change in a range of Middle East states in chapter 4, we may now attempt to develop some general theses about the patterns of social development in the region. Thus, in what follows we shift our optic from the comparative and historical focus of the case studies to a thematic look at the fortunes of the region. We begin with a summary of the problematic fortunes of state formation, attempting to identify the main similarities and differences between the case studies. On the basis of these general patterns, we will then address three important areas of debate about the contemporary Middle East: first, the nature of the state and the issue of democracy; second, the pattern of socio-economic transformation and dependent development; and third, the question of the role of pan-Arabism and Islam. Viewed from the kind of comparative and historical perspective argued for here, the vexed questions of democracy, dependency and cultural specificity appear in a new light. The Middle East no longer appears *unique* in the Orientalist sense of that term, but rather takes its place within those general processes of capitalist development which *everywhere* take determinate and particular forms. Finally, the conclusion brings the various threads of our discussion together in order to assess the current crisis of the state which now characterizes much of the Middle East.

Comparisons and contrasts

While Yapp (1991) is right to stress that there were a number of common features to the pattern of socio-economic and political change across the region, especially in the more populous states, there were also a number of marked differences. As we have seen in chapter 4, important variations related to a number of features, including most importantly: (1) the relation of the state to the landed classes, to the peasantry and to the tribes on the one hand, and to the European colonial powers on the other; (2) the relation of the post-independence state to the world market and the state system; (3) the impact of any large oil rents on the path of political development; and (4) the social location of Islam within the broader pattern of change in these societies. In order to provide a more systematic basis for understanding the different kinds of state formation, let us briefly summarize the salient aspects of these contrasts.

We have seen that the decline of the Ottoman empire (and of Qajar Iran), together with the penetration of European economic and political power, had varied effects on the class structures and state forms of the region. In Turkey no significant landed class ever developed, the social weight of pastoral nomadism and tribal forces was low and European control was primarily economic – Turkey escaped formal colonialism. In both Egypt and Iraq landed classes of big landowners did develop, and British political power was directly imposed. In Egypt it was Muhammad Ali's policy of creating large private estates to produce cotton for the world market that transformed the agrarian structure, whereas in Iraq the settling of tribal chiefs was the work of the Ottoman land laws and the British mandate. Essentially for strategic reasons, Britain sought to maintain a high degree of political and military control in both cases. In Saudi Arabia and the Gulf states, the natural ecology prevented any consolidation of a significant landed class and tribal forms of organization remained the norm. Once again, for state formation the influence of external power was decisive. In the Gulf, British power in effect rendered the Trucial States British protectorates and in Saudi Arabia British resources were crucial to the consolidation of Ibn Saud's rule, and the later discovery of oil soon attracted the support of the United States. Finally, in Iran the situation was different again. The social structure of Iran was mixed: large landed estates coexisted with a high level of pastoral nomadism and tribal organization. And although Iran escaped direct colonial control, it was far from immune from foreign intervention by the British and the Russians.

The connections to the world market and the states system also varied during the formative years of state formation and economic development. Turkey was doubly fortunate: first, in the inter-war years it received diplomatic support from Britain as a barrier to Soviet influence, and the state-led development embarked upon in the 1930s coincided with a more general drift towards economic autarchy; and second, during the Cold War Turkey benefited from economic and military assistance from the United States and its project of import-substituting industrialization was able to take advantage of the global conditions provided by the long boom. In the strategic and economic context of the inter-war years, Turkey's assertion of national independence not only posed no threat to the dominant interests in the international system, but was rather a positive gain for the West. And in the post-war environment of Cold War polarization and US hegemony, Turkey played the role of an important bilateral ally and regional client. Again, Turkey played a positive role in Western strategy.

The Egyptian and Iraqi revolutions were both anti-imperialist in orientation, and were both defined against the interests of the dominant imperialist powers in the region, Britain and the United States. Both states rejected strategic alliances with the West, maintained hostile relations with Israel, courted relations with the Soviet Union and attempted to play an independent role in the regional politics of the Arab world. Egypt was able to gain international assistance from both sides during the Cold War, but was economically disadvantaged by the events of 1956 and suffered a major political setback with the 1967 Arab–Israeli war and the subsequent ascendancy of the conservative oil states in the Gulf and Saudi Arabia. The *infitah* was undertaken before Egypt's import-substituting industrialization had produced any genuine industrial deepening, and Egypt is thus unlikely to be able to replicate Turkey's (albeit meagre) success in this area. However, the turn to the West after 1973 has helped Egypt to become a major recipient of US aid. Iraq's formative years, those of the rise of the Ba'ath after 1968, were those of rapidly rising oil prices. These made significant additions to the resources available to the state and have allowed the regime both to consolidate its repressive apparatus to an enormous degree and have also enabled the state to become a major distributor of economic largesse. After the early 1970s, Iraq allied itself with the Soviet Union.

After the initial consolidation of Ibn Saud's rule with British backing, the external environment of Saudi development has been determined by a pattern of integration into the world market through a single commodity, oil, and by an increasingly strong strategic alliance with the United States. Although there have been tensions and differences of policy between the two states, their fundamental commonality of interests has become ever more clear, especially after 1967 and the defeat of radical nationalist Arab forces. Finally, there is the case of Iran. After the coup in 1953, nationalist and communist forces were weakened and placed on the defensive, and the power of the shah increased as a result of rising oil revenues and the economic, military and security assistance of the United States. This meant that, in marked contrast to the Egyptian and Iraqi cases, the programme of land reform and state-led industrialization was pro- rather than anti-imperialist; and during the attempted augmentation of state power under the shah in the 1960s and 1970s, Iran was the major regional ally of the United States, playing the role of Washington's regional policeman after the Nixon Doctrine and the evacuation of British power from the Gulf. Like the other oil states, the price rises of 1973–4 had a significant, and this time destabilizing, impact on the state.

The size and influence of oil and strategic rents differed widely across the states of the Middle East. Saudi Arabia and the Gulf states lie at one end of the spectrum, with huge levels of oil reserves and production in comparison to their populations and the non-oil sectors of their economies. They are unambiguously rentier economies and rentier states, with oil incomes accounting for around three-quarters of GNP, and oil (as well as oil-financed overseas investments) providing virtually all of the state's revenue. At the other end of the spectrum lie Turkey and Egypt. Turkey has no oil, but nevertheless gained some rents from transit fees. In addition, Turkey derived significant strategic rents in the form of US aid because of its role in the Cold War and benefited from the post-war boom in Western Europe via workers' remittances. Equally, until recently Egypt had little or no oil production, and though now a major source of foreign exchange oil itself does not make Egypt a rentier economy or state. But high levels of US assistance after 1973, aid from the Arab oil states, transit fees, earnings from the

Suez Canal, tourism and workers' remittances have all made Egypt highly dependent on external sources of income for foreign exchange.

Then there are the intermediate and more complex cases of Iran and Iraq. According to Karshenas (1990), in Iran the share of oil revenues in total government income was about 50 per cent in the period 1963–7, rising to over 75 per cent in the period 1973–7. In the latter period, oil income accounted for slightly less than one-third of GNP and for between 80 and 90 per cent of foreign exchange earnings. Thus while it is accurate to refer to a rentier state in Iran during the 1970s, this is not an accurate characterization of the Iranian *economy* as a whole, but rather of its ability to generate foreign exchange. In Iraq, oil accounted for about 30 per cent of GNP prior to the 1973–4 oil price rises and this figure rose to over 60 per cent in the mid-1970s, with oil income already providing more than one-half of total state revenues by the mid-1960s. By the late 1970s, virtually all of Iraq's foreign exchange was earned through oil exports. Thus in the 1960s Iraq was a rentier state but not a rentier economy (except in relation to foreign exchange), but by the 1970s it deserved the latter designation as well.

The other major dimension of comparative variation is related to the social location of Islam within the society at the outset of the project of state formation. This played a large role in determining the subsequent evolution of religion in society. In Turkey, the Sunni *ulema* was highly dependent on the tributary power of the Ottoman state which it served, and it was therefore also bound up with the discrediting of that experience. This left it more or less defenceless against a militantly secularist pattern of social development. Notwithstanding the comparatively recent attempts of the military and the right to mobilize Islam against the left, Islamist forces remain under state control and do not pose a challenge to state power. In Egypt, the lack of any clear association between Islam and decline (imperialist control being a much easier target), in combination with the importance of Islam to Arabic culture, led to a weaker attack on the institutions of Islam, though here too religious institutions – of urban, Sunni Islam and of Sufi orders – were brought under state control. However, the autonomy allowed to Islamic organizations under Sadat (again as a means of combating the left), together with the absence of competitive, secular politics and the depth of the Egyptian economic crisis, is now producing organized Islamic forces which by building alternative forms of welfare and employment pose a serious challenge to state power in many regions of Egypt. (Islamists are also represented in the Labour Party.) In Iraq, the ethnic and religious heterogeneity, combined with the minority status of the Sunni Arab elite, resulted in a strongly secular ideology of state development, stressing Arab nationalist ideology. Any opposition from religious forces has either been co-opted into the clientelist networks of the state or faced savage repression. In Saudi Arabia, we have a different pattern again: modernization was *with* rather than *against* Islam, and this produced a traditional political order buttressed by the Sunni *ulema*. And finally in Iran, the independence of the Shi'ite *ulema* from the state, together with the depth of their penetration of social and material reproduction in the traditional economy and society, contributed to the Islamic character of the revolution and Khomeini's populism.

State forms, politics and democracy

In the light of these contrasts, how can we account for the pattern of state formation and political development in the Middle East? In Turkey, the power of foreign and minority interests was broken by the Kemalist national movement. The absence of any significant landed class and the dependent position of the *ulema*, together with the lack of formal colonialism, facilitated a rapid and successful consolidation of state power in the circumstances created by the First World War. In Egypt and Iraq, the power of local notables and of foreign and minority interests was broken by movements of lower-middle-class army officers once the hold of the colonial powers had declined after the Second World War. In Saudi Arabia and the Gulf there was no notable class, and oil alone provided the resources for such development as there was. In Iran there was a pre-emptive programme of land reform initiated from within the regime, supported by the United States, and thus no revolutionary capture of the state by nationalist or petty bourgeois military-based forces.

What differences of state formation can be observed in these cases? One answer to this question looks to the divergent agrarian structures to explain the relevant differences. In an important study of *The Social Origins of the Modern Middle East* (1987), Haim

Gerber has argued that the different pattern of political development in Turkey on the one hand, and in Egypt and Iraq on the other, relates to the absence of a landed class in the Turkish case and its presence in Egypt and Iraq.[1] Following the path-breaking work of Barrington Moore on *The Social Origins of Dictatorship and Democracy* (1966), Gerber argues that the existence of large landlords in Egypt and Iraq contributed to the repressive character of these states, and hence the need for middle-class, army-based revolutions to overthrow the old order and to inaugurate policies of land reform. Gerber argues that these transformations did not amount to *social* revolutions made by the peasantry, and he explains the lack of communist forms of mobilization, and hence of Stalinist models of development, by the 'absence of an agonizing historical agrarian problem and the consequent ease with which the ancien regime was eliminated' (1987:166).

In other words, on Gerber's reading, the Egyptian and Iraqi revolutions were a form of what Ellen Kay Trimberger has called *Revolution From Above* (1978). According to Trimberger, a revolution from above involves the destruction of an old ruling class, organized and initiated by military and civil bureaucrats, with very little mass participation or violence. Thus whereas social revolutions involve a mass mobilization of the subordinate strata and a period of domestic class struggle, nationalist revolutions from above are usually directed against both a foreign presence and an indigenous elite and generally see 'the rise of a social stratum, originally petty bourgeois, which uses its position of modern knowledge, and its control of the state and the nationalised sector of the economy, to turn itself into an administrative bourgeoisie' (Chaliand 1977:102). That being said, however, we must be careful not to exaggerate the contrast between social revolutions from below and national revolutions from above. For as Fred Halliday and Maxine Molyneux have argued,

> mass action can play a major role in preparing for revolutions from above. It both weakens old regimes and politicizes the actual agents of change, the military bureaucracy. The two forms of challenge to the *ancien regime* are more closely related than a pair of contrasted

---

1 Gerber discusses other cases (notably, Lebanon, Jordan and Syria), but this does not affect the argument that follows. Unfortunately, since he is concerned with the Ottoman empire, Gerber does not attempt to extend his analysis to Iran and Saudi Arabia.

models might suggest, and it is mass action from below that has a prior, instigatory, role. Revolution from above is not so much an alternative to revolution from below as an extension or fulfilment of a mass movement from below, where the latter is, for a variety of reasons, unable to go beyond the stage of creating an atmosphere of national dissidence and to overthrow the established regime. (1981:30, 31)[2]

This was certainly true in the cases of Egypt and Iraq. Trimberger herself thought that Turkey constituted (along with Japan) the leading example of a successful revolution from above, whereas we have seen that Gerber reserves this title for Egypt and Iraq and denies the revolutionary character of the Kemalist experience. This apparent contradiction rests on a basic empirical disagreement between Gerber and Trimberger. Gerber argues that there was no real landed class for the Kemalist project to dispossess, the Ottoman tributary apparatus remained intact, and hence there could not have been a *revolution* (understood as the dispossession of an exploiting class) that destroyed the old ruling class. By contrast, Trimberger claims that in Turkey the *ulema* constituted a traditional aristocracy, that the Kemalists feared opposition from rural notables and that they therefore reinforced landlord control over the peasantry in return for rural support for industrialization. As I read the evidence, Trimberger is mistaken in these claims. This is also the judgement of the fundamental study of *State and Class in Turkey* by Caglar Keyder who concluded that 'Republican Turkey, notwithstanding all the phoenix imagery, represented more of a transformation by coup under war conditions than a revolutionary break with the ancien regime' (1987:199, 200).

If Gerber is correct that the Turkish case differs from those of Egypt and Iraq by virtue of their differing agrarian class structures, is he also right to argue that this is the reason for Turkey's relatively democratic evolution in contrast with Egypt and Iraq? Here I think Gerber is on much weaker ground. In the latter instances, the late Ottoman era and the interlude of European colonialism created an urban-based class of private appropriators who monopolized political power. At the same time, the intermediaries of integration into the world market were in many cases local but

2 We might also note *en passant* that, contra Skocpol (1979), social revolutions do not simply 'happen'; they too are made.

minority groups or Europeans. Prior to the dispossession of these forces, political life was organized by the politics of clientelism in which patrons (notables) operated in the state in order to deliver benefits to their clients (tribes, peasants, urban workers). In return, clients performed labour services and provided political support for their patrons. Thus even where a limited parliamentarism existed, this was combined with a largely unaccountable executive and notable dominance of the latter. To this extent, it is accurate to link notable power with non-democratic forms of rule.

But by Gerber's own account the landed class was weakly placed in Egypt and Iraq, and its political power was swiftly diminished by the army-based revolutions. These transformations involved, first, a strengthening of the repressive apparatus of the state as the military took control of the state institutions. Second, land reform and state control over the clergy destroyed alternative forms of political organization. The fostering of a secular ideology and new incorporative organizations were a third innovation, oriented towards extending the regime's control over the masses. And fourth, the elimination of foreign capital, the start of state-led industrialization and the introduction of agricultural co-operatives aimed to seize the commanding heights of the economy for the state. Thus, after the revolutions, in the apparatus of the newly formed states, the civil and military officials found a new site of organization, surplus appropriation and hence class formation.

Once notable power was broken, then, the pattern of development was in a number of respects *similar* to that pioneered by Turkey in the 1920s and 1930s. In all three cases, as the role of the political power of minorities, foreigners and notables was eclipsed, the state became the main site of accumulation and source of authority within society. In the process, informal clientelism and parliamentary structures were either destroyed or strictly controlled by a mixture of populist mobilization under charismatic leadership, the emergence of state-based clientelism and the imposition from above of bureaucratic forms of control organized by the party-military apparatus. For under whatever ideological and constitutional auspices, the primary functions of the state apparatus have been the consolidation of its rule over and against other principles of authoritative regulation and the mobilization of resources for economic development. As a result of its subordination to these twin functions, party organization has been weak, and where it has not been a direct creation of the state, it has been absorbed into the state apparatus. Corporatist forms, where present, have generally sought to contain class divisions, rather than to represent independently constituted social forces.[3]

To be sure, the army continues to play a more central role in the Egyptian and Iraqi cases than the Turkish experience, but we should not forget that Turkey has thus far been through three military coups (1960, 1971, 1980), that the south-eastern region of the country (populated by Kurds) remains under emergency rule and that the 1982 constitution prohibits the organization of certain political forces. In any case, the Iraqi military remains subordinated to the political control of the Ba'ath Party and the autonomy of Egypt's military has declined since the days of Nasser. What distinguishes the Turkish case in this context is not so much the class structure of its agrarian origins, though this was clearly important, as the degree of political differentiation achieved by Turkey's bourgeoisie as well as the parallel degree of organizational independence achieved by its working class. By contrast, in both Egypt and Iraq, the state sector remains the dominant sector in the economy, thereby frustrating the development of relatively independent social forces outside the state. Of course, in part this is a reflection of the greater degree of transformation involved in the Egyptian and Iraqi anti-landlord revolutions, a greater weighting of the 'social' in relation to the 'national' elements, as compared with the Kemalist coup. (In particular, the forces of the left were better organized, with both Egypt and Iraq having significant Communist Parties before the revolutions, though these were later crushed by nationalist forces.) But it is also in part due to the anti-imperialist, if not anti-capitalist, character of the revolutions, dictated by the greater foreign presence in the economies and polities of Egypt and Iraq than in Turkey, and the subsequent influence of the Soviet model of industrial development on Egypt and Iraq. (Turkish democracy, born in the immediate conjuncture of post-war liberal democracy, took its model from the Western democracies.) And in the Iraqi case, it is above all due to the role of oil in the economy. Moreover, even in the Turkish case, we should not exaggerate the forces sustaining a degree of independent social organization, for, as Keyder reminds us,

3 This reflects the general pattern of post-oligarchic rule in the semi-periphery identified by Nicos Mouzelis in his account of *Politics in the Semi-Periphery* (1986). See also the valuable comparative work of Cammack et al (1988:ch. 3).

no workers' movement brought about the right to organise and strike. . . . [and] The bourgeoisie had matured under conditions of an induced capitalism, occupying their economic space in the wake of a military victory. Their accession to the status of a class-in-itself had occurred under state tutelage without the necessity of a political struggle against pre-capitalist forces. (1987:200, 201)

Never the less, the Turkish experience does represent an evolution towards the structural preconditions for liberal democratic forms of governance. This is so because, contra Gerber, whether a landed class is absent or merely dispossessed is not the end of the story. Just as Moore neglected to analyse the actual route taken to democracy and the role played by modern classes, focusing instead on the earlier class alliances following the commercialization of agriculture, so Gerber fails to consider the role of the central classes of industrial capitalism, the bourgeoisie and the proletariat. In both cases, this has the effect both of antedating the origins of democratic rule and of ignoring the actual class and popular struggles which brought about its development.

In fact, beyond the general considerations about agrarian class relations offered by Moore and Gerber, there are three further fundamental structural preconditions for the consolidation of capitalist democracy.[4] In the first instance, the state apparatus must be able to uphold its authority and monopoly of coercion against other sites of political command, such that the general, public functions of society are decided by a single body of rule-making and coercive enforcement. In the absence of this, the state is drawn into particularistic, often violent, struggles against competing sites of rule. Secondly, there must be a significant degree of separation between the institutions of rule on the one hand, and the mechanisms of domestic surplus appropriation on the other, thus uncoupling the material basis of the power of the ruling class from the formal exercise of state-political power. Without this, the dominant class has a direct material stake in opposing democratic control of the state. And thirdly, the process of rule-making and enforcement must be based on a principle of legitimacy derived from the 'people' and embodying their equal rights to participation. State power that is not legitimated in this way may be able to prevail

---

4 These conditions are minimal structural ones, and thus are neither jointly exhaustive nor without the usual *ceteris paribus* conditions.

against rival centres of authority, it may even be able to govern by consent rather than force, but it cannot govern democratically. Taken together, these features – the emergence of a sovereign public sphere, embodying popular legitimacy, in conjunction with the privatization of command over surpluses – provide the basis for a form of rule in which the state apparatus is formally responsible to elected decision-makers who are chosen by means of a universal and equal franchise.[5]

As we have argued above, the process of capitalist state formation, where it takes a liberal form, can give rise to a separation of the institutions of rule and of surplus appropriation. This is what has happened in the Turkish case. It is important because, as Ellen Meiksins Wood has argued,

> Access to political rights in societies where surplus extraction occurs by 'extra-economic' means and the power of economic exploitation is inseparable from juridical and political status and privilege has a very different meaning from what it does in capitalism, with its expropriated direct producers and a form of appropriation not directly dependent on juridical or political standing. (1990:72)

However, the consolidation of capitalist state power over rival centres of authority, especially in conditions of dependency, can give rise to a situation where rule is secured but it remains deeply imbricated with the appropriation of the surplus. This has been the case in Egypt and Iraq. It is also the pattern found in Saudi Arabia and Iran. In the Saudi case, the consolidation of state power and the initiation of economic development have both centred on oil rents and foreign support and this has resulted in the state standing centre-stage in the control of the surplus. In the Iranian case, the nature of the shah's regime and access to oil and strategic rents

5 In an earlier formulation of this argument (Bromley 1993), I neglected the question of legitimacy. This was a mistake. It is perfectly possible to consolidate state power on the basis of a principle of legitimacy which either circumscribes the exercise of people's rights in the name of some other principle (e.g. Marxism-Leninism) or denies the people political rights (e.g. monarchical Saudi Arabia). See, in particular, the important study by David Beetham, *The Legitimation of Power* (1991). However, I would suggest that the conditions in which a principle of legitimacy consistent with democratic forms of governance is most likely to arise are those in which the institutions of rule and of appropriation have become separated, i.e. where a *civil society* exists. On the capitalist social relations which underpin liberal forms of 'civil society', in which liberal democratic principles of legitimacy can be formulated and given effective force, see Meiksins Wood 1990.

produced a situation where the state stood centre-stage in economic development, even without a military-based, nationalist revolution from above. It is not that the struggle of the bourgeoisie for political differentiation from the state is equivalent to the struggle for democracy; liberalism not democracy has been the historical rallying cry of the bourgeoisie. Rather, it is that liberal civil society provides both the structural underpinning of representative democracy and the terrain on which an organized working class can develop. Historically, the latter have proved to be not capitalism's 'grave-diggers' but its democratizers.

Although it differs in theoretical perspective somewhat from the present study and does not consider the Middle East as such, Dietrich Rueschemeyer, Evelyne Huber Stephens and John D. Stephens' important comparative study of *Capitalist Development and Democracy* argues a very similar general case. Thus they write:

> [There is] a first minimal condition of democracy: democracy is possible only if there exists a fairly strong institutional separation . . . of the realm of politics from the overall system of inequality in society. . . . We retain . . . in our theoretical framework Moore's emphasis on agrarian class relations and on landlord-bourgeoise-state coalitions; but we combine this emphasis with an equally strong focus on the role of the subordinate classes in the new capitalist order. . . . Capitalist development is associated with the rise of democracy primarily because of two structural effects: it strengthens the working class as well as other subordinate classes, and it weakens large landowners. (1992:41, 58)

In sum, the structural preconditions for liberal democracy have been absent from much of the region for most of the post-war epoch. In the Turkish case, stable rule was consolidated early on, a principle of popular legitimacy was established by the secular and nationalist form of Kemalism and significant moves towards the privatization of surplus appropriation were under way by the post-war years. In Egypt, while the secular and nationalist character of the revolution might have established a degree of popular legitimacy, and while the consolidation of the state's authority *vis-à-vis* other potential sources of authority was more or less assured, the deep imbrication of the state in surplus appropriation has posed considerable obstacles to any widening of political participation through genuine democratization. Further, the restrictions that this has imposed on organized political activity have enabled Islamic forces and organizations to challenge the authority and power of the state.

In Iraq none of the conditions for democratic rule exist: state power is imposed by force and is only accepted as legitimate by a minority of the population, even though its principle of legitimacy (Iraqi nationalism, the revolution) is not inconsistent with popular participation; and there is relatively little separation of rule and appropriation. Saudi Arabia provides a classic instance of state formation based on a principle of legitimacy which denies rights of political participation to the people. The Saudi state was able to consolidate its rule against internal rivals relatively easily, but the hereditary monarchy, backed by the *ulema*, cannot legitimate state power in a manner consistent with democratic principles. In addition, the state presently remains dominant in domestic surplus appropriation. In Pahlavi Iran state power was neither fully consolidated against rival centres of authority nor was it legitimated in a fashion consistent with democratic control of the state. The Shi'ite clergy remained an important source of rival authority, never succumbing to state control and never fully supporting the state, and the monarchical nature of the shah's regime, together with the perception of it as a client of the United States, prevented widespread legitimacy being accorded by the Iranian people. Finally, the rentier character of the state directly embroiled the polity in surplus appropriation.

Beyond these structural impediments, a further characteristic of state formation in the Middle East has had adverse implications for the prospects for democratic rule. Given the refractory inheritance of state-building in many cases, the scale of resources devoted to the imposition of state authority has often blocked the potential for future democratization, and this position has been further aggravated in those instances where the expansion of the coercive apparatus was financed by oil and strategic rents. These aspects interact in complex ways. On the one hand, where the state apparatus remains central to surplus appropriation this limits both the material scope for democracy and the ability of popular-democratic forms of legitimation to emerge. On the other hand, the centrality of the state in the process of surplus appropriation may itself owe more to the need to consolidate rule than to any coherent project of socio-economic development.

Finally, the prospects for democracy have been further attenuated by two other features of the pattern of dependent socio-economic development. First, those classes which have historically pushed for liberalization – the private-sector bourgeoise and the middle classes – and for democratization – the working class – have been proportionately small for a given level of development, and they have often emerged in circumstances where the state has been able to impose incorporative forms of political control.[6] And second, in the short to medium term, any reduction in the state's economic role in response to the current economic crisis is certain to widen inequalities between social groups, and this will place further strain on the political system.

But in those instances where a degree of capitalist development has occured outside the direct control of the state apparatus, and has brought with it the tentative organization of a civil society by the bourgeoisie and the working class, some liberalization and controlled experiments in popular participation have emerged (Turkey most obviously, to a more limited extent in Egypt and even in Iran). Where the state has maintained control, blocking the emergence of the organizations of civil society, then the prospects for democratic reform are more limited (the limit cases being Iraq and Saudi Arabia). Thus, the relative absence of democracy in the Middle East has little to do with the region's Islamic culture and much to do with its particular pattern of state formation. For it is the pressures emanating from the character of state formation, and in particular the failure of secular nationalist models of development, which has in turn generated the regimes, the social forces and the particular problems of development that currently shape the region's politics.

Patterns of political economy

If it is these concrete patterns of state formation, and the kinds of political economy that they have brought about, which determine the course of political change, then we should turn first to the political economy of the Middle East in order to explain the current political scene. Across the Middle East as a whole, socio-economic development was impressive in the 1960s and 1970s, thereafter falling off as the limits of domestic patterns of accumulation set in and as the world economic crisis, whose effects were delayed by oil rents, belatedly made its impact felt. Between 1923 and the late

6 This point was noted by Mouzelis (1986).

1980s the region's population increased from 52 to 210 million. By 1968 one-third of the population was urban and by 1989 about one-half. Throughout the region, the inter-war depression reduced the dependence of economies on links with Europe. After the Second World War, between 1950 and 1970, growth averaged about 5 per cent a year, or 2 per cent a year per capita. Over this same period, the state's share of total consumption rose by 50 per cent. The early 1980s saw higher growth based on oil rents, but by the end of the decade war, falling real oil prices, rising debts and internal difficulties restricted the opportunities for growth. Outside of the oil sector, however, the overall performance was not impressive: the region was characterized by rising food imports, as agriculture failed to keep pace with population growth; and the manufacturing sector accounted for a mere 15 per cent of GNP by the mid-1980s, with the Middle East accounting for a lamentable share of world export markets.

Some aspects of the economies we have been concerned with are summarized in tables 1–6 in the Appendix. From these it is clear that only Turkey has a relatively diversified economy and an export performance based on significant exports of manufactured goods. Egypt is the next most diversified economy, also with a degree of its exports accounted for by manufactures. Both have shown a marked reduction on their dependence on primary exports for foreign exchange, though recent oil exports have altered the Egyptian picture to some extent. In these respects, the two non-oil states have broken with their old colonial pattern of integration into the international division of labour, even if Egypt is in danger of lapsing back into this pattern. (Energy and other primary products account for three-quarters of Egypt's exports and manufactures account for two-thirds of its imports.) By contrast, the three oil states are reliant on oil rents for nearly all their foreign exchange, as well as the bulk of their state revenues. Though oil may bring a higher per capita GDP than the non-oil states can muster, and significantly higher than the regional average, by world standards these are not high levels. With the partial exception of Saudi Arabia's presence in the world petrochemical and refined products markets, none of these oil economies shows any signs of making an input into world manufacturing trade. (After oil, Iran's main exports are carpets and pistachio nuts.) And even the relative spread of activity in the Turkish and Egyptian economies only represents very modest levels of overall output.

We have seen that politically and economically breaking the power of the notables, and thereby destroying the political form that this took, was a precondition for launching strategies of development. The absence of notables in Turkey meant that state-led industrialization faced no such obstacles. In Egypt, Iraq and Iran, by contrast, 'land reform was the handmaiden of state-led industrialization strategies' (Richards and Waterbury 1990:151). Though unavowed, the Turkish model was a basic paradigm for these states. In the process, reformers expropriated their political enemies. Finally, in the oil-rich states of Saudi Arabia and the Gulf, oil provided the basis for a rather different path of socio-economic transformation, dependent on the the West not just for the import of capital goods but for skilled manpower and security as well.

Against this backdrop, 'conservative' and 'radical' (Richards and Waterbury) regimes may be distinguished by the model of state-led development adopted. In the conservative, state-capitalist variant, the state seeks to mobilize resources and provide the infrastructure for capitalist development while transferring its own surpluses to the private sector (Turkey since 1950, Iran 1963–79, Egypt since 1973, Saudi Arabia in the 1980s and 1990s). A second type exists where the state retains the surpluses on its own operations, captures a large share of those in the remaining private sector and then attempts to secure for the state more or less complete control over resource mobilization, if not state control over all property (Turkey hesitantly in the 1930s, Egypt nominally after 1961 and Iraq since 1963).

Oil states are found in both camps, some states have moved from the radical to the conservative models, and the main impetus behind the radical variant appears to have something to do with the degree of difficulty and social conflict involved in consolidating state power. Where the latter process has been protracted or violent, then the role of the state has assumed a greater presence throughout society, including the economy. Our comparative survey supports the view advanced by Chaudhry that 'in Iraq, as elsewhere, the deep cleavages between the state and business meant that the regulation of business was tightly entwined with pressing issues of national integration and state building' (1991:21).

The Middle East is now the least food-self-sufficient area in the world. In the new regimes, agriculture has been neglected or harmed by capital-intensive models of industrialization. Agricultural-export-led growth also suffered because it was associated with a position in the international division of labour imposed during the colonial period, and because it emerged under the auspices of a notable class which blocked more general socio-economic change. Other adverse factors have included the declining terms of trade for agricultural products, erratic price movements and a temptation to tax the peasantry heavily. Mineral-export-led growth has been a reasonable strategy for those states which have other resources with which to build a modern economy (Saudi Arabia, Iraq and Iran), although as yet little has been achieved apart from infrastructural development, but for those with little irrigated land, low populations and a lack of other resources the post-oil future may be bleak (the small Gulf states).

Another strategy adopted has been import-substituting industrialization (Turkey, Egypt; and Iraq and Iran based on oil). Setbacks to this model derived from the level of protection granted to infant industries and the proportion of public resources swallowed by unproductive concerns. Over-valued exchange rates and the state subsidization of prices contributed to budget and balance of payments deficits and inflation. Foreign borrowing, or increased dependence on rents, provided a temporary stop gap, but even in the case of the oil states a shortage of foreign exchange constrained the overall growth process. Manufacturing-export-led growth would in principle be a solution to these limits of import-substituting industrialization. Based on achieving international competitiveness by lowering production costs, it would provide the basis for earning foreign exchange. However, there are major political difficulties in implementing such a transition.

To a greater or lesser extent, most of the states in the Middle East are now entering a period of profound uncertainty as they adapt to pressures for structural adjustment and economic liberalization (*infitah*). Structural adjustment is a response to a number of problems. To begin with, at a micro-level, rising deficits in the public sector have occurred as state-owned enterprises have failed to match rising wages by increased productivity. Equally, at the macro-level, the failure of domestic productive activity to keep pace with rising consumption levels has produced deficits on the foreign exchanges. Together, these deficits have generated considerable inflationary pressures. In addition to these problems of financial and monetary stabilization, *infitah* also results from the political limits to state-led growth. Moves towards deregulation and privatization have been encouraged by the emergence of new class forces within and the pressure from the advanced capitalist world mediated by the World Bank and the IMF from without.

At the centre of these difficulties lies the exhaustion and failure of the nationally based strategy of import-substituting industrial development, and thus the political and ideological crises of the regimes which have presided over it. Foreign exchange was not generated but rather drained by the import of capital goods; agriculture fared poorly and food dependence has increased rapidly; non-oil-exporters could only cover the gap between domestic savings and investment by borrowing abroad; operating losses contributed to the state's budget deficits, and, when monetized, this accelerated inflation; and state-led growth did not solve rural – urban disparities or other inequalities. Stagnant economies, growing problems of food security, a rapidly growing and very young population, rising levels of urbanization and large numbers of un- and under-employed youth adds up to a recipe for continuing political instability. This will impose further strains on the already fragile prospects for democratic reform, especially as any significant liberalization will widen socio-economic inequalities.

In sum, then, the political economy of the contemporary Middle East does not present an encouraging picture. It may be that programmes of stabilization and structural adjustment will succeed, but the prospects are not good in the more populous states. (Because of Egypt's central role in regional politics and stability the United States and the international financial institutions will do their level best to ensure that its reform programme is successful.) Given the undoubted fact that the optimism expressed in the 1950s and 1960s that the region could escape from underdevelopment was misplaced, it is difficult to know whether oil has been a blessing or a curse. Certainly, the presence of oil has distorted the pattern of socio-economic development and political evolution in novel ways, it has brought with it the attention of outside powers and it has financed the accumulation of the largest concentration of military power in the Third World. A small elite subsists at levels of luxury fully comparable to those of the West, but for the majority of the population in the region as a whole their poverty is exceeded only by that of the peoples of sub-Saharan Africa and the least developed parts of Asia. Perhaps the lesson of the Turkish experience is that the peoples of the region would have been better served if the oil had never been discovered. The possibility cannot be discounted. At any rate, it is this overarching context of economic crisis and political failure that provides one of the crucial conditions for what is mistakenly referred to as 'Islamic fundamentalism'.

Arabism and Islam

As should be clear by now, the process of state formation in the Middle East has been extremely uneven. But the range of cases considered – secular Turkey and traditional, clerical Saudi Arabia, the very different character of Islamist opposition in Egypt and in Iran, the relative progress towards liberal democracy in Turkey, the revolution in Iran and the bloody and violent repression in Iraq – cannot be reduced to essentialist claims about the incompatibility of pan-Arabism or Islam and the nation-state. Similarities exist between non-Arab Turkey and Iran on the one hand, and Arab Egypt and Iraq on the other; there are differences between Saudi Arabia and Egypt; and finally there are variations between all the (Islamic) states. Too many relevant comparisons and contrasts, unrelated to ethnicity and religion, exist for easy recourse to culturalist and essentialist accounts. Put bluntly, it is my contention that the politics of Arab nationalism are more an effect than a cause of the difficulties of state formation in the Arab Middle East, and that Islamist movements are one kind of response (and not the only one) to the failure of secular models of socio-economic development. To reify Arabism and Islam into obstacles to modernity is, in both cases, to confuse cause and effect.

The phenomenon of 'pan-Arab nationalism' has often been seen as an obstacle to state formation in the Middle East. Specifically, it has been argued that given the strength of pan-Arab forms of identification the Arab states have faced a persistent dilemma as to whether to adopt an Arab nationalist stance and hence pursue programmes of unification or to build a (country-specific) local nationalism (Anderson 1991). Thus it is suggested that the inability to consolidate the latter in the face of popular support for the former has deprived the extant Arab states of legitimacy. In turn, this relative lack of legitimacy is held to account for the coercive character of rule in many Arab states. It is important to be clear about just what is presupposed by this kind of argument. At the most basic level, it assumes the existence of an Arab national identity that pre-dated and outran the process of state formation in the Arab world. The basis of this identity is often argued to lie in the continuity of the Arabic language, which is itself the language of the Koran. It is also assumed that this identity is more or less incompatible with the expression of consent to rule by any kind of organization other than a state covering most of the Arab world. Put thus, it should be obvious that this argument is very largely mythical, little more than a rhetorical ploy of Arab nationalists and Western Orientalists. Let us consider the evidence.

If language is central to Arab nationalism, then we must remember that, for most of the relevant history, the majority of the Arabic-speaking population was illiterate. In addition, while written Arabic does indeed exhibit a high degree of continuity, the spoken word is subject to considerable variation of regional dialect and pronunciation, like any other vernacular language. In this context, what is mistakenly referred to as Arab 'nationalism' should be seen as a proto-national form of identification (among the literate) based on a cultural revival centred on the study of Arabic and developing transport and communication links between the urban centres. But there is no necessary connection, either in logic or in history, between proto-national forms of identification and nationalism proper (that is, the demand for a nation-state of one's own). What gave such forms of identification as there were a firmer anchorage in social reality was opposition to growing foreign penetration (European and Zionist) and Young Turk discrimination against the employment of Arab officials in the Ottoman empire. The latter was to prove decisive. For it was only with the disintegration of the Ottoman empire, and the subsequent birth of *Turkish* reform nationalism, that a future for the Arab provinces outside the caliphate became thinkable. Together with the employment of literate professionals across the Arab regions, and elements of co-operation against foreign rule, especially in relation to Palestine, this forged a pan-Arab identity among some groupings within the petty bourgeoisie. In this respect, Arab nationalism was no different from the other linguistic nationalisms that proliferated towards the end of the nineteenth century. 'The battle-lines of linguistic nationalism', Eric Hobsbawn has forcefully argued, 'were manned by provincial journalists, schoolteachers and aspiring subaltern officials' (1990:117).

Yet, in other ways, (pan-)Arabism proved to be much less, socially speaking, than other unificatory nationalisms. As Hobsbawm's survey admirably shows, there is an important distinction to be drawn between the European nationalisms associated with nation-building, the development of capitalist national markets and the world-wide creation of an *international* economy between the 1830s and the 1880s and the subsequent proliferation of linguistic nationalisms. Moreover, in the colonial world: 'The real and growing force of liberation consisted in the resentment against conquerors, rulers and exploiters, who happened to be recognizable as foreigners by colour, costume and habits, or against those who were seen as acting for them. It was anti-imperial' (Hobsbawm 1990:136, 137). In the Middle East this opposition took a variety of forms: sometimes Islamic, sometimes country-specific nationalism, sometimes Arab nationalist. The latter only became a mass force when it altered its content away from calls for political reform and spiritual renewal towards concrete socio-economic demands for an end to foreign control and for state-led models of transformation. Perhaps even more significant is the fact that Arab nationalist movements were in fact weakest in those places with the most homogenous Arab populations – Egypt and Saudi Arabia – and strongest among minorities in the ethnically and religiously most heterogeneous states – Syria and Iraq. (Indeed, given the importance of *Christians* in the formulation of Arab nationalism, the connection drawn between Arabic and the language of the Koran is at best moot.) Equally, pan-Islamic movements were weak in Islamically homogenous Iran and Turkey. In addition, as Owen (1983) has pointed out, the main sponsors of *pan*-Arabism have been state elites pursuing their own projects in the interstate arena, not their populations. Palestinian nationalism, itself a direct product of conquest (and resistance to it) in a place that did not even have a coherent regional identity, has done as much, if not more, to *divide* as to unite the Arab world. And finally, although labour migration in the wake of the oil boom promoted some solidarities, in general the period since 1967 has witnessed the further discrediting of pan-Arabism, as Egyptian power declined and that of Saudi Arabia rose, as the number of independent Arab states increased and as state power was progressively consolidated. (In this context one should also note that the Arab League far from promoting pan-Arab unification is premised on the recognition of sovereign independence and was established to contain Hashemite bids for hegemony, and later played a similar role in relation to Egyptian designs.) Indeed, the truth is almost certainly the opposite of what pan-Arab nationalists have supposed: it is probably only when state formation has been successfully accomplished and a large degree of *domestic* legitimacy has been secured that pan-Arab integration of any meaningful kind will become feasible. (It is, surely, no accident that the Arab state which has the most claim to a specifically national legitimacy, Egypt, has also been the one state able to make peace with Israel.)

What these considerations strongly suggest is that Arab nationalism did not in any real sense pre-exist the formation of Arab states, except in some intellectual circles, and that it has been more a tool of than an obstacle to state formation. The leaders adopting such ideologies were nationalists 'only because they adopted a western ideology excellently suited to the overthrow of foreign governments' (Hobsbawm 1990:137). Pan-Arabism is little more than an ideology of interstate manouevre. In the Middle East, it has been the processes of state formation that have generated nationalist sentiment, and thus the much-remarked ambivalence of Arab states in relation to local and wider definitions of nationalism reflects aspects of their political development that have little, if anything, to do with primordial loyalties to Arabism. Certainly, state formation has been problematic, including the question of the national identification with the territory of the state, and this has indeed generated difficulties of legitimation, but, as we have seen, it has not been problems of cultural intransigence which have shaped the pattern of political development.

What, then, of Islam? Once again, we are faced with similarly structured arguments about the essential cultural content of Islam, its incompatibility with modernity and hence the failure of the modern nation-state to strike roots in the Middle East. In the contemporary context, this argument comes in two rather different forms. In the first place, a number of writers conform to the culturalist style of analysis that we encountered in chapters 1 and 3. Thus Fouad Ajami writes of *The Arab Predicament* in the following terms: the Arab world is a 'defeated civilization', which because of Islam is 'stubbornly impermeable to any democratic stirrings' (1992:21, 26).[7] Viewed in this way, 1967 represents a defeat of Oriental despotism and tribalism by the modern state, leaving a space for Islamist forces to occupy. A second version of the argument also

---

7 It is important to note that Ajami's argument while *framed* in these essentialist terms also contains important elements of a more sober analysis indicated by such claims as 'the struggle over the role of Islam was an extension of the profane struggle for power' and 'nativism became, as it has classically been and will remain, the rallying cry of those who lost out in the boom' (1992:73, 220; see also 217, 218).

asserts the continuity of Islam but argues for its compatibility with the main features of modernity understood as an industrial division of labour. This is the argument of Ernest Gellner:

> The trauma of the Western impact (appearing in diverse Muslim countries at different points in time, stretching from the late eighteenth to the twentieth centuries) did not, amongst Muslim thinkers, provoke that intense polarization between Westernizers and Populists, *à la Russe*. . . . the dominant and persuasive answer recommended neither emulation of the West, nor idealization of some folk virtue and wisdom. It recommended a *return* to, or a more rigorous observance of, *High* Islam. (1992:19)

Against these kinds of analysis, a number of preliminary points should be noted (see Owen 1992 and Zubaida 1989a). There is a strong tendency in culturalist and essentialist arguments to, in Zubaida's helpful characterization, 'read history backwards', 'seeing the current "revival" as the culmination of a line of development of Islamic politics, rather than as the product of recent combinations of forces and events' (1989b:41). Rather than be seduced by the apparent piety of High Islam we should also pay attention to the ideological mobilization of Islamic purity in blatantly hypocritical ways. Political Islam is by no means the only force in play in contemporary Middle East politics, as secular nationalist and leftist forces remain strong, and Islamic movements therefore compete in a political field not entirely of their own making. This means that political Islam cannot simply represent the religious elements of popular culture, but must instead constitute *new* forms of political mobilization. Moreover, the so-called religious revival in the region is not confined to Islam, but also can be seen in aspects of the politics of the Jewish and Christian communities. In all these cases, a number of general socio-economic and political events appear to have a significant bearing on the politicization of religion, including the trauma of 1967, the worsening economic crisis, the failure of secular nationalist and leftist regimes, and the demonstration effect of the Iranian revolution. Political Islam is itself a thoroughly heterogeneous formation with no pre-given unity: the role played by Islamist forces has varied with the social location of Islamic elements in the process of state formation. And finally, we must remember that Islamist groups are competing *for* (access to) state power and they therefore seek to oppose the configuration of specific regimes rather than the state *per se*.

Drawing on Benedict Anderson's (1983) argument about the creation of a social space in which the 'imagined community' takes a national form, Zubaida argues that, as in general, so in the Middle East.

> Once the new states are established, their very existence promotes the genesis of new 'imaginaires' of the nation: common education systems incorporating the symbols of etatic power as nation; education feeding into employment markets for the most part dominated by the state; national networks of communication and transport; military conscription facilitating the interaction of youths, mostly from the poorer rural classes, with widely different regional and cultural backgrounds. (1989a:148)

The importance of this new national political field is that the very conception and organization of political life now becomes structured through these sets of relations. In this context, two features of the patterns of state formation reviewed above are conducive to the gestation of political Islam in the current period. On the one hand, the very restriction of secular political life often means that 'religious opposition has much greater opportunities of access to the popular locations, through religious venues and channels, notably the mosques' (Zubaida 1989a:161). And on the other, the economic failure of the secular regimes has both pressed the poor strata back into self-help and communal forms of defence and organization, and profoundly damaged the credibility of such regimes. In this context, where Islamist forces and institutions have been able to sustain or to recreate a degree of independence from the state, they provide one basis for popular mobilization against the extant regimes.

These points are reinforced in Nikki Keddie's valuable survey of 'Ideology, Society and the State in Post-Colonial Muslim Societies'.

> The profile of countries with strong Islamist movements nearly always includes the following ... one or more nationalist governments which tried to unify the country by relying more on national than Islamic ideology. . . . rapid economic development and dislocations, which have brought rapid urbanization and visibly differential treatment for the urban poor and the urban rich ... virtually all have profited from oil economies at least at second hand ... a

longer and more radical break with an Islamically-orientated past government and society than is true of a country like Yemen. Most have experienced a heavy Western impact and control and Western and secularly orientated governments. (1988:17)

Islamism, then, is probably best understood as a form of populist mobilization in which middle strata seek to mobilize the working class, and in particular the unorganized urban poor, against foreign influence and a failed political establishment. Drawing on charismatic leaders and the available networks of popular activity, it does not question the status of private property, in fact it is generally pro-market, and it focuses on moral and political renewal. In Egypt its slogan is, simply, 'Islam is the way'. In the Middle East, populism takes a religious form not because it is an atavistic throwback, nor because of the scriptural character of High Islam, but because Islam is constitutive not only of popular culture but also of many of the quotidian features of social life (Gilsenan 1990), and because the failed regimes have been attempting to modernize under *secular* nationalist ideologies. It is these refractory problems of state-building and economic development, rather than 'religion', 'oil' or 'neo-colonial' forms of control, which need to be addressed and which currently make the political future of the Middle East so bleak.

Conclusions and prospects: a crisis of the state?

That movements which proclaim adherence to a text from the seventh century have no chance of introducing anything beyond further chaos and repression is all too obvious. Islam is in general a reactionary force in the region, especially in political fields where secular liberal forces, whether nationalist or socialist, are already established. That populist Islamic forces seek to repress such secular currents is itself evidence of their retrograde character. Moreover, the populist character of Islamist movements should not be confused with a democratic impulse. (Both Zubaida (1989a) and Hooglund (1992) have drawn attention to the relatively high degree of political participation under Iranian populism, as compared with many other regimes in the region, but the theocracy in Tehran is not a democracy: basic liberal rights are denied and those who step outside tolerated bounds are systematically repressed.) Thus, it is when measured against liberal nationalist and socialist tendencies, rather than in terms of ahistorical judgements about religion, that political Islam has to be judged a regressive development.

The reactionary forms of political mobilization of Islamic movements in contemporary Egypt have recently been underlined in an important essay by Zubaida, who concluded that:

> if the quest for civil society is one which seeks a framework for the exercise of human rights and social autonomies, then the model presented by the Islamic sector falls short. It reproduces under modern conditions the authoritarian and patriarchal framework of the associations of kinship, village and religious community at a time when such communities have been effectively loosened and dispersed by the socioeconomic processes of modernity. . . . These illiberal forces are increasingly represented in government apparatuses, both formally, in the constitutional commitment to the *shari'a* enshrined by Sadat, and informally, in terms of networks and sympathies. (Zubaida 1992:9)

This had added significance, given the centrality of Egypt to the rest of the Arab world: it is the most populous Arab state; it is the only Arab state at peace with Israel and aligned strongly with the United States; it is currently embarked upon an ambitious and extremely difficult reform programme supported by the West; and it forms a bridge between the Maghreb, the Arab East and Arab Africa. The failure of economic reform in Egypt and a further regression away from secular rule would have serious reverberations from the Atlantic to the Gulf. However, a repetition of the Iranian experience is unlikely in the Egyptian case because of the different social roles of the clergy and the state on the one hand, and the relations between these forces on the other hand. An Algerian 'solution' is more likely. Still, were political Islam to achieve state power in the Arab Middle East, the much-discussed Islamic threat to the West would not even remotely consist in any challenge that it might mount in terms of political and economic competition, but would arise from the very real prospect of large numbers of people running away to less impoverished and repressive regions. A return to clerically prescribed Islam does not and cannot offer an alternative *social system* to capitalism. The application of *shari'a* law and Islamic and other traditional practices to the regulation of social and moral life do not constitute an alternative social order, either domestically or internationally. The idea sometimes advanced that the West is in some sense in competition or rivalry with the Islamic world, in the way that it was with the communist world, is simply risible.

Although talk of a pan-Islamic alternative is profoundly misleading, the crisis of the state in large parts of the Middle East and the scope which this has given to political Islam is real enough. As we have seen, the pattern of state formation in the Middle East, and the pattern of dependent political economy that this has engendered, have resulted in formations which (oil aside) have been unable to compete in the international system. If programmes of reform gain momentum and prove durable elsewhere in the world – in Latin America, in Central and Eastern Europe and elsewhere in Asia – the pressure for change in the Middle East will only increase. Against a domestic background of falling real oil prices, increasing food insecurity, rapidly growing and young populations, and a general failure of programmes of industrialization, such international pressures are all the more intractable. Barring a major and sustained fall in the real oil price, the major oil- and (increasingly) gas-producing states can probably muddle through with more or less success at least in the medium term. It is the intractability of economic reform in the basically non-oil states, in circumstances where the stability of the incumbent regime is scarcely distinguishable from the bases of state power, that the immediate problems are found in their sharpest form.

A comparison of the prospects for economic reform in Turkey and Egypt might help to make this clear. Both of these states have received favourable assistance from the United States, essentially for strategic reasons, and by the same token have also been dealt with fairly leniently by the international financial institutions (the IMF and the World Bank). The objective need for reform is far greater in Egypt than in Turkey: Turkey is a net exporter of agricultural produce, Egypt imports around one-half of its food; the Turkish population has grown more slowly than Egypt's, and the rate of growth of the urban population is much higher in Egypt; and Turkey had begun its state-led industrialization much earlier than Egypt and therefore had already achieved a degree of industrial deepening before it faced the need for reform. These differences are vividly illustrated by the relative size of the respective public sector deficits, expressed as a percentage of GDP: 26.3 per cent in Egypt in 1986 and 6.1 per cent in Turkey in 1990.

However, notwithstanding these contrasts, Turkey has undergone a significant degree of structural adjustment, while in Egypt the reform programme has made little or no real progress. Clearly, Turkish reforms had a stronger base from which to start and in any case may still not succeed, but one other factor seems to be very important in accounting for the difference. This has been brought out in a valuable comparative study by John Waterbury.

> The lesson of the Egyptian example is that the kind of crisis that triggered structural reform in Turkey and Mexico has been postponed because of Egypt's ability to collect strategic and other rents. In that context the coalitional entitlements built up since 1956 have been protected, and existing arrangements defended especially by organised labour, the top bureaucrats, and the military. . . . [Whereas in Turkey] During the period of military rule, . . . the fragile and costly coalitions that had dominated the 1970s were smashed so that opposition to the economic reforms was minimal. (1992:201, 208)

In other words, the inability of the Turkish state to turn to a 'rentier quest' of the kind we have seen in Egypt (notwithstanding international assistance), and hence the seriousness of the economic and political crisis, prompted a coup by the military which, in turn, destroyed the social bases of the old coalition that had been blocking reform. In the Egyptian case, the ability to earn foreign exchange through rents (oil, canal fees, tourism and so forth) has blocked the reform process. If Waterbury's assessment of the relevance of this is correct, then how much more of an obstacle do oil rents constitute in the genuine oil states?

Thus just as the European social democracies ran into problems in the late 1970s and the state socialist economies entered systemic crisis in the late 1980s, so the long-awaited crisis of the state and its protected economic spaces in the Middle East is dawning. Long delayed by oil and other rents, the crisis is now making its belated appearance, and, given the degree of protection in these economies from the full competitive blasts of the world market, the crisis is likely to be much more serious than that which overtook the social democratic states, if less severe than the systemic crisis of the state socialist bloc. Moreover, the longer the inevitable reckoning is delayed, the further the region will fall behind the performance of the rest of the world economy. In the long run, even the oil economies (at least those with significant populations) are unlikely to be able to escape this logic.

Finally, with the demise of the Cold War and the consequent end of superpower bipolarity, one important stabilizing factor in the region has passed from the scene. To be sure, the United States is not about to desert its key regional allies, but in the post-Cold War climate of domestic retrenchment the ability to dispense large sums of foreign aid may well diminish. Equally, the growing demands made on the international financial institutions and the private markets by the former Eastern bloc will further constrict the availability of capital in the Middle East. As yet, there is no prospect of a stable new regional order emerging, and whether the current reassertion of United States influence in the region can hold the ring must be open to serious doubt.

Conclusions

In an earlier work on the relationship between US power in the international system and the world oil industry (Bromley 1991b), I argued that the analysis of these question had to take into account the connections between the state system and the global, capitalist economy. In particular, I criticized approaches which distinguished the state system and the world economy analytically and then proceeded to treat them as substantially independent of one another. Against this, I sought to develop a historical and theoretical account which recognized the varying relations between the socio-economic and the state in order to account for the specificity of US power in the international system. In some respects, the argument presented here is both an extension and a self-criticism of that work. For while the principal arguments of that book still seem to me substantially correct, it had two connected limitations. Substantively, I took for granted the reproduction of those regimes which supported US power in the Middle East, and I tended to treat them as merely responsive to outside influences. This was always a gross simplification and it was connected to the main unresolved theoretical problem with my account: in response to the predominant intellectual tendency to separate the state system from the world economy, I sought to show their deep interconnections theoretically and practically. Thus I argued that the power of the United States in the international system derived not simply from its resources but also from its *capitalist* character, and I suggested that the character of the state, both domestically and internationally, differed systematically between the capitalist and the state socialist world.

The problem with this way of formulating things is that it attempts to put back together what should never have been separated. Rather than argue that analytical distinctions should not be confused or conflated with substantive questions, it now seems to me that it is more helpful to pose these issues historically. For as soon as we step outside the advanced capitalist world, it is obvious that the separation of 'economics' and 'politics' is wholly specific to developed capitalist relations of production. And even in this part of the capitalist world, this separation is both the subject of continuous struggle and the outcome of the contingent reproduction of specific social relations. That is to say, the purely political, sovereign state of capitalism, and hence its associated state system, is intrinsically bound up with the privatization of command over surplus appropriation characteristic of capitalist relations of production. Both the 'state' and the 'market', in their historically specific modern forms, are particular to capitalism. If our analytic distinctions assume this separation,[1] then we both misread the history of capitalist society, as large parts of its reproduction are simply assumed, and falsely apply historically specific categories backwards into the pre-capitalist world.

As we have seen above, in the Middle East the struggle to consolidate these forms has been a large part of what the history of these societies has been about. It remains unfinished business. This was also true for earlier periods of European history, and it continues to be true in significant parts of the Third and (former) Second Worlds. Put differently, once we focus on the *process* of state formation and capitalist development (as well as on the social character of pre-capitalist forms of society), rather than on interactions of 'state' and 'economy', then we need categories which are empirically open and which can grasp the fact that the separation of the political and the economic is a determinate, historical and contingently reproduced accomplishment. This ongoing process is both logically and historically prior to the questions which dominate most social and political theory, and its theoretical and historical comprehension is the primary task of any understanding of modernity. This book has been an attempt to rethink the evolution of one part of the world with these concerns in mind.

1 As most recent social theory does with its focus on 'allocative' and 'authoritative' resources (Giddens 1985), or by distinguishing the overlapping networks of ideological, economic, political and military power (Mann 1986).

How might the argument presented here be taken forward and developed? Most obviously, the kind of approach deployed above can be extended both to cover more societies in the Middle East and to detail the transformations more fully. There is a need for more comparative and more historically informed work. This is true generally, that is more detailed accounts of more states are called for, but also in particular, in the need to rethink a range of substantive questions of Middle East politics: the Arab-Israeli conflict, relations between ethnic and religious groups more generally, the nature of interstate relations, the role of the superpowers, etc. In the light of the analysis of state formation offered here, these important questions need to be reassessed. Moreover, this kind of work should not confine itself to the Middle East. Geographically defined 'regions' have no pre-given unity, and these arguments, if correct, apply equally to other regions of the modern world: this kind of analysis therefore needs to be tested against developments in the rest of the Third World and against the history of European societies. The academic separation in the social sciences between general theorists and area specialists runs against this, but it is too important to allow such intellectually disabling barriers to stand in the way.

At the risk of pre-empting my critics, I should point out that the analysis can also be extended in theoretical terms. I have argued that it is relations of surplus appropriation which provide the key to understanding the main trajectories of social change. But I have implicitly concentrated on relations of surplus appropriation between social classes, and the relationship of these to the emergence of the state, and have neglected the unequal appropriation of social labour between men and women. Yet it is clear that patterns of command in the division of labour between men and women are systematically structured and that they change in the course of social development. Most visibly, the emergence of a particular form of state involves struggles around, and hence transformations in, the nature of the 'public'–'private' divide and the intersection of this with gender inequality and power. (Given the overtly patriarchal nature of political Islam, this is a pressing political question as well as a theoretical issue in contemporary Middle East societies.) The methodology suggested here could, I believe, be extended to analyse these questions, not in the sense that 'gender' is a similar category, or should be assimilated, to that of 'class', but along the lines of examining gender relations in terms of the unequal appropriation of social labour within the sexual division of labour. The limitation of much historical materialist analysis (the present study included) is not that it cannot deal with gender (and other) inequalities but that its notion of the production and reproduction of material life is too narrowly conceived. I have tried to show that an empirically open historical materialism is perfectly capable of generating a theory of the state, indeed that only such an approach can adequately explain the historically specific form of the state, and it ought to prove possible to extend this kind of analysis to include the sexual division of labour.

The analysis of state formation presented here, then, has wider implications beyond the study of the Middle East and beyond the dimensions of power here considered. The theoretical and methodological approach that I have developed can be used more generally in the historical and structural specification of the social forms of modernity. If this agenda were to be developed, then not the least of its benefits would be a definitive end to assumptions about the peculiar nature of the Middle East.

Appendix:
The
Middle East Economies,
Some Comparisons

Table 1 Population, per capita GDP and growth, 1990

	Population (millions)	1990 GDP/capita ($)	Average annual growth rate 1965–90 (%)
Turkey	56.1	1,630	2.6
(Poland)		(1,690)	
Iran	55.8	2,490	0.1
(Mexico)		(2,490)	
Egypt	52.1	600	4.1
(Zimbabwe)		(640)	
Iraq	18.9	—	—
Saudi Arabia	14.9	7,050	2.6
(Greece)		(5,990)	
Middle East and North Africa	256.4	1,790*	
OECD	776.8	20,170*	
World	5,283.9	4,200*	

* Weighted averages

Table 2 Structure of production, 1990 (%)

	GDP 1990 ($bn)	Agriculture	Industry	Manu-facturing	Services
Turkey	96.5	18	33	24	49
Iran	116	21	21	8	58
Egypt	33.2	17	29	16	53
Iraq	—	—	—	—	—
Saudi Arabia	80.9	8	45	9	48

Table 3 Structure of manufacturing, 1990 (%)

	Food, beverages, tobacco	Textiles and clothing	Machinery, transport and equipment	Chemicals	Other
Turkey	17	15	14	14	41
Iran	23	19	12	7	37
Egypt	31	16	9	8	35
Iraq	—	—	—	—	—
Saudi Arabia	—	—	—	—	—

Table 4 Structure of merchandise exports, 1990 (%)

	Fuels, minerals and metals	Other primary commodities	Machinery and transport equipment	Other manu-factures	Textiles and clothing
Turkey	7 (9)	25 (89)	7 (0)	61 (2)	37 (1)
Iran	98 (88)	1 (8)	0 (0)	1 (4)	0 (4)
Egypt	41 (8)	20 (71)	0 (0)	39 (20)	27 (15)
Iraq*	98 (95)	0 (4)	1 (0)	1 (1)	0 (0)
Saudi Arabia	88 (98)	1 (1)	0 (1)	11 (1)	0 (0)

* 1989 figures
Figures in ( ) are for 1965.

Table 5 Structure of merchandise imports, 1990 (%)

	Food	Fuels	Other primary commodities	Machinery and transport equipment	Other manu-factures
Turkey	7 (6)	21 (10)	11 (10)	31 (37)	30 (37)
Iran	12 (16)	0 (0)	5 (6)	44 (36)	38 (42)
Egypt	31 (26)	2 (7)	10 (12)	23 (23)	34 (31)
Iraq*	27 (24)	0 (0)	5 (7)	29 (25)	39 (44)
Saudi Arabia	15 (30)	0 (1)	4 (5)	39 (27)	42 (37)

* 1989 figures
Figures in ( ) are for 1965.

Table 6 Structure of manufacturing exports to OECD, 1990 (%)

	Textiles and clothing	Chemicals	Electrical machinery and electronics	Transport equipment	Other
Turkey	70	4	5	2	20
Iran	93	0	0	0	7
Egypt	53	5	1	18	24
Iraq*	1	19	2	9	69
Saudi Arabia	0	47	5	10	38

*1989 figures
Sources: World Bank: *World Development Report 1992* and *World Development Report 1991*.

Bibliography

Abrahamian, E. 1991: Khomeini: Fundamentalist or Populist? In *New Left Review*, no. 186.

Ahmad, A. 1992: *In Theory: Classes, Nations, Literatures*. London: Verso.

Ahmed, A. 1992: *Postmodernism and Islam*. London: Routledge.

Ajami, F. 1992: *The Arab Predicament* (2nd edn). Cambridge: Cambridge University Press.

Amin, S. 1978: *The Arab Nation*. London: Zed Press.

Amin, S. 1989: *Eurocentrism*. London: Zed Press.

Anderson, B. 1983: *Imagined Communities*. London: Verso.

Anderson, L. 1990: Policy-Making and Theory Building. In Sharabi, H. (ed.).

Anderson, L. 1991: Legitimacy, Identity, and the Writing of History in Libya. In Davis, E. and Gavrielides, N. (eds).

Anderson, P. 1974a: *Passages From Antiquity to Feudalism*. London: New Left Books.

Anderson, P. 1974b: *Lineages of the Absolutist State*. London: New Left Books.

Asad, T. 1986: *The Idea of an Anthropology of Islam*. Washington DC: Georgetown University Press.

Asad, T. and Owen, R. (eds) 1983: *Sociology of "Developing Societies": The Middle East*. London: Macmillan.

Aulas, M. 1988: State and Ideology in Republican Egypt. In Halliday, F. and Alavi, H. (eds).

Azim, A. 1989: Egypt: The Origins and Development of a Neo-colonial State. In Berberoglu, B. (ed.).

Bayly, C. 1988: *Indian Society and the Making of the British Empire*. Cambridge: Cambridge University Press.

Bayly, C. 1989: *Imperial Meridian*. London: Longman.

Beblawi, H. 1990: The Rentier State in the Arab World. In Luciani, G. (ed.).

Beetham, D. 1991: *The Legitimation of Power*. London: Macmillan.

Berberoglu, B. (ed.) 1989: *Power and Stability in the Middle East*. London: Zed Press.

Brenner, R. 1986: The Social Basis of Economic Development. In Roemer, J. (ed.).

Brittain, V. (ed.) 1991: *The Gulf Between Us*. London: Virago Press.

Bromley, S. 1991a: Crisis in the Gulf. In *Capital and Class*, no. 44.

Bromley, S. 1991b: *American Hegemony and World Oil*. Cambridge: Polity Press.

Bromley, S. 1993: The Prospects for Democracy in the Middle East. In Held, D. (ed.).

Brown, L. 1984: *International Politics and the Middle East*. London: I. B. Tauris.

Brubaker, R. 1984: *The Limits of Rationality*. London: George Allen and Unwin.

Bull, H. and Watson, A. (eds) 1984: *The Expansion of International Society*. Oxford: Oxford University Press.

Burawoy, M. 1989: Two Methods in Search of Science: *Skocpol versus Trotsky*. In *Theory and Society*, vol. 18.

Burrell, R. (ed.) 1989: *Islamic Fundamentalism*. London: Royal Asiatic Society.

Bush, R. et al. (eds) 1987: *The World Order*. Cambridge: Polity Press.

Cammack, P. et al. 1988: *Third World Politics*. London: Macmillan.

Carr, E. 1966: *The Bolshevik Revolution 1917–1923*, vol. 3. Harmondsworth: Penguin.

Chaliand, G. 1977: *Revolution in the Third World* (tr. D. Johnstone). Hassocks: Harvester Press.

Chaudhry, K. 1991: On the Way to Market: Economic Liberalization and Iraq's Invasion. In *Middle East Report*, no. 170.

Collins, R. 1986: *Weberian Sociological Theory*. Cambridge: Cambridge University Press.

Cook, M. 1983: *Muhammad*. Oxford: Oxford University Press.

Crafts, N. 1985: *British Economic Growth During the Industrial Revolution*. Oxford: Clarendon Press.

Crone, P. 1980: *Slaves on Horses*. Cambridge: Cambridge University Press.

Crone, P. and Cook, M. 1977: *Hagarism*. Cambridge: Cambridge University Press.

Crone, P. and Hinds, M. 1986: *God's Caliph*. Cambridge: Cambridge University Press.

Davis, E. 1991: Theorizing Statecraft and Social Change in Arab Oil-Producing Countries. In Davis, E. and Gavrielides, N. (eds).

Davis, E. and Gavrielides, N. 1991: Statecraft, Historical Memory, and Popular Culture in Iraq and Kuwait. In Davis, E. and Gavrielides, N. (eds).

Davis, E. and Gavrielides, N. (eds) 1991: *Statecraft in the Middle East.* Miami: Florida International University Press.

Eisenstadt, S. and Roniger, L. 1984: *Patrons, Clients and Friends.* Cambridge: Cambridge University Press.

Esposito, J. 1988: *Islam.* Oxford: Oxford University Press.

Esposito, J. 1991: *Islam and Politics.* Syracuse, New York: Syracuse University Press.

Farhi, F. 1989: Class Struggles, the State, and Revolution in Iran. In Berberoglu, B. (ed.).

Farouk-Sluglett, M. and Sluglett, P. 1990: *Iraq Since 1958.* London: I. B. Tauris.

Foran, J. 1991: The Strengths and Weaknesses of Iran's Populist Alliance. In *Theory and Society*, vol. 20.

Fromkin, D. 1991: *A Peace To End All Peace.* Harmondsworth: Penguin.

Gallagher, J. and Robinson, R. 1953: The Imperialism of Free Trade. In *Economic History Review*, second series, vol. VI, no. 1.

Gellner, E. 1981: *Muslim Society.* Cambridge: Cambridge University Press.

Gellner, E. 1988: *Plough, Sword and Book.* London: Collins Harvill.

Gellner, E. 1992: *Postmodernism, Reason and Religion.* London: Routledge.

Gerber, H. 1987: *The Social Origins of the Modern Middle East.* Boulder, Colorado: Lynne Rienner.

Gibb, H. 1949: *Islam.* Oxford: Oxford University Press.

Giddens, A. 1976: Introduction. In Weber, M. *The Protestant Ethic and the Spirit of Capitalism* (tr. Talcott Parsons). London: Harper Collins.

Giddens, A. 1985: *The Nation-State and Violence.* Cambridge: Polity Press.

Gilsenan, M. 1988: State and Popular Islam in Egypt. In Halliday, F. and Alavi, H. (eds).

Gilsenan, M. 1990: *Recognizing Islam.* London: I. B. Tauris.

Godelier, M. 1986: *The Mental and the Material.* London: Verso.

Goody, J. 1986: *The Logic of Writing and the Organisation of Society.* Cambridge: Cambridge University Press.

Haggard, S. and Kaufman, R. (eds) 1992: *The Politics of Economic Adjustment.* Princeton, New Jersey: Princeton University Press.

Hall, J. 1985: *Powers and Liberties.* Harmondsworth: Penguin.

Hall, J. (ed.) 1986: *States in History.* Oxford: Basil Blackwell.

Halliday, F. 1974: *Arabia Without Sultans.* Harmondsworth: Penguin.

Halliday, F. 1987: The Middle East in International Perspective. In Bush, R. et al. (eds).

Halliday, F. 1988: The Iranian Revolution: Uneven Development and Religious Populism. In Halliday, F. and Alavi, H. (eds).

Halliday, F. and Alavi, H. (eds) 1988: *State and Ideology in the Middle East and Pakistan*. London: Macmillan.

Halliday, F. and Molyneux, M. 1981: *The Ethiopian Revolution*. London: Verso.

Hawthorn, G. 1991: 'Waiting for a Text?': Comparing Third World Politics. In Manor, J. (ed.).

Held, D. (ed.) 1993: *The Prospects for Democracy: North, South, East, West*. Cambridge: Polity Press.

Hindess, B. 1977: Humanism and Teleology in Sociological Theory. In Hindess, B. (ed.).

Hindess, B. (ed.) 1977: *Sociological Theories of the Economy*. London: Macmilan.

Hobsbawm, E. 1954: The Crisis of the Seventeenth Century. In *Past and Present*, nos 5–6.

Hobsbawm, E. 1960: The Seventeenth Century in the Development of Capitalism. In *Science and Society*, vol. XXIV, no. 2.

Hobsbawm, E. 1962: *The Age of Revolution, 1789–1848*. London: Weidenfeld and Nicolson.

Hobsbawm, E. 1975: *The Age of Capital, 1848–1875*. London: Weidenfeld and Nicolson.

Hobsbawm, E. 1987: *The Age of Empire, 1875–1914*. London: Weidenfeld and Nicolson.

Hobsbawm, E. 1990: *Nations and Nationalism Since 1780*. Cambridge: Cambridge University Press.

Hodges, R. and Whitehouse, D. 1983: *Mohammed, Charlemagne and the Origins of Europe*. London: Duckworth.

Hooglund, E. 1992: Iranian Populism and Political Change in the Gulf. In *Middle East Report*, no. 174.

Hourani, A. 1991: *A History of the Arab Peoples*. London: Faber and Faber.

Ibn Khaldun 1967: *The Muqaddimah*. London: Routledge and Kegan Paul.

Ingham, G. 1984: *Capitalism Divided?* London: Macmillan.

Ismael, T. 1986: *International Relations of the Contemporary Middle East*. New York: Syracuse University Press.

Issawi, C. 1982: *An Economic History of the Middle East and North Africa*. London: Methuen.

al Jabar, F. 1991: Roots of an Adventure, The Invasion of Kuwait: Iraqi Political Dynamics. In Brittain, V. (ed.).

James, L. 1990: *The Golden Warrior*. London: Weidenfeld and Nicolson.

Johnstone, D. 1989: Turkey's Other NATO Link. In *Middle East Report*, no. 160.

Jones, E. 1981: *The European Miracle*. Cambridge: Cambridge University Press.

Karshenas, M. 1990: *Oil, State and Industrialisation in Iran*. Cambridge: Cambridge University Press.

Keddie, N. 1988: Ideology, Society and the State in Post-Colonial Muslim Societies. In Halliday, F. and Alavi, H. (eds.).

Kedourie, E. 1987: *England and the Middle East*. London: Mansell Publishing.

Kedourie, E. 1992: *Politics in the Middle East*. Oxford: Oxford University Press.

Keyder, C. 1987: *State and Class in Turkey*. London: Verso.

Keyder, C. 1988: Class and State in the Transformation of Modern Turkey. In Halliday, F. and Alavi, H. (eds).

Keylor, W. 1984: *The Twentieth-Century World*. Oxford: Oxford University Press.

al-Khafaji, I. 1992: State Terror and the Degradation of Politics in Iraq. In *Middle East Report*, no. 176.

al-Khalil, S. 1990: *Republic of Fear*. London: Radius Hutchinson.

Kiernan, V. 1969: *The Lords of Humankind*. London: Century Hutchinson.

Kiernan, V. 1980: *State and Society in Europe 1550–1650*. Oxford: Basil Blackwell.

Kiernan, V. 1982: *European Empires From Conquest to Collapse*. London: Fontana.

Korany, B. and Dessouki, A. (eds) 1991: *The Foreign Policies of Arab States* (2nd edn). Boulder, San Francisco: Westview Press.

Korany, B. et al. (eds) 1993: *The Many Faces of National Security in the Arab World*. London: Macmillan.

Kriedte, P. 1983: *Peasants, Landlords and Merchant Capitalists*. Leamington Spa: Berg.

Lacoste, Y. 1984: *Ibn Khaldun*. London: Verso.

Lapidus, I. 1988: *A History of Islamic Societies*. Cambridge: Cambridge University Press.

Lawson, F. 1993: Neglected Aspects of the Security Dilemma. In Korany, B. et al. (eds).

Lenczowski, G. 1980: *The Middle East in World Affairs*. Ithaca: Cornell University Press.

Lewis, B. 1988: *The Political Language of Islam*. Chicago: The University of Chicago Press.

Louis, W. 1984: The Era of the Mandate System and the Non-European World. In Bull, H. and Watson, A. (eds).

Luciani, G. 1990: Allocation vs. Production States: A Theoretical Framework. In Luciani, G. (ed.).

Luciani, G. (ed.) 1990: *The Arab State*. London: Routledge.

Mann, M. 1984: The Autonomous Power of the State. Reprinted in Hall, J. (ed.) 1986.

Mann, M. 1986: *The Sources of Social Power, Vol I*. Cambridge: Cambridge University Press.

Manor, J. (ed.) 1991: *Rethinking Third World Politics*. London: Longman.

Mansfield, P. 1991: *A History of the Middle East*. Harmondsworth: Penguin.

Marr, P. 1985: *The Modern History of Iraq*. Boulder, Colorado: Westview Press.

Marshall, G. 1982: *In Search of the Spirit of Capitalism*. London: Hutchinson.

Marsot, A. 1984: *Egypt in the Reign of Muhammad Ali*. Cambridge: Cambridge University Press.

Meiksins Wood, E. 1981: The Separation of the Economic and Political in Capitalism. In *New Left Review*, no. 127.

Meiksins Wood, E. 1990: The Uses and Abuses of Civil Society. In Miliband, R. and Saville, J. (eds).

Miliband, R. and Saville, J. (eds.) 1990: *Socialist Register*. London: Merlin Press.

Mitchell, T. and Owen, R. 1990: Defining the State in the Middle East, MESA Bulletin 24.

Moghadam, F. 1988: Nomadic Invasions and the Development of Productive Forces: An Historical Study of Iran (1000–1800). In *Science and Society*, vol. 52, no. 4.

Momen, M. 1989: Authority and Opposition in Twelver Shi'ism. In Burrell, R. (ed.).

Mommsen, W. 1974: *The Age of Bureaucracy*. Oxford: Basil Blackwell.

Moore, B. 1966: *The Social Origins of Dictatorship and Democracy*. Harmondsworth: Penguin.

Mouzelis, N. 1986: *Politics in the Semi-Periphery*. London: Macmillan.

Owen, R. 1972: Egypt and Europe. In Owen, R. and Sutcliffe, B. (eds).

Owen, R. 1981: *The Middle East in the World Economy 1800–1914*. London: Methuen.

Owen, R. 1983: Arab Nationalism, Unity and Solidarity. In Asad, T. and Owen, R. (eds).

Owen, R. 1992: *State, Power and Politics in the Making of the Modern Middle East*. London: Routledge.

Owen, R. and Sutcliffe, R. (eds.) 1972: *Studies in the Theory of Imperialism*. London: Longman.

Picard, E. 1990: Arab Military in Politics. In Luciani, G. (ed.).

Polanyi, K. 1944: *The Great Transformation*. Boston: Beacon Press.

Poulantzas, N. 1978: *State, Power, Socialism*. London: New Left Books.

Richards, A. and Waterbury, J. 1990: *A Political Economy of the Middle East*. Boulder, Colorado: Westview Press.

Riley-Smith, J. 1977: *What Were the Crusades?* London: Macmillan.

Robinson, R. 1972: Non-European Foundations of European Imperialism. In Owen, R. and Sutcliffe, B. (eds).

Rodinson, M. 1987: *Europe and the Mystique of Islam*. London: I. B. Tauris.

Roemer, J. (ed.) 1986: *Analytical Marxism*. Cambridge: Cambridge University Press.

Rondot, P. 1961: *The Changing Patterns of the Middle East 1919–1958*. London: Chatto and Windus.

Rosenberg, J. 1990: Notes on 'bringing the state back in'. Mimeo. Paper presented to a seminar at the LSE.

Rueschemeyer, D., Huber Stephens, E. and Stephens, J. D. 1992: *Capitalist Development and Democracy*. Cambridge: Polity Press.

Runciman, W. 1983: *A Treatise on Social Theory, Vol. I*. Cambridge: Cambridge University Press.

Said, E. 1985: *Orientalism*. Harmondsworth: Penguin.

Said Zahlan, R. 1989: *The Making of the Modern Gulf States*. London: Unwin Hyman.

Salame, G. 1989: Political Power and the Saudi State. In Berberoglu, B. (ed.).

Salame, G. 1990: 'Strong' and 'Weak' States: A Qualified Return to the *Muqaddimah*. In Luciani, G. (ed.).

Sayer, D. 1983: *Marx's Method*. Brighton: Harvester Wheatsheaf.

Sayer, D. 1987: *The Violence of Abstraction*. Oxford: Basil Blackwell.

Sayer, D. 1991: *Capitalism and Modernity*. London: Routledge.

Sayigh, Y. 1993: Arab Military Industrialization: Security Incentives and Economic Impact. In Korany, B. et al. (eds).

Sharabi, H. (ed.) 1990: *Theory, Politics and the Arab World*. London: Routledge.

Sivard, R. 1986: *World Military and Social Expenditures 1986* (5th edn). Washington, D.C: World Priorities.

Skocpol, T. 1979: *States and Social Revolutions*. Cambridge: Cambridge University Press.

Stivers, W. 1982: *Supremacy and Oil*. Ithaca, New York: Cornell University Press.

Stork, J. 1989: Class, State and Politics in Iraq. In Berberoglu, B. (ed.).

Therborn, G. 1978: *What Does The Ruling Class Do When It Rules?* London: New Left Books.

Tibbi, B. 1990: *Islam and the Cultural Accommodation of Social Change*. Boulder, Colorado: Westview Press.

Tilly, C. 1990: *Coercion, Capital and European States, AD 990–1990*. Oxford: Basil Blackwell.

Tilly, C. 1991: War and State Power. In *Middle East Report*, no. 171.

Trimberger, E. 1978: *Revolution From Above*. New Brunswick: Transaction Books.

Turner, B. 1974: *Weber and Islam*. London: Routledge and Kegan Paul.

Vatikiotis, P. 1987: *Islam and the State*. London: Routledge.

Waterbury, J. 1992: The Heart of the Matter? Public Enterprise and the Adjustment Process. In Haggard, S. and Kaufman, R. (eds).

Wickham, C. 1985: The Uniqueness of the East. In *Journal of Peasant Studies*, vol. 12, nos 2–3.

Wolf, E. 1982: *Europe and the People Without History*. Berkeley: University of California Press.

World Bank 1991: *World Development Report*.

World Bank 1992: *World Development Report*.

Yapp, M. 1987: *The Making of the Modern Near East 1792–1923*. London: Longman.

Yapp, M. 1991: *The Near East Since the First World War*. London: Longman.

Zubaida, S. 1989a: *Islam, the People and the State*. London: Routledge.

Zubaida, S. 1989b: Reading History Backwards. In *Middle East Report*, no. 160.

Zubaida, S. 1992: Islam, the State and Democracy: Contrasting Conceptions of Society in Egypt. In *Middle East Report*, no. 179.

Index